MW01076405

From Trump to Biden and Beyond

Earl A. Carr Jr.
Editor

# From Trump to Biden and Beyond

Reimagining US–China Relations

*Editor*
Earl A. Carr Jr.
Strategy Department
Pivotal Advisors
New York, NY, USA

ISBN 978-981-16-4296-8        ISBN 978-981-16-4297-5   (eBook)
https://doi.org/10.1007/978-981-16-4297-5

Cover credit: © Alex Linch shutterstock.com

This Palgrave Macmillan imprint is published by the registered company Springer Nature
Singapore Pte Ltd.
The registered company address is: 152 Beach Road, #21-01/04 Gateway East, Singapore
189721, Singapore

*This book is dedicated to*
*My Mom and Dad, who instilled in me the values of integrity, an*
*unwavering commitment to excellence, faith in God, and the belief that to*
*whom much is given much is required.*

*Johanna, my wife,*
*An incredible woman, mother, and confidant, whose unwavering love and*
*steadfast support have remained essential to me and our family.*

*Francis and Mia, my son and daughter,*
*The joy, wonder, and energy you bring means the world to me.*

# FOREWORD

The nature of U.S.–China relations is very much in flux. Although the relationship has always been some combination of cooperation and competition, there is a growing consensus in the United States that the relationship today is defined largely by competition. The policy approach of "constructive engagement," followed by U.S. administrations for some forty years, is now discredited—unfairly so, but discredited just the same. In its place, the Trump administration offered an alternative vision of how the United States should approach China. It viewed China as a strategic rival determined to spread its malign influence across the globe as it promoted values inimical to those adhered to by the United States. Given that perspective, there was little interest in any kind of bilateral cooperation—even when there was a common need.

The Biden administration has inherited this foreign policy legacy. One central question for the new administration is what parts of that legacy will be rejected and what parts retained. These decisions should be informed by an analysis of whether the Trump administration's approach to China produced positive results for the United States. While still in the early days of the Biden administration, we were already seeing significant policy continuity with respect to China. No one should expect to see a wholesale reset of U.S.–China relations. It is safe to say that the bilateral relationship will remain a sharply contentious one.

This volume offers valuable suggestions for the new U.S. administration. There is, of course, no shortage of books about U.S.–China relations. In fact, there seems to be a new such book every day. But in that crowded field, what sets this volume apart from the crowd is the diverse background of its contributors. The ten chapters of this book tap into the rich and multidisciplinary experience of a broad range of subject matter experts: current and former academics, economists, and venture capitalists. They hail from across the globe (United States, China, Japan, Taiwan, UAE, Panama, Jamaica, South Korea, and Malawi) and collectively speak multiple languages and dialects. This is not your typical list of contributors for a volume of this sort. That geographic diversity and freshness of perspective are matched by the wide range of topics covered in this book, including some that typically receive less attention, such as U.S.–China competition in Latin America and the Caribbean, in Africa, and in the Gulf. Moreover, this book is recent enough that it offers some initial assessments on the Biden administration's first steps toward China, as well as insights on key topics likely to define U.S.–China relations moving forward. These include the evolving role of the Quad and the change in rhetorical emphasis from "Asia-Pacific" to "Indo-Pacific" that began in the Trump administration and remains intact under President Biden's leadership.

The United States cannot afford to make mistakes in its approach toward China. The stakes are too high, not just for the United States but for the entire world. As the title of this volume suggests, we need to reimagine how our two countries interact and work together. The policy proscriptions in this volume are a helpful step in that direction.

Shanghai, China                                      Kenneth Jarrett
U.S. Consul General, Shanghai (2005–2008)
President, American Chamber of Commerce
in Shanghai (2013–2018)

# Acknowledgments

Writing a book is a challenging and truly rewarding endeavor. It is collective process that has allowed me to reflect on the relationships I have developed throughout the United States, Asia, Europe, Latin America, and the Caribbean. First and foremost, I would like to thank my parents whose support and encouragement gave me the confidence to complete this edited book volume. To my beloved wife Johanna Pan-Carr, I owe an incredible gratitude, who along with my twelve-year-old son Francis and ten-year-old daughter Mia stood by with exceptional grace (well, most of the time) as I missed dinner or a family activity to meet the insatiable demands of completing this book project. Working alongside my fellow extraordinary coauthors allowed me to realize the tremendous respect for their unwavering commitment to intellectual integrity, professionalism, and friendship. To all of my dedicated and respected coauthors: Jeeho Bae, Winslow Robertson, Asad Hussaini, Carolyn Kissane, Jackson Ewing, Junya Ishii, Kevin Chen, Kwei-Bo Huang, Matt Harris, Owa Kankhewende, Ricardo Barrios, and Yaser Faheem, the honor and privilege to work with each of you for the last seven months on this book project has been a truly humbling experience that I will always cherish. One of the defining moments in writing this book volume came during March of 2021, when I felt completely exhausted and burnt out from working a fulltime job, maintaining a family, and often writing at night from 11 pm to 2 am. I owe an incredible gratitude to Winslow and Jeeho, who, at my hour of greatest need, stepped in and breathed new life into this project and whose contribution ensured the completion of this book volume. I will forever be indebted to you both! A special thanks to Michael Tang and Pengyu Lu who read and edited several chapters.

Special notice must be given to Margery Thompson, who edited portions of the book and whose great expertise and experience greatly augmented the book's quality. I would also like to acknowledge Jin Liqun, president of the Asian Infrastructure Bank, for allowing us to arrange a an exclusive zoom call where we had the opportunity to discuss U.S.–China relations in an open and transparent manner. I am in deep gratitude to my friend and dear mentor General Clint Hinote, whose steadfast guidance also included taking time to discuss portions of the book and incorporate his perspectives as a war-gaming strategist. I must acknowledge Gerard Johnson and Keith Collister who reviewed our chapter on Latin America and The Caribbean and gave insightful comments and quotes given their extensive knowledge of the region. I would be remiss not to acknowledge my father Earl Carr Sr. who also read and commented on Chapter 4 (China's presence in the Caribbean) to which I am exceptionally grateful. To my dear friend and mentor Dick Day and my dear sister Carolyn, your comments and reflections on China's engagement in Africa, a continent you both know better than most were insightful. Additional extraordinary mentors include: Jim Turner, Elizabeth Economy, Jerome Cohen, & Professor Li Qingsi, who's knowledge on China has contributed enormously to this book project and to my own personal and professional edification.

A tremendous acknowledgment is due to Shining Sung and Yue-Sai Kai, with whom I had a chance to discuss portions of the book and who have lent their support in so many ways. I also want to thank Pivotal Advisors and in particular CEO Tiffany McGhee, President Chadwick Roberson, and the exceptional Global Research Team (Owa, Koji, Jeeho, Aries, and Yaser) that I have the pleasure of working with every day for their support and encouragement and for keeping me sane especially during a pandemic. I would also like to thank my dear friend Benjamin Lee, whose friendship,guidance, generosity have been truly invaluable. A tremendous acknowledgment is due to Fiona Zhou, President of the Global Institute for Financial Professionals, and to the Association of Diplomatic Studies and Training Professionals (ADST) for their kind support.

Special thanks to Ambassador Gina Winstanley, whose unwavering mentorship over the many years has enabled me to engage on significant policy analysis on East Asia, to the great benefit of this book. And tribute must be paid to Jacob Dreyer, along with Arun Kumar Anbalagan and the extraordinary editorial team at Palgrave and Springer Nature. I am especially grateful to Kenneth Jarrett for writing the Foreword to this edited book volume and for his instrumental friendship and guidance. Thank you Kotaro for your friendship and for introducing me to Junya san. I must also acknowledge Tom Rowe and the ICAP Fellows community whose support has been essential. A special tribute must be paid to the late Emita Samuels, whose tenacious spirit and vitality touched the lives of so many; your legacy and voice lives strong in all ICAP Fellows. I must also recognize the late Maggie Torchon, whose remarkable life inspired me to be a bridge between the United States and China and to pay it forward by mentoring young professionals. Thank you for inspiring me to dream.

In closing, to all of my siblings: (Sherrill & Bobbie, Shawn, Carolyn, Linda, Lisa, Lydia, Alicia, Ernest, Theo & Amanda) your encouragement, love, and faithfulness has sustained my thirst for knowledge and commitment to excellence. To Elmer Huh, Mark Campisano, Craig Broderick, Benjamin Lee, and Jim Turner, my faithful mentors, I can see further because I stand on the shoulders of your guidance, faithfulness, and truth. To Paul, Peyton, Curtis, Yi-Jen, Xunyoung, and the Chung Family (Hilton, Suzie, Logan & Cassidy), My Friends: If it were not for your friendship, fellowship, and generosity, I don't know how I would have gotten through the pandemic. And to Vera, who inspired, encouraged, and challenged me to make writing this book a goal, a humble Thank you.

# About This Book

The past four years have witnessed a tumultuous time in U.S.–China bilateral relations, exemplified by the closure of the Chinese Consulate in Houston, the subsequent closure of the U.S. Consulate in Chengdu, and the abrupt ending of the Fulbright and Peace Corps programs in China—all hallmarks of decades of public-private partnerships, relationships, and history. In the past two decades of geopolitical rivalry between Beijing and Washington, the United States comes off as playing defense vis-à-vis China playing offense. The Biden administration inherited a foreign policy and a diplomatic strategy on life support, with core allies questioning America's resolve and commitment to the region especially in light of the abrupt US withdrawal from Afghanistan and China eager to fill this void. This worsening of bilateral relations will take years to rebuild. On April 28, 2021, President Biden delivered to U.S. Congress and the nation his administration's accomplishments of his first 100 days in office. Consistent throughout his speech was preparing the United States for competition with China, which he argued is needed to "win the 21st century." He noted that China's President Xi is "deadly earnest about [China] becoming the most significant, consequential nation in the world."

To fully address these challenges and regain credibility both at home and abroad, the Biden administration will need to recalibrate its values, objectives, and thinking as it redefines the most important bilateral relationship in the world. But first, the United States must get its own house in order. The U.S. government must develop strategic partnerships with the private sector to enhance foreign direct investment in critical high-tech sectors and also train and retrain the workforce effectively. Doing so will create an effective ecosystem in which the United States will see advanced innovation, continue to employ millions of highly skilled and educated workers, and further the competitiveness of its high-tech sector, not only to confront China but to more effectively compete with it. America needs to define a winning strategy, which at its core begins at home.

Priority must also be placed on rebuilding political capital between Washington and Beijing and deescalating the current adversarial tone. For example, having a clear policy on listing Chinese companies on U.S. markets can help to rebuild trust between U.S. and Chinese investors and clarify expectations on regulatory guidelines. At the same time, US consumers and investors alike must develop a more nuanced under-standing of the geo-political risk in investing in emerging economies like China. Rebuilding and coordinating relations with U.S. allies in the region will help to present real alternatives to China's Belt and Road Initia-tive, as well as to the Regional Comprehensive Economic Partnership (RCEP), and the China–EU Investment Treaty, which, as of the early 2020s, both exclude the United States. In addition, the United States will have to re-envision its policy on Chinese economic engagement with Latin America—all against the backdrop of a global pandemic and the huge economic destruction it has caused. How the United States and China deal with oil and natural gas will have critical implications for the main-land's rapacious energy needs well into the next decade. It will also impact how the U.S. reengages with the Middle East on strategic energy and security-related interests.

Last, identifying common fundamental interests on issues like climate change and transnational crime will establish the foundation by which to engage on more difficult issues like national security, intellectual prop-erty rights, and trade. More important will be identifying a set of mutual shared core interests to help guide and prioritize U.S. foreign policy decision-making. Using a variety of both firsthand and secondhand quan-titative and interactive data, charts, and geopolitical analysis, the authors of this volume aim to highlight the central themes and issues defining U.S.–China relations now and well into the future and seeks to inform policymakers, academics, and key stakeholders.

Drawing upon the expertise and experiences of scholars, economists, former diplomats, and other outside experts, the editors have compiled a book geared toward providing policy recommendations for the next administration. Edited by Earl Carr with Winslow Robertson and Jeeho Bae, this book provides pragmatic proposals for how the United States should develop its policy toward China to more effectively compete, respond, and responsibly engage with current realities that best safeguard and promote America's values, security, economic engagement, and interests.

# INTRODUCTION

It was Napoleon who said, "*Let China sleep, for when she wakes, she will shake the world.*" Analysts argue that China could overtake the United States as the world's largest economy in 2026, measured by GDP[1] and that, coupled with an industrious population of 1.4 billion, many would argue, the "middle kingdom" of today is clearly awoken. It is often said that beauty is in the eye of the beholder, so, for some, China is a crown jewel, highly sought after for data and consumers. Facebook can only dream of catching China's WeChat. On May 15, 2021, on its first attempt, China's space program landed a rover on Mars. The achievement of the Tianwen-1 mission makes China the third nation after the United States and Soviet Union to land on the red planet.[2] If that was not impressive, as of June 2020, 226 of the world's 500 most powerful supercomputers were located in China, twice as many as its nearest competitor, the

---

[1] Evelyn Cheng and Yen Nee Lee, "New Chart Shows China Could Overtake the U.S. as the Largest Economy Earlier than Expected," *CNBC,* February 1, 2021, https://www.cnbc.com/2021/02/01/new-chart-shows-china-gdp-could-overtake-us-sooner-as-covid-took-its-toll.html.

[2] Natasha Khan, "China Lands on Mars in Crowning Moment for Space Program," WSJ, May 16, 2021. https://www.wsj.com/articles/china-lands-on-mars-in-crowning-moment-for-space-program-11621040108.

United States, with 113 supercomputers.[3] China is fast closing the once significant lead the United States maintained on Artificial Intelligence (AI) research. And if that weren't enough, in April 2021, in a first for the second-largest economy, China established its own digital currency,[4] which serves two primary objectives. First, a cyber *Renminbi* enables Beijing to track spending in real time. Second, it allows the Chinese government to trace money that isn't linked to the dollar-denominated global financial system.

In infrastructure, China claims at least a million bridges, including most of the world's highest. Of the world's one hundred tallest skyscrapers, forty-nine are in China.[5] In 2014, Bill Gates noted a remarkable statistic: China had used more cement in the previous three years than the United States had during the entire twentieth century.

In the realm of foreign policy and what many scholars have referred to as Chinese soft power or "sharp power," China's recently developed more assertive approach represents a clear departure from the past. According to the Lowly Institute, in 2019, China overtook the United States in the number of diplomatic posts abroad, more than any other country in the world, with 276 embassies and other representative offices globally.[6] As of 2021, this number has increased to 284. More significant is that within the last five years 2016–2021, China has increased its foreign diplomatic missions (i.e. Embassies, Consulates & Virtual Missions) abroad by 7% going from 263 to 284, while the US during that same corresponding

[3] Thomas Alsop, "Number of top 500 Super Computers in the World," *Statista*, July 3, 2020, https://www.statista.com/statistics/264445/number-of-supercomputers-worldwide-by-country/.

[4] James T. Areddy, "China Creates Its Own Digital Currency, a First for Major Economy," *Wall Street Journal*, April 5, 2021, https://www.wsj.com/articles/china-creates-its-own-digital-currency-a-first-for-major-economy-11617634118.

[5] James T. Areddy, "What The US Can Learn From China's Infatuation with Infrastructure," *Wall Street Journal*, April 3, 2021, https://www.wsj.com/articles/what-the-u-s-can-learn-from-chinas-infatuation-with-infrastructure-11617442201.

[6] "China now has more diplomatic posts than any other country," *BBC News*, November 27, 2019, https://www.bbc.com/news/world-asia-china-50569237.

period has decreased its foreign diplomatic missions by 8% going from 271 to 252 (see infographic below).

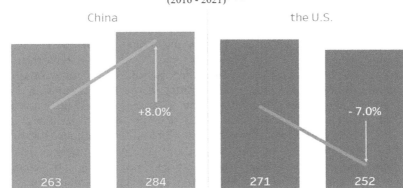

Comparison of the number of Overseas Diplomatic Missions Between The U.S. and China (2016 - 2021)* **

China — +8.0% — 263 (2016) — 284 (2021)

the U.S. — - 7.0% — 271 (2016) — 252 (2021)

\* Diplomatic missions include 1) Embassies, 2) Consulates, 3) Permanent Mission's, and other representation such as virtual offices such as The Maldives, Madagascar etc, for the US.
\*\* Data sourced included the U.S. State Department website, the Chinese Ministry of Foreign Affairs, and interviews with US Foreign Service officers as of August 28th, 2021.

China's more assertive foreign policy strategy was supported by the significant number of overseas visits made by senior Chinese officials. The foreign travels of President Xi Jinping, China's supreme leader, significantly demonstrate the nation's strategic priorities. Between 2013, when he became China's president, and 2020, Xi Jinping made 98 in-person visits to 69 foreign countries,[7] compared to the 103 visits made by Presidents Barack Obama and Donald Trump throughout this same period. China's leaders paid special attention to Asia, Russia, the United States, Europe, Latin America, and Central Asia.

While China is perceived as strong and worthy to be emulated, however, on issues like human rights they are vilified, in particular regarding Xinjiang and the plight of the Uyghurs, or the issue of Tibet and the Dalai Lama. The significant wealth inequality and the poor quality of health and education, particularly in China's rural areas, are also causes for concern. It is a nation whose contradictions are only compounded by the quality of information available from it. As a young research marketing

[7] "What do Overseas Visits Reveal about China's Foreign Policy Priorities?" *Center for Strategic and International Studies*, March 29, 2021, https://chinapower.csis.org/diplomatic-visits/#easy-footnote-bottom-4-7368.

specialist at McKinsey & Co., the editor, Earl Carr, arrived in Shanghai in 2006. He was astounded that as one of the world's leading consulting firms, McKinsey had purchased the best research and data that money could buy; yet questions nevertheless remained over the quality of data in China.

The continued rise of China coupled with the enduring preeminence of the United States has many worried about what the future holds: inevitable confrontation or constructive dialogue. Craig Broderick, senior director at Goldman Sachs, puts it this way: "The U.S.–China relationship will be the defining international interaction of this and subsequent generations. As articulated by Thucydides in the fifth century BC, the emergence of a powerful military rival to an established power is one of the most complex policy challenges for either side to navigate." The United States and China determine the outcome and influence transnational and domestic issues. For example, many Asian American leaders believe that the intensifying rivalry between Washington and Beijing is contributing to the heightened suspicion, prejudice, and violence against their communities in ways that could continue to intensify even after the pandemic begins to subside.[8] Sino–U.S. relations also impact immigration policies which in turn determines policy for thousands of students that ultimately brings intellectual capital, technology, and more.

This collaborative volume seeks to explore these issues, with the notion of "reimagining" U.S.–China relations a critical theme throughout the chapters. The authors collectively acknowledge that Sino–U.S. relations have important implications for East Asia and, more importantly, for the global community. One of the highlights of working on this book was an exclusive zoom call with Jin Liqun, president of the Asian Infrastructure Bank (AIIB) based in Beijing, discussing the significance of our book within the context of U.S.–China relations and getting his perspective on a plethora of issues. These ranged from coal and the environment to Western perceptions of the AIIB to U.S.–China rivalry in Africa and Latin America and more. The eighty-minute discussion was extremely rich and insightful. In another valuable discussion three-star Air Force general Clint Hinote provided his views on what the cost of a military conflict

---

[8] David Nakamura, "Beyond pandemic, Asian American leaders fear U.S. Conflict with China will fan racist backlash." March 17th, 2021. https://www.washingtonpost.com/national-security/biden-china-asian-american-racism/2021/03/17/69eb4bc6-873d-11eb-82bc-e58213caa38e_story.html.

between the United States and China might be on human capital and loss of life, not to mention the impact on global and or regional economies.

The ten chapters of this volume incorporate a truly multidisciplinary group of authors and subject matter experts. In total, the authors represent nine economies (United States, China, Japan, Taiwan, UAE, Panama, Jamaica, South Korea, and Malawi) and collectively speak seven languages (Chinese, Urdu, Arabic, Spanish Japanese, Korean, and Afrikaans) and two dialects (Patwa and "Tai Yu" or 台语). The geographic diversity is also striking. Nine of the thirteen authors live and reside in the United States, while the others live in Spain, Japan, Taiwan, and the United Arab Emirates. As a result, unlike previous books and/or analyses that can often present a homogenous and/or parochial perspective, we have incorporated a diverse range of views and backgrounds, which have served to greatly inform our thoughts. The mandate of each contributor was to address, within the scope of the assigned chapter, several core questions of practical value to policymakers, scholars, and practitioners.

With any book on China, incorporating a regional focus can be a particularly daunting challenge. Our analysis did not incorporate a focus on Europe, as we wanted to highlight China's more targeted foreign policy and commercial ambitions in East Asia, Africa, the Middle East, Latin America, and the Caribbean. Nevertheless, it is important to mention that the EU-China Comprehensive Agreement on Investment (CAI) of December 30, 2020, took nearly seven years to negotiate. It is also noteworthy that Europe concluded this agreement despite objections from the incoming Biden administration, which had asked to be consulted on specifics in the agreement. Equally significant is that in 2020 China surpassed the United States to become the European Union's largest trading partner, driven in part by Europeans' insatiable appetite for Chinese medical equipment and electronics during the Covid-19 pandemic. Another limitation of our analysis is that we did not include Central and Southeast Asia, both vital regions that have significant trade and economic linkages with the mainland but which fell outside the scope of our book.

In Chapter 1, "How the U.S. and China Can Redefine Competition and Cooperation through Manufacturing, Tech, and Innovation," a core component seeks to explain how the United States and China are running different playbooks. The U.S. playbook is a free-for-all of distinct corporate partnerships, strategic initiatives, and mergers and acquisitions.

China, meanwhile, is running a strategic and highly coordinated play-book that includes the direct and massive government support of national champion technology companies.[9] The chapter's authors, Earl Carr and Matt Harris, argue that we can characterize the current geopolitical rivalry between Beijing and Washington as the United States playing defense with China playing mostly offense. It is vital that the U.S. government develop strategic partnerships with the private sector to enhance foreign direct investment in critical high-tech sectors and train and retrain the workforce effectively. In this way it will create an effective ecosystem in which the United States will see advanced innovation, continue to employ millions of highly skilled and educated workers, and further the competitiveness of the U.S. high-tech sector not only to confront China, but also to more effectively compete with China.

In Chapter 2, "'Welcome, but Verify': The Future of Chinese Companies Listed on the U.S. Stock Exchanges," Dr. Kevin Chen notes that for almost three decades, hundreds of Chinese companies have come to the United States to raise capital. Many of the most important companies from China, both private sector and state-owned, are currently traded on American stock exchanges, including the venerable New York Stock Exchange and the technology-heavy Nasdaq Exchange. The total market capitalization of these companies approached $2 trillion by the end of 2020. Since the beginning of the Trump administration in 2017, these U.S.-listed Chinese company shares have been the focus of financial market participants and regulators globally. The volatile relationship between Beijing and Washington under the Trump administration had a direct impact on a large number of new IPOs of Chinese companies listing or trying to list on American exchanges. And the U.S. media produced some major headlines about accounting fraud and other irregularities, Luckin Coffee being a case in point. As a result, U.S. regulators forced several companies to delist. Furthermore, at the end of 2020, the U.S. government delisted three major Chinese telecommunication companies, citing their military involvement. U.S. members of Congress have called for a wholesale ban on these companies. Both U.S. and Chinese regulators have taken some steps to scrutinize this sector. In this chapter, Dr. Chen reviews the historical development and current situation of

---

[9] Louise Lucas, "China government assigns officials to companies including Alibaba," *Financial Times*, September 23, 2019, https://www.ft.com/content/055a1864-ddd3-11e9-b112-9624ec9edc59.

Chinese companies listed on U.S. stock exchanges and best business practices. He outlines practical approaches for the next decade for Chinese companies aiming to list on U.S. exchanges, to whom we suggest: "Welcome, but Verify." It is essential to American institutional investors, to retail investors, and to New York's status as a global financial center to welcome listing high-quality Chinese companies on American stock exchanges. However, stricter compliance with United States accounting rules, market disclosure requirements, and investor-protection regulation are equally needed.

In Chapter 3, "Competitive Energy and Climate Statecraft between China and the United States," Dr. Carolyn Kissane explores how energy and climate statecraft are part of a new dynamic with complementary synergies. China is a bit of the Jekyll and Hyde when it comes to climate change; it is the world's largest emitter of carbon emissions while also leading in the production of the technologies to address climate. China's fourteenth Five-Year Plan (2021–2026) puts climate at the heart of its economic and political strategy.

Author Ricardo Barrios, in Chapter 4, "Reimagining U.S. Engagement with Latin America and the Caribbean in Response to a Risen China," astutely observes that the Trump administration's reactive approach to Latin America and the Caribbean (LAC) hearkened back to an earlier, more heavy-handed model of American foreign policy that is unsuited to compete with Beijing's increasingly sophisticated approach to the region. The approach was in fact counterproductive, as China's presence in the region has only increased since Trump. Long considered outside Beijing's influence, the region has warmed to China. This is evident in a string of diplomatic switches in which several countries severed ties to Taiwan most notably Panama and the Dominican Republic. Moreover, the participation of nineteen countries from Latin America and The Caribbean in the Belt and Road Initiative have many policy makers in the U.S. concerned. Even traditional U.S. partners Colombia and Mexico have seemingly come around to viewing China as a partner to be courted, at least in the economic domain.

In Chapter 5, "U.S. Strategy vis-à-vis China's Presence in the African Continent: Description and Prescription," Owakhela Kankhwende and Winslow Robertson take a non-traditional approach in assessing the U.S.–China rivalry in Africa. They describe how Africa is becoming more populous, youthful, urban, mobile, educated, and networked. The demographic evolution and emerging political, economic, and security changes are increasing Africa's significance to U.S. national interests. The authors argue that President Biden should approach the continent as a single region, dismantling the artificial divide between sub-Saharan and North Africa; reconceptualize how it uses high-level engagement; and deepen its partnerships with Africa's multilateral institutions. Moreover, Washington should encourage U.S. private companies to increase their Africa activity, in particular companies in sectors that align with U.S. comparative advantage in the region or that coincide with U.S. national security goals.

In Chapter 6, "Rethinking Strategic Alignment with the Gulf States," Yaser Faheem and Asad Hussaini analyze how China has actively engaged countries in the Gulf Cooperation Council (GCC), in particular, the United Arab Emirates (UAE) and the Kingdom of Saudi Arabia. The intricate relations between the United States, the GCC, and China are emblematic of both strategic and cooperative objectives. As the GCC powerhouses Saudi Arabia and the UAE seek to diversify their economies and attract more foreign investment, enhancing and bolstering trade and economic relations with other regional powers have become core priorities. The GCC, China, and the United States have strategic choices that can and will redefine the future. Given the Gulf's inherent reliance on the security umbrella of the United States to establish an effective deterrent against Iran, the GCC states may inevitably find themselves engaged in a balancing act due to increasing animosity between their primary security and commercial benefactors.

Chapter 7 by Jeeho Bae is entitled, "Reshaping U.S.-South Korea-Japan Trilateral Relations." The Republic of Korea (ROK), while relying heavily on China as its biggest trade partner, is an indispensable U.S. ally in the region. A core focus of the Trump administration's foreign policy toward South Korea centered on asking Seoul's government to pay more for defense costs to support the U.S. military base in South Korea. At the same time, the United States hesitated to intervene in the trade conflict between the ROK and Japan, which demonstrated a lack of U.S. leadership. The author argues that U.S. policies on the Korean peninsula must reshape and rebuild the alliance in East Asia and focus priorities on foreign policy, high-technology cooperation, and trade.

In Chapter 8, "Pathways for U.S.–China Climate Cooperation under the Biden Administration," Jackson Ewing posits that President Biden would do well to immediately restart the U.S.–China Climate Change Working Group—scuttled by President Trump—to provide a forum for substantive cooperation at national levels. The frequent and regular-ized interactions that it facilitated in the past were essential for building trust and for avoiding platitudes in favor of tangible micro and macro outcomes. Moving forward, such interactions will prove essential for clar-ifying differences, finding areas of common purpose, and developing the middle ground that can again provide the foundation for effective international climate progress.

The final two chapters focus on the most critical geopolitical issues with significant implications for East Asia. If there is one quintessential geopo-litical flashpoint that keeps policy makers, senior executives, and ordinary citizens alike up at night it is the issue of Taiwan. In Chapter 9, "The U.S. and Unresolved Cross-Strait Relations: From Trump to Biden," Kwei-Bo Huang addresses the issue of cross-strait relations. Professor Huang argues that the United States should encourage both sides of the Taiwan Strait to carry out a "surprise-free" policy and work with the United States for a win-win-win situation that will also benefit the Indo-Pacific region.

In the tenth and final chapter, "Indo-Pacific Diplomacy, the Quad, and Beyond: Democratic Coalition in the Era of U.S.–China Global Competition," Junya Ishii notes that, as the United States and China are competing over dominance in various areas, U.S. allies and partners are forming multilayered coalitions like the Free and Open Indo-Pacific (FOIP) and the Quad. These multidimensional coalitions will engage military, security, technology, supply chain, governance (democracy and human rights), and economic development issues. The 10 chapters in this book highlight the most salient issues impacting  US-Sino relations. If there was ever an inflection point which could determine the future trajec-tory of bilateral relations it is now. This edited volume finds that the bene-fits of engaging China, politically, economically and socially, far outweigh the negative externalities. There is no substitution for building mutual trust. The US, China, and the global community have far too much at stake for the world's two largest economies to not harness the full poten-tial of globalization. That is not to say that the US and China cannot acknowledge differences on values, political systems, and strategic core interests. As Jerome Cohen one of the leading Sinologists notes while the Biden Administration has defined US Foreign Policy towards China using the 4 C's (Cooperation, Competition, & Confrontation) frame-work, another important C is criticism and that should be extended both ways when warranted. In the final analysis, contrary to the current rhetoric in Washington and Beijing, the authors argue that investing time, energy, and political will in finding common ground on transnational issues like the environment, trade, and cross Strait relations can, will, and must reap dividends in laying the foundation to build stronger bilateral relations.

# Contents

# Notes on Contributors

**Jeeho Bae** is a senior research analyst at Global Research Team at Pivotal Advisors. He is specialized in data analytics and global research in the East Asia region. Jeeho holds a master's degree in Data Analytics and Visualization at the Katz School at Yeshiva University, a master's degree in International Affairs at the Milano School at The New School, and a bachelor's degree with a major in Chinese Literature and a minor in International Relations at Chonnam National University in South Korea.

**Ricardo Barrios** is a specialist in Chinese foreign policy, with a focus on Latin America and the Caribbean. He is currently an analyst at RWR Advisory Group. He holds a Master's in International Politics from Peking University and a Bachelor's in Politics and East Asian Studies from Oberlin College.

**Earl A. Carr Jr.** is the Chief Global Strategist at Pivotal Advisors based in New York City. Mr. Carr possesses over twenty years of experience working in the private sector and non-profit business organizations. Earl is also an Adjunct Instructor at New York University's Center for Global Affairs. Mr. Carr received his undergraduate degree from The College of William & Mary in International Relations and his Master's degree in International Affairs from American University. Earl is a Board member at The Association for Diplomatic Studies & Training (ADST) and Board Director at The Global Institute of Financial Professionals (GIFP). He is a Senior Advisor to The International Career Advancement Program

(ICAP). Mr. Carr is a member of The National Committee on United States–China Relations and a columnist at Forbes.com.

**Kevin Chen** is Chairman and CEO of Edoc Acquisition Corporation. Chief Economist and CIO of Horizon Financial. Adjunct Associate Professor, New York University. A guest speaker at Harvard University, Fordham University, Pace University, and IESE Business School. Former member of the Adjunct Advisory Committee and former Interim Head of the Private Sector Concentration program of Ms. Global Affairs, New York University. Member of the Economic Club of New York. Fellow of the Foreign Policy Association. Member of the Bretton Woods Committee. Editorial Advisory Board Member of the Global Commodity Applied Research Digest (GCARD) at JP Morgan Center for Commodities (JPMCC) at the University of Colorado Denver Business School.

**Jackson Ewing, Ph.D.** is a Senior Fellow at Duke University's Nicholas Institute of Environmental Policy Solutions, Adjunct Associate Professor at the Sanford School of Public Policy, Faculty Lead for the Duke Kunshan University Environment Program, and Senior Adviser to the Asia Society Policy Institute. Based in the Asia-Pacific from 2005 to 2014, Dr. Ewing previously served as a Director of Asian Sustainability at the Asia Society Policy Institute and as a MacArthur Fellow and head of the Environment, Climate Change and Food Security Program at Singapore's S. Rajaratnam School of International Studies. He has worked throughout Asia and internationally with actors in government, the private sector, civil society, and international organizations. He has authored more than 100 publications, and holds a B.A. in Political Science from the College of Charleston, and a M.A. and Ph.D. from Australia's Bond University.

**Yaser Faheem** works as a Geopolitical & Market Research Analyst with the Global Research Team at Pivotal Advisors. Having spent most of his time in the Middle East & South Asia, he carries his regional expertise to help provide valuable research on investment opportunities in these regions. Additionally, he has a background in Corporate Communications as well as Digital & Social Media Strategy having previously worked at Fleishman Hillard—a top tier multinational Communications Agency. Yaser recently received his Master's degree in International Relations & Futures Policy from New York University's Center for Global Affairs. He completed his undergraduate degree in Mass Communication at United Arab Emirates University in Abu Dhabi.

**Matt Harris** is on the investment team at Draper Associates where he invests in frontier technology companies all over the world. Matt joined the Draper Associates team in 2020. He was formerly a Vice President at The Blackstone Group where he focused on providing growth financing to global energy companies. Matt has a bachelor's degree in business administration and finance from Texas A&M University. He is based in Austin, Texas where he lives with his wife and two daughters.

**Dr. Kwei-Bo Huang** is an Associate Professor of Diplomacy at National Cheng-Chi University (NCCU), as well as Director of Center for Global and Regional Risk Assessment at NCCU College of International Affairs, Taipei, Taiwan, Republic of China (ROC). He was Vice Dean at NCCU College of International Affairs from spring 2018 to spring 2020. He was also a Fulbrighter at SAIS, Johns Hopkins University and a visiting fellow at The Brookings Institution. He earned his master's degree from Department of Political Science at the George Washington University and his doctorate from Department of Government and Politics at University of Maryland, College Park.

**Asad Hussaini** is a principal at a Single-Family Office based in Dubai that focuses on North American Real Estate. Asad serves on the Board of the Emirates German Foundation, Emirates Swiss Real Estate Company, Gravity Hospitality Group, ANSAB Transport and Aviatrans Holding Canada and is on the advisory board of Tau Investment Management in New York and Peninsula Real Estate in the UAE. He started off his career in his family business Zafco Group—a global tire manufacturer, distribution and retailing company with a presence in 105 countries. He was educated at Georgetown University in Washington D.C.

**Junya Ishii** is a senior analyst focusing on politics and economy of the Asian region and the U.S. foreign policy toward Asia at Sumitomo Corporation Global Research. Prior to the current position, he worked for the Ministry of Foreign Affairs of Japan as a diplomat and for Clifford Chance and Anderson Mori and Tomotsune as a lawyer. He holds a J.D. from Tokyo University and a M.A. in international relations from Stanford University.

**Owakhela Kankhwende** is currently in the Master of Science in Business Analytics program at Fordham University Gabelli School of Business. He also is a Research Analyst with the Global Research Team at Pivotal Advisors. His undergraduate degree was in the Economics Major at New York University.

**Dr. Carolyn Kissane** serves as the Academic Director of the graduate programs in Global Affairs and Global Security, Conflict and Cybercrime at the Center for Global Affairs. She is a Clinical Professor, Director of the SPS Energy, Climate Justice and Sustainability Lab, and Coordinator of the Energy and Environment concentration at the Center. Dr. Kissane received her Ph.D. from Columbia University.

**Winslow Robertson** is a Ph.D. candidate in Managing People in Organizations at IESE Business School focusing on ideology and management. He is the founder/managing member of the China-Africa strategic consultancy Cowries and Rice. Winslow earned his M.A. and B.A. in History from Syracuse University and James Madison University respectively.

# LIST OF FIGURES

# CHAPTER 1

# How the United States and China Can Redefine Competition and Cooperation Through Manufacturing, Tech, and Innovation

*Matt Harris and Earl A. Carr Jr.*

---

Louise Lucas, "China Government Assigns officials to companies including Alibaba," *Financial Times*, September 23, 2019, https://www.ft.com/content/055a1864-ddd3-11e9-b112-9624ec9edc59.
The views and opinions expressed in this chapter are those of the author and do not reflect the official policy or position of any organizations with which the author is affiliated.

---

M. Harris (✉)
Draper Regina Ayot, West Lake Hills, TX, USA
e-mail: matt@draper.vc

E. A. Carr Jr.
Strategy Department, Pivotal Advisors, New York, NY, USA
e-mail: earl@pivotal-advisors.com

© The Author(s), under exclusive license to Springer Nature Singapore Pte Ltd. 2021
E. Carr Jr. (ed.), *From Trump to Biden and Beyond*,
https://doi.org/10.1007/978-981-16-4297-5_1

**Abstract** As we stand at the brink of the fourth industrial revolution the United States and China are running different playbooks. This chapter examines how the United States playbook is a free-for-all of distinct corporate partnerships, strategic initiatives, and M&A. China, meanwhile, is running a strategic and highly coordinated playbook that includes the direct and massive government support of national champion technology companies. More importantly though, many have juxtaposed the current U.S. and China relationship to the Cold War. This is a misleading and dangerous comparison. The U.S.SR was a three-legged stool with two legs already wobbling. Gary Rieschel, Founder and Managing Partner of Qiming Venture Partners notes, "In any competition, there are moves and countermoves. It has been decades since the United States has had an economic competitor that required any significant change in United States thinking. Japan was that competitor in the 80s. China has become that competitor in the twenty-first century, and on a more comprehensive basis. Our responses to this should not eliminate the opportunity for future cooperation in areas of our mutual best interest." Moreover, we can equate the current geopolitical rivalry between Beijing and Washington as the United States playing defense and China playing more offense.

**Keywords** China · U.S. · Sino–U.S. · Competition · Cooperation · Manufacturing · Technology · Innovation · R&D · Research & Development

During President Biden's inauguration on January 20, 2021 the United States defined a different strategy with China. In some ways the new strategy uses similar tactics as the previous administration, such as maintaining trade tariffs, while in other ways it is different, such as seeking to establish meaningful collaboration on issues like climate change. U.S. Trade Representative Katherine Tai said "yanking off" the tariffs imposed by former President Donald Trump in March 2018[1] could hurt U.S. companies, traders, manufacturers, and their workers who have

---

[1] Office of the United States Trade Representative, *President Trump Announces Strong Actions to Address China's Unfair Trade*, (Washington, DC: Office of the United States Trade Representative, 2018), https://ustr.gov/about-us/policy-offices/press-office/press-releases/2018/march/president-trump-announces-strong.

adapted to the post-tariffs trade environment.[2] At the same time President Biden invited Xi to attend the Virtual Climate Summit from April 22–23.[3] What has not changed over the last several years is a growing recognition on Capitol Hill that the China the United States faces today is fundamentally different than in the past and thus requires a more resilient, focused, and consistent approach.

It's important to note that as we stand at the brink of the fourth industrial revolution the United States and China are running different playbooks. The United States playbook is a free-for-all of distinct corporate partnerships, strategic initiatives, and M&A. China, meanwhile, is running a strategic and highly coordinated playbook that includes the direct and massive government support of national champion technology companies. Chinese electronics giant Xiaomi in March announced it will be entering the electric vehicles market promising to spend around $10 billion over the next decade.[4] The corporate partnerships and M&A in the United States are between industrial incumbents and high-flying technology firms. The industrial companies with mechanical and customer know how are partnering with firms that have the capabilities and cultures to operate digitally. Ty Findley, Managing Partner at digital industrial venture capital fund Ironspring Ventures, commented,

*There is no doubt that the global Industry 4.0 race is on. The current pandemic has really put a spotlight on why having a robust, modern and secure U.S. manufacturing base is critical to both national security and economic prosperity. The U.S. launched the "Manufacturing U.S.A" initiative in 2013 and China launched its "Made in China 2025" plan in 2015 – it will be very telling to watch how these differing strategies play out.*

[2] Jonathan Ponciano, "Trade War: Biden Administration Not Ready to 'Yank' China Tariffs, But Open to Talks," *Forbes*, March 28, 2021, https://www.forbes.com/sites/jonathanponciano/2021/03/28/trade-war-biden-administration-not-ready-to-yank-china-tariffs-but-open-to-talks/?sh=2864ae025e8b.

[3] Katheryn Watson, "Biden Invites World Leaders Including Putin and Xi to Climate Summit," *CBS News*, March 26, 2021, https://www.cbsnews.com/news/biden-invites-putin-xi-40-world-leaders-climate-summit/.

[4] Dan Strumpf, "Xiaomi Budgets $10 Billion to Add Electronic Vehicles," *Wall Street Journal*, March 31, 2021, https://www.wsj.com/articles/xiaomi-enters-electric-vehicle-market-with-10-billion-investment-11617118767.

Analysis of 37 Internet of Things tech/industrial company partnerships (2016 - 2019)

| Partnership Objective | Number of Partnerships | Example Tech company | Example Incumbent | Description |
|---|---|---|---|---|
| Codevelopment | 20 | IBM | ABB | Codevelopment of ABB IoT solutions for utilities, transport, industry, infrastructure verticals |
| Joint go-to-market campaigns | 4 | Microsoft | Avnet | Join GTM to drive adoption of IoT platform |
| Promote common data and technology standards | 7 | Cisco | Rockwell Automation | Promotion of common networking standards for industrial environments |
| Drive adoption of IoT across the value chain | 3 | Amazon | Ford (via Automatic") | Drive adoption of IoT across mobility players (e.g., fleet management, ride hailing) |

Source: BCG research and analysis
"Autonomic (owned by Ford) is building a transportation mobility cloud platform.

**Fig. 1.1** Analysis of 37 Internet of Things tech/industrial company partnerships (*Source* Massimo Russo and Gary Wang, "Orchestrating the Value in IoT Platform-Based Business Models," *BCG Henderson Institute*, June 2020, https://image-src.bcg.com/Images/BCG-Orchestrating-the-Value-in-IoT-Platform-Based-Business-Models-Jun-2020-n_tcm9-252129.pdf)

Examples of U.S.-based corporate partnerships in one vertical of industrial technology, the internet-of-things, are shown in a Fig 1.1.

The U.S. government dedicated 2.3% of the federal budget in 2020 to R&D alongside what is clearly a private market-led effort.[5] Meanwhile, the Chinese playbook clearly includes a belief in first-mover advantages. Moving first increases the chances that Chinese AI will get smarter faster and that Chinese digital platforms[6] will reap the benefits of scale, big data, and network effects. In the 14th Five-Year plan, (2020–2025) China is targeting annual increases of 7% or more on R&D spending in each of the next 5 years. In other words, spending could reach 2.8% of GDP by 2025, up from an estimated 2.3 to 2.4% for 2020. In 2019, total spending on R&D rose 12.5% over the previous year, to 2.21 trillion yuan ($322 billion) according to the National Bureau of Statistics in China, dwarfing

[5] "Federal Research and Development (R&D) Funding: FY 2020," *Congressional Research Service*, March 18, 2020, https://fas.org/sgp/crs/misc/R45715.pdf.

[6] Earl Carr, "Is China Threatening America's Dominance in the Digital Space?," *Forbes*, June 20, 2020, https://www.forbes.com/sites/earlcarr/2020/06/20/is-china-threatening-americas-dominance-in-the-digital-space/?sh=450d82bc3cd4.

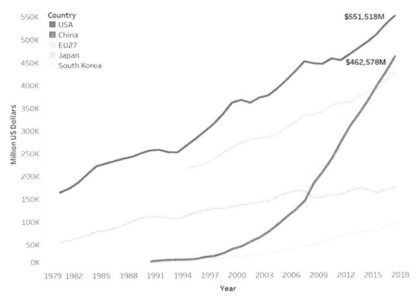

**Gross domestic spending on R&D, the US and China (1981 - 2018)**

**Fig. 1.2** AGross Domestic Spending on R&D, the U.S. and China (1981–2018) (*Source* "Gross Domestic Spending on R&D," *Organization for Economic Co-operation and Development*, accessed January 20, 2021, https://data.oecd.org/rd/gross-domestic-spending-on-r-d.htm)

what is being spent in the United States and elsewhere.[7] If current trends continue, after **2030**, China will be the largest spender on research & development (Fig. 1.2).

The People's Republic of China's ultimate objective is to reduce its dependence on foreign technology and promote Chinese high-tech manufacturers and standards in the global marketplace. Semiconductors are an area of particular emphasis, given their centrality to nearly all electronic products. China accounts for about **60 percent** of the global demand for semiconductors but only produces some **13 percent** of the

[7] Bloomberg News, "Unraveling the Mysteries of China's Multiple Budgets," *Bloomberg*, March 13, 2020, https://www.bloomberg.com/news/articles/2020-03-13/unraveling-the-mysteries-of-china-s-multiple-budgets-quicktake.

global supply. China's Made in 2025 sets specific targets: by 2025, China aims to achieve 70 percent self-sufficiency in high-tech industries, and by 2049—the hundredth anniversary of the People's Republic of China—it seeks a dominant position in global markets. More importantly, Beijing seeks to leverage soft power or "sharp power" to exert economic leverage to achieve political objectives around the world.[8] In a speech President Xi delivered in early 2020, published in the Chinese Communist Party's leading journal "Qiu Shi" he said, China "must tighten international production chains' dependence on China" with the aim of "forming powerful countermeasures and deterrent capabilities."[9] The phrase "powerful countermeasures and deterrent capabilities" can be equated to this notion of "Dual Circulation" economic strategy. So, on the one hand, President Xi advocates supporting Chinese consumer spending and increasing import substitution to reduce the Chinese economy's dependence on foreign trade. On the other hand, Xi advocates strengthening other countries' dependence on Chinese technology, so that China can threaten to cut off their supply when necessary, as a form of deterrence. However, Xi criticizes other countries for "weaponizing" or "politicizing" supply chains in the context of the COVID-19 pandemic.

The playbooks in motion in the United States and China will have ripple effects across the world and through time they will fundamentally alter the way we, our children, and our grandchildren live, work, and relate to each other. As it stands today, this is a competition between the United States and China that is threatening to create a bifurcated global system particularly in areas such as 5G.

---

[8] "Is China's Soft Power Strategy Working," *Center for Strategic and International Studies*, August 26, 2020, https://chinapower.csis.org/is-chinas-soft-power-strategy-working/.

[9] Ben Murphy, "Translation: Certain Major Issues for Our National Medium- to Long-Term Economic and Social Development Strategy," *Center for Security and Emerging Technology*, November 10, 2020, https://cset.georgetown.edu/wp-content/uploads/t0235_Qiushi_Xi_economy_EN.pdf.

## A Roadmap for Leadership in Manufacturing, Tech, & Innovation

Preserving American leadership will require reconstituting a national manufacturing arrangement that is both safe and reliable—particularly in critical high-tech sectors.

There are five key steps that America, led by the new Biden Administration but working closely with the private sector, and non-profit organizations must take to maintain and increase its global lead in industrial technology. The first is to identify the minimum viable industrial capacity needed to deal with national emergencies and to be globally competitive. An obvious area of focus is semiconductors and microchips, which are indispensable to technological progress but made largely in Taiwan, a significant economy and ally of the United States which China believes to be a renegade province and has threatened to use military force to reunify with the Mainland. Active pharmaceutical ingredients (APIs) are another clear example. Approximately 80 percent of the API's used to procure drugs in America are believed to come from China and other countries like India. Next, America should procure access to reliable and abundant supplies of natural resources and integrate supply chains in a way that promotes the environment, sustainability, and good governance across the world. China has long been procuring these resources but doing it in a way that in many circumstances have promoted servitude and left little room for real partnerships. Education is a critical sector that the United States and China must collaborate more on. On April 28, 2021, President Biden addressed the U.S. Congress and the nation sharing his administration's accomplishments of his first 100 days in office. Consistent throughout his speech was preparing the United States for competition with China, which he argued is needed to "win the twenty-first century." He noted that China's President Xi is "deadly earnest about [China] becoming the most significant, consequential nation in the world."[10] Beyond the rivalry, Biden said he "welcomes" healthy competition with China, and that the United States is not "looking for conflict."[11] If the United States is to maintain its edge in cultural innovation it must

---

[10] "Remarks by President Biden in Address to a Joint Session of Congress," *White House*, April 29, 2021. https://www.whitehouse.gov/briefing-room/speeches-remarks/2021/04/29/remarks-by-president-biden-in-address-to-a-joint-session-of-congress/.

[11] Ibid.

also support international exchanges particularly in study abroad at both the high school, college, and graduate school level as well as increase professional exchanges between the United States and China. Congress should earmark funding to support these exchanges as they plant the seeds of innovation, cultural competency but more importantly life-long friendships which become invaluable in building the foundation of global trade, business, and economic linkages between the United States and China. The United States should also take a different approach and use this as an opportunity to rebuild multilateral institutions in Europe, fortify alliances in Asia and The Middle East, re-engage countries in Latin America and reimagine free trade agreements and commercial ties based on equity and respect on the continent of Africa. Third, America must build up a domestic base of the required talent via retraining and education. A study by McKinsey rated employee training among the top three factors reducing American competitiveness in manufacturing. The skills gap in the United States is large and takes many forms— it is unlikely that the problem can be solved by a single institutional actor. The problem is better approached multilaterally to create opportunities like apprenticeships focused on baseline skills, specialized digital training, and technical training. This also requires providing scholarships and modifying immigration policies to enable our world-class universities to attract, train, and harness the power of global talent. Fiona Zhou, President of The Global Institute of Financial Professionals, an NGO which provides certificate training programs in both the United States and China notes, "as the landscape for global talent becomes more intense professionals and employers will find that attaining continuing educational programs throughout ones career will become second nature in order to stay ahead of the competition." Fourth, investments must be made in hotbeds of innovations via public–private partnerships, research grants, and even in the earliest stages of venture capital. This also includes restoring critical federal funding for R&D, as there is no substitute for the government to lead by example. Last, de-emphasize weaponizing trade policy as this has both short and long-term implications in limiting market access and raising costs for American MNC's and United States innovation capabilities.

A starting point for America could be to revive the now-defunct Obama-era organization called the National Network of Manufacturing Innovation or Manufacturing USA. Manufacturing USA was a joint coordinated effort between DoE, NIST, NSF, and DoD to build specialized innovation sites around the country. The effort failed because it didn't go far enough to include private sector capital, expertise, and dynamism. Manufacturing USA was meant to more effectively compete with China's Five-Year Plan as it relates to technology and, properly revived, it can fulfill its mission. Infrastructure is another case in point. At Biden's first press conference as president he noted that "China spends three times more on infrastructure than the U.S."[12] Figures from the Council on Foreign Relations put United States spending at 2.4% of GDP, compared with 8% in China.[13] Bullet trains that travel about 100 miles between Shanghai and Hangzhou attain speeds of up to 215 miles an hour, covering the distance in about 65 min. It takes more than an hour and a half to go about as far on an Amtrak route which Mr. Biden knows well, between Wilmington, Del., and Washington.

President Biden in March of 2021 published his Interim National Security Strategic Guidance. The document puts China in a category potentially capable of combining its economic, diplomatic, military, and technological power to mount a sustained challenge to a stable and open international system.[14] It is critically important that the United States and China develop codes of conduct and be intentional about communicating and building mutual trust and mitigating risk and misunderstanding as the human and or economic cost for any kind of military conflict would be catastrophic for both nations, East Asia and the global community. The bottom line is: many have juxtaposed the current U.S. and China relationship to the Cold War. This is a misleading and dangerous comparison for the United States. The U.S.SR was a three-legged stool with two legs already wobbling. China is a full and sturdy chair, this is not a Grand Father Chair and this is not your grandparent's cold war. Gary Rieschel, Founder and Managing Partner of Qiming Venture Partners notes, "In any competition, there are moves and countermoves. It has been

---

[12] The White House, *Remarks by President Biden in Press Conference*, (Washington, DC: The White House, March 2021), https://www.whitehouse.gov/briefing-room/speeches-remarks/2021/03/25/remarks-by-president-biden-in-press-conference/.

[13] James McBride and Anshu Siripurapu, "The State of US Infrastructure," *Council on Foreign Relations*, April 8, 2021, https://www.cfr.org/backgrounder/state-us-infrastructure.

[14] The White House, *Interim National Security Strategic Guidance*, (Washington, DC: The White House, March 2021), https://www.whitehouse.gov/wp-content/uploads/2021/03/NSC-1v2.pdf.

decades since the U.S. has had an economic competitor that required any significant change in U.S. thinking. Japan was that competitor in the 80 s. China has become that competitor in the twenty-first century, and on a more comprehensive basis. Our responses to this should not eliminate the opportunity for future cooperation in areas of our mutual best interest." Moreover, we can equate the current geopolitical rivalry between Beijing and Washington as the United States playing defense and China playing more offense. If the U.S. government strategically develops partnerships with the private sector to enhance FDI in critical high-tech sectors and train and retrain the workforce effectively, this will create an ecosystem in which the United States will see advanced innovation, continue to employ millions of highly skilled and educated workers, and further the competitiveness of our high-tech sector to not just confront China, but to more effectively compete with China. America needs to define a winning strategy, which at its core begins at home. The United States needs to focus on its game, knowing that the best defense is a good offense. Failing to do so could risk the United States permanently losing its global technological leadership to China.

# CHAPTER 2

# "Welcome, but Verify": The Future of Chinese Companies Listed on the U.S. Stock Exchanges

*Kevin Chen*

**Abstract** The U.S.-listed Chinese companies have been the focus of Wall Street, Washington, and beyond. There have been plenty of new developments in this sector. Firstly, Chinese companies have launched many successful new IPOs on the U.S. stock exchanges. Secondly, accounting fraud and other irregularities in this sector have created major headlines. Regulators in the United States have forced several Chinese companies to delist. United States. Congressmen and Senators have called for a blanket ban on these companies. Through this chapter, we intend to review the historical development and current situation of Chinese companies

The views and opinions expressed in this chapter are those of the author and do not reflect the official policy or position of any organizations with which the author is affiliated

K. Chen (✉)
New York University, New York, NY, USA
e-mail: kc105@nyu.edu

listed in the United States, and outline some realistic approaches for the next decade. It needs to be stated clearly that there are tremendous benefits created by the Chinese companies that come to trade on the U.S. stock exchanges. A more collaborative and reciprocal relationship would be an achievable goal for the White House's new administration. Chinese companies should continue to be welcomed to the American stock exchanges, just like all other foreign companies. However, American accounting standards need to be applied rigorously. Management and controlling shareholders need to be held accountable for illicit behavior.

**Keywords** Chinese Listed · Companies · U.S. Stock Exchange · Delist · IPO · Chinese companies · Regulators

Since the beginning of the year 2020, the shares of U.S.-listed Chinese companies have been the focus of financial market participants and regulators globally. There have been plenty of new developments in this sector. Firstly, Chinese companies have launched many successful new IPOs on the U.S. stock exchanges. Secondly, accounting fraud and other irregularities in this sector have created major headlines. Regulators in the United States have forced several Chinese companies to delist. U.S. Congressmen and Senators have called for a blanket ban on these companies. Regulators in China and the United States have also taken cautious steps to scrutinize this sector. Through this chapter, we intend to review the historical development and current situation of Chinese companies listed in the United States and outline some realistic approaches for the next decade of Chinese companies listing in the U.S. stock exchanges.

## THE FOUR LISTING BOOMS OF CHINESE COMPANIES ON THE U.S. STOCK EXCHANGES

Chinese companies listed on the U.S. stock exchanges impact a very special sector of the U.S. stock market. They are commonly defined as businesses with main operating income from the Chinese mainland. The very first batches of them were mostly listed on the New York Stock Exchange (NYSE), but more recently, many of them chose the Nasdaq Stock Market for their listings. Some even chose smaller exchanges like Chicago or Boston for potential listings. The sector also includes Chinese companies listed in Hong Kong and then traded in the U.S. stock market in the form of American Deposit Receipts (ADRs). Many of the largest controlling shareholders (usually defined as more than 30 percent) or the actual controller are directly or indirectly affiliated with mainland Chinese private enterprises or individuals. There are a large number of domestic household names in China's stock market, but it is likely that U.S. investors are unfamiliar with them. From Tencent, Alibaba, to Industrial and Commercial Bank of China, to PetroChina and Sinopec, Chinese companies listed in the United States actually cover the Chinese economy's major industry sectors, from large state-owned enterprises to private enterprises. Therefore, when Chinese investors participate in U.S. stock market investment and trading, they often prefer to trade these stocks. For American institutional and retail investors who want to participate in Chinese economic growth, these stocks provide a convenient way to invest or speculate, without having to go to open a brokerage account in China or Hong Kong.

Since the 1990s, about 500 Chinese companies have publicly listed in the United States (U.S.CC, 2019). So far, about 160 companies are still listed on the three largest U.S. exchanges, with a market capitalization of about $1.3 trillion. The earliest batch of Chinese-owned companies listed in the United States were predominately State-Owned Enterprises (SOEs). They include: Shanghai Petrochemical listed on the New York Stock Exchange in 1993, Hua Neng Energy listed in 1994, China Southern Airlines and China Eastern Airlines listed in 1997, PetroChina listed in 2000, Sinopec listed in 2001 and so on. For the first time, the listing of these mega-cap state-owned enterprises (SOE) has given institutional investors in the United States an opportunity to participate in the rapid growth of China's economy. American investment legends, including Warren Buffett and George Soros, have also been involved in restructuring and investing capital in the IPOs of these large (SOE's). It can be said that the public listing of these Chinese enterprises has helped China reform its image and join the international capital market as well as introduce foreign capital.

The second batch of Chinese-listed stocks is closely linked to America's dotcom bubble of 2000. Chinese internet companies including Sina, NetEase, Sohu and others listed on the Nasdaq in the year 2000. These companies belonged to the first generation of the new Chinese Internet Portal. These private enterprises made global investors aware of the development of the internet in China, simultaneously bringing in capital to help domestic scientific and technological innovation to achieve rapid development. The listing of China Telecom in 2002, Agricultural Bank of China in 2003, and ICBC ADRin New York in 2006 also represented the pace of continued privatization of large Chinese (SOE's).

With Chinese search engine Baidu's United States listing in 2005, Chinese companies began a new round of listing booms in the United States. I remember Wall Street investment bankers on roadshows touting companies as China's "Google," China's "Amazon," China's "Netflix," or China's "Facebook." It can be said that this was the third batch of Chinese companies listing in the United States, beginning from 2005 and ending in 2008 during the global financial crisis, when the global financial market listing freeze ended. During this period, many more well-known Chinese companies began listing in the United States. In addition to Baidu, there were New Oriental education, Focus Media, 51Job online job market, and so on. China, as a huge market, grafts the mature business models that already exist in the United States, whether its search engines or job sites, and the chances of success are relatively high. Of course, with the occurrence of the 2008 financial crisis, many Chinese-owned enterprises have also experienced operational difficulties, performance decline, and their stock prices have fallen sharply. Some companies were even asked to delist because of persistently low share prices, hovering in single digits.

A new period of global economic growth, which began in 2010, has also led to a fourth round of listings of Chinese stocks in the United States. There is no doubt that Alibaba's listing on the New York Stock Exchange in 2014 was a highlight of the 4th wave. Alibaba's IPO raised a world record $25 billion. The most prominent location in the lobby of the New York Stock Exchange is a historic photograph of Alibaba's celebration on the trading floor when it went public. Mr. Ma's speech at the Economic Club of New York demonstrated the high popularity of Chinese entrepreneurs on Wall Street. This round of listing boom covers many industries: e-commerce industry giant JD.com, online education giant Good Future, video-on-demand industry iQiyi, fun headlines, online insurance unicorn 360 financial, internet loans companies, health care providers, electric vehicle manufacturers, cloud computing, coffee chains and so on. This round of listed Chinese companies are mainly private enterprises, new start-ups, but also spin-off units like Weibo, Tencent Music, and other business units from already listed Chinese companies. From the start of 2020 to date, despite the Covid-19 outbreak, the listing of Chinese shares on the U.S. stock market does not seem to have been affected in any respect. In terms of the number of IPOs, capital raised, and performance post IPOs, 2020 has actually exceeded all previous years.

## BENEFITS CREATED BY CHINESE COMPANIES LISTED ON AMERICAN STOCK EXCHANGES

There are tremendous benefits created by the Chinese companies that trade on U.S. stock exchanges. Like all other publicly traded companies, they pay a listing fee, hire professional service providers like lawyers, accountants, marketers, and bankers. This sector has probably directly and indirectly created thousands of high-paying jobs in the United States. In addition, these companies pay various taxes and contribute to the American economy. Their shareholder meetings tend to attract a large number of attendees.

From a macro point of view, a vibrant group of new Chinese companies joining New York Stock Exchange and Nasdaq helped in maintaining New York City as the financial capital of the world. The capital formation function of the stock listing tends to create huge amounts of wealth, which contribute to the economy. The number of publicly traded companies have also been in decline in the United States for the past twenty years. According to World Bank, the number of public traded companies in the U.S. peaked in 1996 at 8,090. Since then, by 2018, due to merger acquisition, bankruptcy, management buyout, etc., the number is at 4,307. That represents an almost 50% decrease in the number of publicly traded companies (Fig. 2.1).

As the second-largest economy in the world, with relatively high growth, China has produced some of the most critical private enterprises for the new millennium. It is vital for many of these companies to come trade in U.S. stock exchanges.

## CRISES FACED BY THE CHINESE COMPANIES LISTED IN THE UNITED STATES

Over the last three decades, nearly 500 Chinese companies have listed in the United States. So far, one-third of them have continued normal business operations. The other two-thirds no longer trade due to the following cases: privatization, de-listing, or bankruptcy. There is no doubt

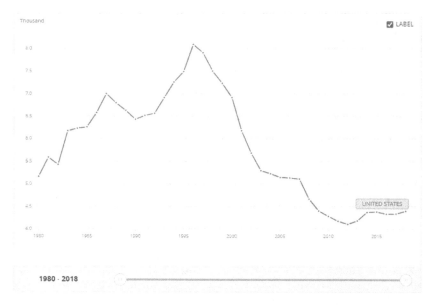

**Fig. 2.1** Number of publicly traded Companies in the United States (1980–2018) (*Source* "Listed domestic companies, total—United States," *The World Bank*, accessed January 10, 2021, https://data.worldbank.org/indicator/CM.MKT.LDOM.NO?locations=US)

that China's reform and opening, capital market development, scientific and technological innovation have played a significant role. For institutional investors in Europe and the United States, china's equity stocks as a whole have also helped them achieve substantial wealth benefits. Investors involved in long-term investments in Alibaba, ICBC, or Tencent Music have all received very high returns. However, it is undeniable that in the past two decades, Chinese companies have also had many crises, which has led to losses for many investors. Reasons for the multiple crises in the Chinese companies listed in the United States include the following:

### Systemic Risk Factors in the U.S. Stock Market

Chinese companies are an integral part of the U.S. stock market, so if the U.S. economy is in recession, China's stock is likely to fall even more.

As a result, investors need to keep a close eye on U.S. employment data, manufacturing data, real estate data, and other U.S. macroeconomic data, as well as other overseas economies such as Europe and Japan. If Brazil, Russia, India, and other emerging markets experience risk events, illiquidity, and other issues, it will also impact the price stability of Chinese stocks since China's equity stocks are broadly classified as global emerging market equity investment. Thus, Chinese companies in the U.S. experienced a major crisis in 2008 when the sub-prime crisis hit.

### *The Issue of Trust in the Chinese Companies' Financial Reports*

The issue of trust in China's listed companies in the United States has been a concern for investors, as there have been many accounting fraud cases. Chinese companies have faced an unprecedented crisis of confidence in the U.S. stock market. The Securities and Exchange Commission (SEC) listing more than 200 de-listing, many of them by Chinese companies. In 2011, a United States accounting firm reported a Chinese client to the U.S. SEC on alleged financial fraud, noting that several other companies were also suspected of fraud. Since March 2019, more than 20 stocks have been exposed to audit problems. Nearly 20 companies have been suspended or delisted, followed by the relevant brokerages issued a warning. Chinese stock integrity crises began to cause collective panic and selling by investors. Also, Chinese companies' legal structure is often opaque, which often result in U.S. investors questioning the governance structure. In 2020, the U.S. SEC issued a specific financial disclosure of China's shares and other notices and again prompted the risk of China's shares. The information asymmetry in financial markets between China and the United States often created excessively negative perceptions. In early 2017, there was news of an evaluation and re-licensing of Internet portals by the Ministry of Broadcasting and Television in China. Chinese internet stocks in the United States fell 15 percent on the day because the news was interpreted as a systemic risk by U.S. institutional investors (Fig. 2.2).

### *Hunted by Short Sellers*

In the U.S stock exchanges, if you are bearish on a stock, you can short the stock meaning you can bet that the stock will decline and profit from that expectation if it occurs. Any investor with a securities trading account

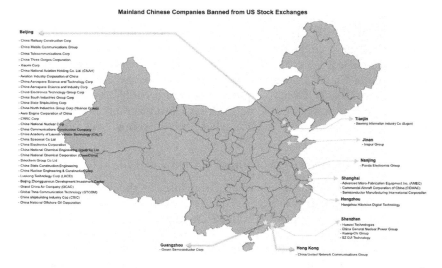

**Fig. 2.2** Mainland Chinese Companies Banned from U.S. Stock Exchanges[1]) (*Source* "DOD Releases List of Additional Companies, In Accordance with Section 1237 of FY99 NDAA," The Department of Defense, the United States, January 14, 2021, https://www.defense.gov/Newsroom/Releases/Release/Article/2472464/dod-releases-list-of-additional-companies-in-accordance-with-section-1237-of-fy/. On May 12th The U.S. Department of Defense agreed to remove Chinese smartphone maker Xiaomi from a government blacklist which reverses a key Trump-era action and clears the way for the future American investment into the company. "Pentagon Agrees to remove Chinese Smartphone Giant Xiaomi from Trump -Era Blacklist," *Forbes*, May 12, 2021. https://www.forbes.com/sites/siladityaray/2021/05/12/pentagon-agrees-to-remove-chinese-smartphone-giant-xiaomi-from-trump-era-blacklist/?sh=4308327548c4)

[1] The infographic was created by Koji Kanao, Technology Director at Pivotal Advisors, and Yijie Liu, Research Analyst at Pivotal Advisors

can either go long or go short. Hedge funds are often the leading operators of shorting. U.S. stocks do not limit the percentage of rise and fall of the stock price, so the volatility of Chinese stocks in the United States is likely to be extremely large.

There are two ways to short a stock: one can borrow a certain amount of stock from a third-party institution and sell it at the current market price, or one can buy the "put option" of a stock and bet that the stock goes down. When the share price falls, short sellers can repurchase it at the price after the fall and return the borrowed stock. The difference between selling and buying is the profit from the investment after paying fees from the securities firm. If investors own "put options," which is the right to sell at the specified price before a specific date, they can profit from the drop as well. This method is less risky than the first approach, and the loss is limited to the option's cost. When a stock is suspended, the shorter's gain is the share price at the time of the sale, which is deducted from the borrowing fee at the suspension time. If the stock never resumes trading and its share price is equivalent to zero, the shorter's return is theoretically 100%. Notable short sellers like Muddy Water, Citron Research, and others have issued many bearish reports on Chinese companies.

These companies targeted by short sellers share many commonalities:

1. **High price-to-earnings ratios.** Most of the companies that encounter shorting are among the most expensively priced stocks.
2. **Small market capitalization.** Most of the targets of the short sellers are valued between $50 million and $500 million.
3. **Many of the companies targeted by short sellers are in the process of issuing new stocks.** Because of the SEC rules for registration, the newly issued stocks could be traded immediately. It might lead the subscribers, before the allocation, to choose to short the stocks, and then on the day of subscription with the subscription of new shares to close arbitrage.
4. **During the trade negotiations between China and the United States in 2019, due to the impact of a lot of negative news, Chinese companies in the United States also encountered a lot of shorting.**

Of course, the financial fraud of Luckin Coffee in early 2020, and the subsequent suspension of the company from Nasdaq, should not be under stated. Luckin Coffee belonged to a large-cap blue chip in the Chinese stock market and was often benchmarked against Starbucks. Consumer stocks are the European and American institutional investors' favorite long-term investment target. Luckin Coffee, on the other hand, once had a large fan base in the European and American markets, but now has joined many other questionable companies at home in China.

## "Welcome, but Verify": The Future of Chinese Companies in the United States

There has been a lot of discussion over the past two decades about the future of Chinese stocks on Wall Street. Pessimists have repeatedly predicted that this sector will disappear from Wall Street. However, after each crisis, there is a new round of listing booms. The author is extremely optimistic about China's equity stocks' overall prospects, which will still be an important part of China and the United States' capital markets. The current total market capitalization of $1.3 trillion will only continue to rise, not disappear. KE Holdings (BEKE), China's largest housing platform operating under the Lianjia and Beike brands, raised $2.1 billion in August 2020 in the largest U.S. IPO from a Chinese issuer since 2018 and posted the best first-day pop of 71% for a billion-dollar IPO since 2000. It has achieved a market capitalization of more than $75 billion. A total market capitalization of more than $3 trillion over the next decade is a conservative expectation.

The core reason for the continued growth and development of Chinese companies listed in the United States is that the existence and development of these Chinese companies is in both China and the U.S.' mutual interest—there is no doubt that it is a win–win situation. First, for Wall Street, the continued growth of China's stock market has increased trading opportunities and helped the three largest United States exchanges gain global standing. Over the past three decades, the number of publicly traded companies in the United States has fallen from more than 8,000 to 4,000. U.S. institutional investors urgently need newly listed companies to invest in the target. Many Chinese stocks are high-growth enterprises in Internet, finance, medical health, consumer goods, and other industries that have huge growth potential. Many U.S. buyer institutional investors have difficulty opening an account in Shanghai or Shenzhen to buy A-shares, with exchange rate risk, tax uncertainty, overseas account opening, and others posing operational obstacles. The United States listing provides an incredibly convenient channel for U.S. pensions, university endowments, and other institutions to invest in China and participate in China's economic growth.

For China's economy, the continuous introduction of foreign investment for medium- and long-term healthy growth is essential. Especially in recent years, there has been a net outflow of capital items in China, and foreign exchange reserves have declined. As an important way to attract international capital into China, China's equity stocks have an irreplaceable position. And in the face of some counter-globalization voices in recent years, China's stock market's activeness in the U.S. capital market can bring very positive voices.

More importantly, is the brand effect of Chinese companies listed in the U.S. China's outstanding enterprises in various industries have constantly been going abroad to become genuine, global multinational companies.

Of course, strengthening the supervision of Chinese companies in the United States is also in line with protecting investors' interests. Over the past two decades, many Chinese companies' financial fraud has seriously damaged the image of Chinese companies. Some of the companies' management infringed on the rights and interests of small shareholders. They were not willing to pay dividends nor buy back shares. These bad governance habits are gradually being changed. The improvement of corporate governance structure is also very worthy of promotion to improve the image of Chinese companies listed in the United States, to improve the valuation of Chinese companies listed in the United States, and to create several successful private enterprises in China. We believe that in the next decade, Chinese companies in the United States will continue the process of survival of the fittest, many high-quality Chinese general stocks will continue to come to the New York Stock Exchange or the Nasdaq to list. Simultaneously, some of the problem enterprises will also face more stringent supervision or even be delisted from the market.

A more collaborative and reciprocal relationship would be an achievable goal for the White House's new administration. Chinese companies shall continue to be welcomed to the American stock exchanges, just like all the other companies from Asia, Europe, Latin America, or Africa. However, American accounting standards need to be applied rigorously. Management and controlling shareholders need to be held accountable for illicit behavior.

"Trust, But Verify" is a Russian proverb that President Reagan used during his negotiations with the Soviet Union. We suggest "Welcome, But Verify" as the core approach for the Chinese companies in the U.S. capital market.

# CHAPTER 3

# Competitive Energy and Climate Statecraft Between China and the United States

*Carolyn Kissane*

**Abstract** Looking back at the last four years of media headlines, a picture of an adversarial relationship between China and the United States appears as the central narrative; a bilateral relationship that is highly stressed. This narrative includes tough rhetoric focusing on the ongoing trade war, threats of technological decoupling, and the use of harsh economic statecraft in the form of sanctions and high tariffs. Ties with Beijing were tense and contentious under the last U.S. administration, where strong man and militaristic language was the norm. Think of U.S.–China trade war, and the verbiage against China. Former President Trump made China a target of harsh rhetoric with the aim to limit China's growing global power. What U.S. foreign policy failed to consider

The views and opinions expressed in this chapter are those of the author and do not reflect the official policy or position of any organizations with which the author is affiliated.

C. Kissane (✉)
NYU Center for Global Affairs, New York, NY, USA
e-mail: carolyn.kissane@nyu.edu

© The Author(s), under exclusive license to Springer Nature Singapore Pte Ltd. 2021
E. Carr Jr. (ed.), *From Trump to Biden and Beyond*,
https://doi.org/10.1007/978-981-16-4297-5_3

was how far ahead China was in many of the areas the United States had historically led on, and how China was undergoing its own national and international security repositioning. It was and remains a contest for power, but where does energy and climate come in, are these areas also prone to discontent?

**Keywords** Energy · Statecraft · China · U.S. · Energy Security · Renewable energy · Net-zero · Climate change

## INTRODUCTION

Looking back at the last four years of media headlines, a picture of an adversarial relationship between China and the United States appears as the central narrative; a bilateral relationship that is highly stressed. This narrative includes tough rhetoric focusing on the ongoing trade war, threats of technological decoupling, and the use of harsh economic statecraft in the form of sanctions and high tariffs. Ties with Beijing were tense and contentious under the last U.S. administration, where strong man and militaristic language was the norm. Think of U.S.–China trade war, and the verbiage against China.[1] Former President Trump made China a target of harsh rhetoric with the aim to limit China's growing global power. What U.S. foreign policy failed to consider was how far ahead China was in many of the areas the United States had historically led on, and how China was undergoing its own national and international security repositioning. It was and remains a contest for power, but where does energy and climate come in, are these areas also prone to discontent?

The geopolitics of energy, traditional hydrocarbons such as oil, natural gas and coal, and now also, for renewable energy and the inputs required to foster deep decarbonization, are experiencing a period of discontinuity. Chinese leadership in clean energy investment continues to alter the clean energy landscape.[2] Demands for deep decarbonization and climate

---

[1] Richard Fontaine, "Why Biden Won't Reset on China," *Australian Financial Review*, January 28, 2021, https://www.afr.com/world/north-america/why-biden-won-t-reset-on-china-20210128-p56xhx.

[2] Llewelyn Hughes and Jonas Meckling, "The Politics of Renewable Energy Trade: The US–China Solar Dispute," *Energy Policy* 105 (C), 2017, pp. 256–262.

change mitigation and adaptation are driving new policies and practices, in the United States, China, and around the world. The proverbial energy deck of cards is being reshuffled and new hands will allow different states to wield outsized influence in geopolitics, this is especially true for China and the United States because of their towering influence as the largest consumers and producers of many different sources of energy and the technologies that support the ongoing evolution of the global energy transition.

The world's two superpowers remain connected on energy trade, and an increasingly co-dependent relationship for energy and climate security, or what Ryan Hass refers to as U.S.–China competitive interdependence.[3] An area in need of examination is how energy and climate statecraft are part of a new dynamic between the world's two superpowers. While both China and the United States remain the behemoths of the energy world, it is important to recognize how their priorities diverge and also merge. The United States witnessed an energy renaissance with extraction potential for oil and natural gas catapulting the United States into one of the world's largest oil and gas producers, while China is rich in coal, it remains increasingly deficient in oil and gas, making it susceptible to energy insecurity. In response, China has shifted gears to make the production and export of renewable energy technologies part of its larger grand strategy, employing smart energy statecraft in the process.[4]

Will the next four years under the Biden administration usher in a new era of cooperation and possible collaboration with China? Will the United States and China change direction to work more closely with the other? The glass half full camp might think so, but there's also a strong probability the relationship will remain frayed and decisively competitive; both will use the other as the target of blaming and shaming, but even under this scenario the two countries have a number of issues where even if they are not on the same page, the connections are many, namely, energy and climate change. When Biden's foreign policy emphasizes standing "shoulder to shoulder with U.S. allies and key partners" what does that

[3] Ryan Hass, *Stronger: Adapting America's China Strategy in an Age of Competitive Interdependence*, (Yale University Press, 2021).

[4] Morgan Bazilian, Benjamin Sovacool, and Todd Moss, "Rethinking Energy Statecraft: United States Foreign Policy and the Changing Geopolitics of Energy," *Global Policy* 8 (3), June 28, 2017.

mean for China?[5] Dramatic changes in policy and practice are underway with the Biden administration—with energy and climate being high-rung priority areas for the United States. And also, for China.

This chapter aims to look at the last four years and possibilities for the next decade of the energy relationship between China and the United States. The United States and China have been in competition for years, but the last four, were an especially acute time for great power competition and rivalry. Can we reimagine the relationship under a more cooperative lens or will hegemonic power competition stand in the way? The jury is still out. This chapter seeks to explore how shifting global dynamics are fostering new approaches to energy and climate statecraft. Specifically, the chapter explores energy security and grand strategy and the rapidly changing geopolitics of renewable energy and climate change. Each of these will be explored to better understand the ways energy and climate statecraft impact U.S.–Sino relations.

## FUELING THE WORLD'S HUNGRY GIANTS: ENERGY SECURITY AND GRAND STRATEGY

China and the United States are energy superpowers. Both countries' economies are inextricably tied to energy, for economic growth, national and international security. Both employ what is best described as an all of the above energy strategy, focused on securing hydrocarbons while also developing and strengthening domestic production of clean and renewable energy technologies. The United States and China are the largest energy consumers, and represent the top two countries for fossil fuel demand, oil and gas. China is the world's largest consumer and producer of coal, and China is taking a firm lead on green energy production. To understand the position of the two largest energy users it is critical to consider what energy security is and how it fits within each country's grand strategy? Daniel Yergin defines energy security as "the capability to assure adequate, reliable energy supplies at reasonable prices in ways that do not jeopardize major national values and objectives."[6] This definition integrates economic, security, and ideological elements in addition

---

[5] Elise Labott, "Biden Puts a Kinder, Gentler Spin on America First," *Foreign Policy*, February 5, 2021, https://foreignpolicy.com/2021/02/05/biden-foreign-policy-speech-america-first/.

[6] Daniel Yergin, *The Prize*, (New York: Simon & Schuster, 1994), 67.

to the core necessity of ensuring access to adequate supplies. However, energy security today is about more than access, supply, and affordability. Meghan O'Sullivan goes further with her definition of energy security. She integrates how countries can account for things beyond energy access into their foreign policy. She defines energy security as "having access to affordable energy without having to contort one's political, security, diplomatic, or military arrangements unduly."[7] While the mid-twentieth century version of energy security centered on access and supply, especially for oil and gas, the twenty-first century is moving toward O'Sullivan's more nuanced and multilayered understanding of energy security to include access to critical resources, and to ensure energy security does not preclude environmental security. Energy security today is not synonymous with energy independence. Energy independence is often cited as a goal for individual countries, but it is a fallacy and a myth; it is impossible to ever be energy independent, and national energy security is always tied to resources and trade with other countries. Jason Bordoff describes energy security in this way, "Energy security comes from being more, not less, connected with the rest of the world."[8] China and the United States are the two greatest examples of energy interdependence, and their own policies and strategies reveal the importance of connections and interdependence and the critical role of secure trade and access to the resources required to sustain and support national economies.

Rapidly increasing energy demand has made China influential in world energy markets. Despite structural changes to China's economy during the past few years, China's energy demand is expected to increase, and government policies support cleaner fuel use and energy efficiency measures.[9] China consumed an estimated 14.5 million Barrels Per Day (b/d) of petroleum and other liquids in 2019, up 500,000 b/d, or nearly 4%, from 2018.[10] In 2017 China surpassed the United States as the

[7] Meghan O'Sullivan, "The Entanglement of Energy, Grand Strategy, and International Security," *Handbook of Global Energy Policy*, ed. Andreas Goldthau, (Malden: Wiley-Blackwell, 2013).

[8] Jason Bordoff, "The Myth of Energy Independence Has Gone up in Smoke," *Foreign Policy*, September 18, 2021, http://foreignpolicy-com.proxy.library.nyu.edu/2019/09/18/the-myth-of-u-s-energy-independence-has-gone-up-in-smoke/.

[9] "China," *U.S. Energy Information Administration*, September 30, 2020, http://eia.gov/international/analysis/country/CHN.

[10] Ibid.

largest importer of oil, coming in at 7.2 million barrels a day (mbd), and six years later, China continues to hold the top spot; in 2021 imports closer to 14 mbd. The Middle East, Latin America, Africa, and Russia are regions China depends on to feed its oil appetite, and it also imports energy from the United States. According to the EIA, 67.3 percent of China's crude oil supply in 2019 came from imports.[11] This dependence on foreign energy is likely to increase. Some estimates have suggested that by 2040 around 80 percent of China's oil needs will be sourced from elsewhere.[12] Today the U.S. ships LNG and oil to China illustrating China's diversified energy strategy, and its aim to limit over-dependency on one country or region of the world.

China employs all of the above strategy toward its own energy security. It aims not to be dependent on any one country, and takes a diversified approach toward oil imports.[13] China depends on critical sea lanes for its oil and LNG, and they want to diminish vulnerabilities, a driver behind the country's ambitious electric vehicle policies. Today there are over 100 Chinese companies making electric cars and buses. The Chinese car manufacturer BYD is now the largest producer of electric vehicles in the world, with another six Chinese firms also ranking in the top 20. Aside from China's development of alternatives to critical hydrocarbons it continues to seek deals and arrangements to secure oil and gas. China recently signed a U.S. $400 billion-dollar twenty-five-year cooperation agreement with Iran that involves China securing oil for loans it will grant to Iran.

China has deployed a multi-pronged global energy strategy that ensures continued economic growth and energy security.[14] These twin drivers, coupled with an increasingly distant global energy supply chain,

[11] "Country Analysis Executive Summary: China," *EIA*, September 30, 2020, https://www.eia.gov/international/content/analysis/countries_long/China/china.pdf.

[12] Tsvetana Paraskova, "China Set to Become More Dependent on Oil Imports," *Oilprice.com*, December 5, 2017, https://oilprice.com/Energy/Crude-Oil/China-Set-To-Become-More-Dependent-On-Oil-Imports.html.

[13] "Energy in China's New Era," *The State Council Information Office of the People's Republic of China*, December 2020, http://www.scio.gov.cn/zfbps/32832/Document/1695135/1695135.htm.

[14] Lirong Wang, "Sea Lanes and Chinese National Energy Security," *Journal of Coastal Research*, Winter 2015.

require China's leadership to include energy as a priority in decision-making abroad. China has been working to diversify both its domestic power mix and the sources of its imports, preventing any one supplier or technology from gaining too much influence within its economy. China must make strategic decisions about the material of its energy investments. Put simply, China's relative abundance of coal provides the country with a degree of energy security derived from central government policy control that imported gas simply does not.[15]

Trump, early in his presidency in 2017, was the first president to move America's energy narrative from one of seeking independence to achieving dominance. In November 1973, President Nixon launched Project Independence and pledged to wean the United States off of foreign oil and every U.S. president since Nixon has pledged energy independence as a national target. In 2020, for the first time since 1973 the United States exported more oil abroad than it imported. The United States can produce up to 12–13 (mbd) and is producing close to 100 billion cubic feet per day. In simpler terms, the United States could be called a petro-power. This power also translates into its relationship with China. China is a taker of U.S. oil and LNG and in 2019 Phase One of the U.S.–China Trade Deal included the requirement of China purchasing over $59 billion in U.S. energy, specifically in the purchase of U.S. liquefied natural gas.[16] What is interesting here, is China was already importing oil and gas from the United States, and economists have argued rather than strengthening U.S. energy exports to China, the deal only drove China to strategically position itself away from reliance on U.S. energy. The deal, and the energy trade between the U.S. and China illustrates how both are in some ways tethered to the other.

The United States and Trump's narrative shift from energy independence to dominance matters, and it was a direct aim at China which is natural resource dependent on imports, but what Trump didn't gamble on was China's move to reduce import dependencies, and build out its

---

[15] Carolyn Kissane, "The Quest for Energy Security China, the United States and the Future of Central Asia," *China, the United States, and the Future of Central Asia*, ed. Denoon.

[16] Chad Brown, "Anatomy of a Flop: Why Trump's Phase One of US-China Trade Deal Fell Short," *Petersen Institute for International Economics*, February 8, 2021, https://piie.com/blogs/trade-and-investment-policy-watch/anatomy-flop-why-trumps-us-china-phase-one-trade-deal-fell.

own export model for renewable and clean energy technologies. Anyone who understands energy markets and trade knows energy independence was an inspiring sound bite, but it could never be a reality. The United States still imports oil but now imports more from our northern and southern neighbors Canada and Mexico than from the Middle East, and specifically Saudi Arabia. China depends on imports from Saudi Arabia, Russia, the Gulf and Brazil, and many other oil-producing countries. Trump prioritized fossil fuel production and positioned the United States as an oil and gas producing energy power, while diminishing the importance of renewable energy in the context of U.S. energy statecraft.

The idea of energy dominance in the United States called for using oil and liquefied natural gas exports for leverage and influence. The energy cushion was meant to allow the United States to engage in different ways with old and new allies. The problem is the timing. Trump's energy vision was stuck in the past and not in the energy realities of today and the rapidly unfolding future of energy. The United States is rich in energy resources, both hydrocarbons and renewables, but today it is imperative to support more decarbonized sources of energy, and China being oil and gas deficient saw this space as a strategic opening. China's dependency on fossil fuel imports is helping to drive its move toward being the export market of choice for renewable energy and the technologies required to reach deep decarbonization. Under U.S. President Biden, the United States is now moving toward prioritizing less carbon-intensive forms of energy, and using a "whole of government approach" to address climate change and the energy transition. Energy security in the first quarter of the twenty-first century still involves fossil fuels, but the urgency of addressing climate change means energy security intersects with climate security, and new sources of energy are beginning to challenge the old energy status quo.

## SECURITY AND (IN)SECURITY: BELT AND ROAD INITIATIVE AND SOUTH CHINA SEA

In 2013 China launched the Belt Road Initiative, considered by many to be the cornerstone of economic and energy statecraft for the country. Its aim is to promote more interconnected, Chinese-funded physical and digital infrastructure across many regions of the world.[17] The United States views BRI as China seeking to advance its geopolitical ambitions, and increasing dependency on Chinese infrastructure and human capital. China's BRI, which Beijing hopes will reorient the global economy from U.S.–Europe to China, features energy as a key pillar. China's energy dominance is strengthened not only through its manufacturing capacity but also via its role as a leading energy project financier and developer. Under the umbrella of its Belt Road Initiative (BRI) China accelerated its development and funding for coal-fired power plants abroad, despite its concerted domestic efforts to reduce coal-fired contribution to its power mix through coal-to-gas fuel switching. From Kenya to Pakistan, China has been financing and building coal-fired power plants in a bid to ensure continued demand for its coal and thereby maintain the livelihoods of the large coal mining community; an example of domestic demands impacting geopolitics.[18] China has shifted gear after criticism around its exports of high emitting carbon energy projects, such as coal. China has reframed BRI to also have a green agenda.[19] An instrument of influence and power China has employed is through financing of overseas energy projects. Between 2017–2020 China financed $49 billion worth of energy projects, while between 2013–2016 financed $73 billion,[20] with many of these projects in Africa, Asia, and Latin America, regions where China seeks a stronger and more impactful foothold.

The Chinese-Turkmen national gas pipeline, Line D is an example of a BRI project. The project reduces Turkmenistan's dependence on Russia by providing the landlocked country with an alternative transit route for natural gas, and China gains competitive advantage by locking Turkmenistan into long-term loans for gas, and ultimately diminishes U.S.

[17] Daniel Kliman, Rush Doshi, Kristine Lee, and Zack Cooper, "Grading China's Belt and Road," *Center for a New American Security*, April 8, 2019, http://cnas.org/public ations/reports/beltandroad.

[18] Carolyn Kissane, "The Upending of the Geopolitics of Energy: Disruption Is the New Normal," *The Future of Global Affairs: Managing Discontinuity, Disruption and Destruction*, eds. Christopher Ankersen and Waheguru Pal Singh Sidhu, (New York: Palgrave Macmillan, 2020).

[19] Jonathan Elkind, "Toward a Green Belt and Road," *Columbia University Center on Global Energy Policy*, April 25, 2019, https://www.energypolicy.columbia.edu/research/commentary/toward-real-green-belt-and-road.

[20] Kevin P. Gallagher, "China's Global Energy Finance," *Global Development Policy Center, Boston University*, https://www.bu.edu/cgef/#/2020/EnergySource.

influence in a strategically important region. This is just one example of the many projects China has invested in across BRI participating countries. One of the main criticisms of China and its BRI ambitions is that it is a means of exporting carbon-emitting technologies, and ultimately, a way for China to export stranded carbon as it transitions away from coal toward cleaner less carbon-emitting sources of energy. This argument comes out of the push to export coal-fired technologies and power plants to countries across Asia which ultimately contributes to pollution and growing reliance on Chinese produced energy production plants.

Maritime trade routes are the cornerstone of the energy market and more broadly, global trade. Almost 80 percent of all trade is by sea, with up to one-third passing through the South China Sea. Over 64 percent of China's maritime trade transited the SCS in 2016, while nearly 42 percent of Japan's maritime trade passed through the SCS in the same year.[21] A region where tensions remain high, and where the United States recognizes a threat to the free flow of trade is in the South China Sea. China has expanded its reach through the construction of new islands and establishment of military bases remains a point of heated potential for conflict. The United States has assured allies such as Japan and Vietnam it will protect their sovereignty and interests in the region, but there is concern over China's larger motivations and fears over possible obstruction or blockades of the maritime trade which passes through the South China Sea.

Maritime security has been the purview of the United States which has since the end of WWII served to secure the seas. The fear of China obstructing trade in the South China Sea is overblown. China would only be harming its own interests and security if it were to in any way impede the free flow of goods and trade. What is more of an unknown is China's quest to extract and nationalize the resources in the region. Estimates put the amount of recoverable oil reserves to be over 30 billion barrels, and an event more abundant amount of natural gas deposits. Is extraction and control of natural resources behind the simmering tensions in the SCS? The CNOOC Chairman Wang Yilin, for instance, has justified the "mission" of its first deep-water oil rig 981 on August 8, 2012 not just on commercial reasons. The commissioning of the oil rig was described as

---

[21] China Power Team, "How Much Trade Transits the South China Sea?," *China Power*, August 2, 2017, updated January 25, 2021, https://chinapower.csis.org/much-trade-transits-south-china-sea/.

a "mobile national territory" to help "ensure our country's energy security, advance maritime-power strategy and safeguard our nation's maritime sovereignty."[22] The United States is the only countervailing force that has the naval capabilities to contain China's claims and assertions in the region.

## CHINA: THE WORLD'S GREEN GIANT?[23]

Chinese President Xi Jinping came to power with a new set up strategic goals and priorities. A shift in foreign policy and economic statecraft, as illustrated in the Belt Road Initiative, a more focused and outward pivot toward taking on the United States in technological and military competition and forging a green domestic and international agenda. "Since assuming office in 2012, Chinese President Xi Jinping has turned to a new strategy: a pivot to renewable energy." China dominates the solar-panel market, and is rapidly expanding and capturing market share in the production of clean energy technologies, from batteries, wind turbines, and electric vehicles. Beginning in 2015, China's central government began promoting the development of electric vehicles as part of "Made in China 2025," a government backed push for the nation to pursue and lead in key technologies like artificial intelligence and electric vehicle (EV) over the following decade.[24] "The goal is not just to reduce China's dependence on foreign oil and gas but also to avoid putting the country at an economic disadvantage relative to the United States, which will see its own growth boosted by its exports of oil and gas to China."[25]

In the absence of U.S. global clean energy and climate leadership under Trump, China stepped in to take the lead. While the U.S. stepped back from global leadership in green energy and nuclear technology,

[22] Frank Umbach, "The South China Sea Disputes: The Energy Dimension," *The Institute for Strategic, Political, Security and Economic Consultancy*, July 2017, https://ethz.ch/content/dam/ethz/special-interest/gess/cis/center-for-securities-studies/resources/docs/ISPSW-494_Umbach%20(2).pdf.

[23] Ibid.

[24] Eli Binder, "China's EV Startup Boom," *The Wire: China*, April 25, 2019, https://www.thewirechina.com/2021/02/07/chinas-ev-startup-boom/.

[25] Amy M. Jaffee, "Green Giant: Renewable Energy and Chinese Power," *Foreign Affairs*, March/April, 2018, https://www.foreignaffairs.com/articles/china/2018-02-13/green-giant.

China positioned itself not only as a global manufacturer of green technology but as an innovator and technical partner. China holds 30 percent of global renewable energy patents; 150,000 compared to the United States' 100,000. It is the world's leading producer of solar panels, wind turbines, batteries, and EVs. China has been the top investor in clean energy projects for nine of the last ten years, according to the Frankfurt School of Finance and Management. Over the last two decades China has invested more than $244 billion in energy projects across the globe. It has helped develop over 12.6 gigawatts of solar in South and South East Asia over the last fifteen years. China and domestic entities have produced, engineered, financed, and developed renewable energy projects from Argentina and Brazil to Mexico, Scotland, Ethiopia, and Turkey. These and other programs have been rolled out as part of a deliberate effort to rebrand China as the world's environmental champion. China is hedging its bets positioning itself as the energy manufacturer, financier, and expert for the emission-free, low emission energy future.[26]

President Xi Jinping put forward a new energy security strategy focusing on a vision of innovative, coordinated, green, open, and shared development focusing on reforming the ways energy is consumed, to build a clean and diversified energy supply system, to implement an innovation-driven energy strategy, to further the reform of the energy system, and enhancing international energy cooperation. 2060 net-neutral pledge will require an absolute overhaul of its current energy system. In 2013, China declared a war on pollution and since then particulate pollution has decreased, the University of Chicago estimates that "between 2013 and 2016 air pollution improved by 21 to 42 percent in China's most populated areas."[27] And in 2018 China launched a three-year plan of action for "winning the war to protect blue skies" aimed at significantly reducing the concentration of pollution in the air, reduce the number of days of heavy pollution, and improve the quality of the environment.[28]

---

[26] Carolyn Kissane, "The Upending of the Geopolitics of Energy. Disruption Is the New Normal," *The Future of Global Affairs*, eds. Ankersen and Sidhu.

[27] Michael Greenstone, "EPIC-China," *Energy Policy Institute at the University of Chicago*, https://epic.uchicago.edu/area-of-focus/epic-china/.

[28] "Guowuyuan guanyu yinfa da ying lantian baowei zhan san nian xingdong jihua de tong" 国务院关于印发打赢蓝天保卫战三年行动计划的通知, [Three Year Plan of Action for Winning the War to Protect Blue Skies], *State Council, People's Republic of China*, 2018, http://www.gov.cn/zhengce/content/2018-07/03/content_5303158.htm.

China's energy conundrum is best understood by looking at its past growth trajectory. The country has moved hundreds of millions out of poverty and moved to be the world's manufacturing giant. This growth required building new cities and supporting heavy industry. China accounts for around half of global consumption of steel, copper, aluminum, and cement. The structure of Chinese growth has locked in high levels of energy intensity. This combination of an energy-intensive growth model and a carbon-intensive energy supply created an enormous carbon footprint.[29] Over the last twenty years, $CO_2$ emissions in China grew six times as fast as in the rest of the world, and China accounted for almost two-thirds of the growth in global $CO_2$ emissions.

The United States, under the new Biden administration, has committed to achieving net-zero by 2050. Xi Jinping in October 2020 pledged that China will reach net-neutrality by 2060. In a virtual meeting at the UN he stated,

> "Covid-19 reminds us that humankind should launch a green revolution. Humankind can no longer afford to ignore the repeated warnings of nature. As major economies work to reach their net-zero goals, they will have to buy more solar panels, batteries and critical minerals and the main supplier is China."[30]

China is the Jekyll and Hyde when it comes to climate change; it is the world's largest emitter of carbon emissions while also leading in the production of the technologies to address the urgency of climate change.[31] China's 14th Five-Year Plan puts climate at the heart of its economic and political strategy between 2021–2026. Moreover, like the United States, where states are integral to making climate policies work, China requires all government departments and local governments to come up with plans for climate change.

---

[29] Virgil Bisio, Charles Horne, Ann Listerud, Kaj Malden, Leyton Nelson, Nargiza Salidjanova, and Suzanna Stephens, "The U.S.-China 'Phase One' Deal: A Backgrounder," *U.S.-China Economic and Security Review Commission*, February 4, 2020, https://www.uscc.gov/research/us-china-phase-one-deal-backgrounder.

[30] Ibid.

[31] Carolyn Kissane, "Welcome to the Era of Competitive Climate Statecraft: In Trade, Finance, Development, and Security, Governments Are Racing to Get Closer to Net-zero," *Foreign Policy*, February 8, 2021, https://foreignpolicy.com/2021/02/08/welcome-to-the-era-of-competitive-climate-statecraft-united-states-china/.

Chinese leaders recognize the challenge of needing to maintain economic growth while confronting the country's serious energy and environmental challenges. It is an enormous task, but one that also offers the country the opportunity to capture the world's movement toward greener energy technologies and what is now called the race to net-zero. Serving as the world's leader in clean energy technologies is part of an economic competitive strategy, and offers China expanded export opportunities. China is using its manufacturing power not only meet global demand for renewable energy but also its own installation and distribution of renewable energy in China. Between 2019 and 2024, China will account for 40 percent of global renewable capacity expansion, driven by improved system integration, lower curtailment rates, and enhanced competitiveness of both solar PV and onshore wind. During the same period, China is forecast to account for almost half of global distributed PV growth, overtaking the EU to become the world leader in installed capacity this year, 2021.[32]

Biden's overall climate plan calls for a more powerful federal role in scaling up research and commercialization of next-wave energy technologies, even as it looks to speed up deployment of existing low-carbon sources. Can the Biden administration usher in a new era of climate diplomacy between China and the United States, one where climate change can play an increasingly important role? Does China want to work with the United States and share the leadership role around climate stewardship? John Kerry, the Biden administration's climate envoy with a new seat on the National Security Council has said he wants to work with China, knowing that China's involvement is an imperative in addressing global carbon emissions. Kerry has said, "Obviously we have some very serious differences with China on some very, very important issues. But climate is a critical standalone issue that we have to deal on," he added. After this comment from Kerry, the next day in Beijing, Chinese Foreign Ministry spokesperson Zhao Lijian argued that climate issues can't be separated from the overall state of the two countries' relationship, saying "unlike

---

[32] "Renewables: 2019," *IEA*, October, 2019, https://www.iea.org/reports/renewables-2019.

flowers that can bloom in a greenhouse despite winter chill, (any such cooperation) is closely linked with bilateral relations as a whole."[33]

China's energy strategy and means to achieve greater energy security are strategic. By taking the global lead in producing green energy, Beijing aims to make itself an energy exporter to rival the United States, but for the United States, the strategy has focused on the export of hydrocarbons until now. Biden calls for a transition away from U.S. reliance on fossil fuels and toward building out the technologies and infrastructure for a net-zero economy but the United States is late to the game. Over 100 countries now have a net-zero-net-neutral pledge and China wants to be the go to for the technologies, but also the mineral resources required across the clean energy supply chain. The United States, historically out front with patents, and innovation, is finding out China is no longer a second-tier player, it is playing to win the new green great game.

## CONCLUSION

Energy and climate will play a significant role in the continuing unfolding of the U.S.–China relationship. Both are using a stronger hand of the government to further each country's energy transition but it will be a long time before either country achieves the European Union's Green Deal plan to decouple GDP from emissions. China and the United States share similar energy security goals, and each has taken divergent policy priority paths, but maybe for the first time, both align around net-zero and net-neutrality. 2050 is the year the United States aims to be net-zero and for China net-neutrality is 2060.

It is possible to reimagine coordination in the face of global threats, specifically climate change, but it is also possible to envision an even more deteriorated relationship than what exists today. China and the United States are moving into a new twenty-first century form of energy and climate competition, this is true, but it is also imperative to recognize the "competitive interdependence" between the two countries.[34] Competition between the United States and China will not wane, it will continue

[33] Jullian Brave Noisecat and Thom Woodroff, "The United States and China Need to Cooperate- for the Planet's Sake," *Foreign Policy*, February 4, 2021, https://foreignpolicy.com/2021/02/04/united-states-china-climate-change-foreign-policy/.

[34] Ryan Hass, *Stronger: Adapting America's China Strategy in an Age of Competitive Interdependence*, (Yale University Press, 2021).

and in some areas such as technology, the stakes are high for both sides. Competitive energy and climate statecraft between the United States and China may prove beneficial in deploying more decarbonized technologies and scaling innovation, that is the optimistic view of competitive climate statecraft, though it is also possible both sides could play a zero-sum game and not engage in areas of coordination and cooperation that is required to address the urgency of climate change and emerging global threats, as was witnessed with the lack of cooperation around managing the Coronavirus.

When Biden spoke at the Munich Security Conference in February 2021 he said the United States and its allies, "must prepare together for a long-term strategic competition with China."[35] China's foreign minister Wang Yi responded to United States threats of continued sanctions and export controls in another way, "A good mannered gentleman never thrusts his knife and fork into the food on someone else's table."[36] China is not holding out for an improved relationship with the United States; rather, it seeks to advance the state's role in the economy beyond the control it currently exerts, and to develop strategic technologies (also included is technological independence and indigenous innovation). China is leveraging its already well-tested economic statecraft into competitive energy and climate statecraft. "Beijing is playing a more sophisticated game, using technological innovation as a way of advancing its goals without having to resort to war."[37] Cooperation could prove beneficial for both China and the United States, and advance security for both sides, but if bets were on the table, the odds look more like the two countries will retain fiercely competitive stances. U.S.–China tensions will increase, there is bipartisan consensus in the United States to go harder on China, and in China, there's a deep and concerted effort to lessen dependence on the United States and circumvent the United States where possible, making the geopolitics of energy a new global great (and green) game.

[35] Yuan Yang and Demetri Sevastopulo, "China Calls on Biden to end Sanctions and Stop Meddling," *Financial Times*, February 22, 2021, https://www.ft.com/content/bbdcf8b3-422a-4235-9767-035206c92191.

[36] Ibid.

[37] Christopher Darby and Sarah Sewall, "The Innovation Wars," *Foreign Affairs*, March/April, 2021, http://foreignaffairs.com/articles/united-states/2021-02-10/technology-innovation-wars.

# CHAPTER 4

# Reimagining U.S. Engagement with Latin America and the Caribbean in Response to a Risen China

*Ricardo Barrios*

**Abstract** Although still based on the commodities trade, China's relations with the countries of Latin America and the Caribbean (LAC) have grown increasingly complex over the past two decades, as demonstrated by the changing trends in investment and finance to the resource-rich region. There, Chinese entities continue to be active in key sectors, including extractives and agriculture, which make China a major economic partner to many of the region's largest economies, including Argentina, Brazil, and Chile. In comparison with the past, between 2017–2020, the region also played a larger role in China's foreign policy, which has come to include the region more frequently in its programs, such as

---

The views and opinions expressed in this chapter are those of the author and do not reflect the official policy or position of any organizations with which the author is affiliated.

---

R. Barrios (✉)
RWR Advisory Group, Washington, DC, USA

© The Author(s), under exclusive license to Springer Nature Singapore Pte Ltd. 2021
E. Carr Jr. (ed.), *From Trump to Biden and Beyond*,
https://doi.org/10.1007/978-981-16-4297-5_4

the Belt and Road Initiative (BRI). In comparison to much of Asia, where the hardline stance adopted by the administration of Donald J. Trump was received favorably by countries which look toward Washington as a security partner, LAC countries broadly rejected the administration's antagonism toward Beijing. This was on the one hand a consequence of the administration's heavy-handed approach to LAC, which only exacerbated Washington's long-term neglect of the region, and on the other hand the result of China's already significant presence in many of its countries.

**Keywords** China · Latin America · Caribbean · United States · Development finance · International rivalry

China's gains in Latin America and the Caribbean (LAC) during the administration of President Donald J. Trump were made thanks to, not in spite of, the United States' opposition to China's presence in the region. In comparison to most of Asia, where the Trump administration's hardline stance toward China was received favorably by countries which look toward Washington as a security partner, LAC countries broadly rejected the administration's antagonism toward Beijing. This was on the one hand a consequence of the administration's heavy-handed approach to LAC, which exacerbated Washington's long-term neglect of the region, and on the other hand the result of China's already significant presence in many of its countries.

China's policy toward LAC is primarily guided by domestic economic factors, i.e., the search for commodities, which are plentiful in the region. Whether its soybeans in Brazil and Argentina, copper in Chile and Peru, or oil in Venezuela and Ecuador, these fungible goods remain the decisive factor in determining where, in what sectors, and through what means China engages with any given country. As is the case with explaining China's behavior, this economic dimension is central to explaining why many LAC countries consider China an important partner. Separated from China by the Pacific Ocean, LAC countries' relationship with China remains largely positive today, even as China's increasing assertiveness in Asia has caused some countries there to reconsider their reliance on China's economic dynamism.

Nonetheless, after nearly two decades, the negative aspects of China's economic activities have become evident in LAC too. In Jamaica, an aluminum refinery owned by Chinese company Jiuquan Iron and Steal Company (JISCO) released pollutants that sickened local communities.[1] Along the Pacific Coast, Chinese fishing vessels have taken to fishing around the protected area of the Galapagos Islands, threatening local wildlife.[2] Across the region, the ready accessibility of financing from Chinese state lenders provided financial alternatives to governments—like that of former president Rafael Correa in Ecuador—which ran afoul of creditors and were subsequently denied access international credit markets. Nonetheless, in that case too, the continuation of Ecuador's debt troubles today and its newly found reliance on Chinese finance make clear that Chinese institutions provide an alternative, but not necessarily an answer, to many of the region's problems.

It is difficult to argue that China made absolute gains in LAC during the Trump administration. However, the president's detrimental rhetoric, his administration's contempt for regional norms, and its lack of coherent policies toward the region often worked against it, thereby bolstering China's relative stature in the region at Washington's expense. If the Trump administration can be said to have had an LAC policy, it seems to have been primarily organized around the goal of excluding China from the hemisphere, and its main channel was the condemnation of Chinese activities, often without providing an alternative to stand in place for the benefits these activities bring to the region.

Opposition to China's presence in LAC is neither a feasible policy for the United States, nor a palatable alternative for the countries of LAC, which have come to embrace the Chinese market. Based on that, it seems that the future of U.S.–China relations in LAC will be based on a competitive logic, with Washington and Beijing each attempting to increase their own abstract influence in a series of undefined contests. While acknowledging that such competition could have negative consequences for the

---

[1] Jevon Minto, "Aluminium Refinery Sickens Jamaicans," *Dialogo Chino*, March 22, 2019, dialogochino.net/en/extractive-industries/25227-aluminium-refinery-sickens-jamaicans.

[2] Mat Youkee, "China Wary of Image Crisis after Galapagos Fishing Scrutiny," *China Dialogue Ocean*, August 28, 2020, chindialogueocean.net/14750-china-wary-of-image-crisis-after-galapagos-fishing-scrutiny.

region—as a cursory review of the region's Cold War history demonstrates—this same competitive element already evident in the U.S.–China relationship could catalyze difficult changes to the United States' inadequate foreign policy toward the region, as well as the ossified development institutions that have failed to compete with Chinese analogues.

This chapter provides an overview of China's activities in LAC between 2017–2020, simultaneously identifying the main patterns that characterized the relationship during this period. It also places them within the broader context of the past two decades of China–LAC relations. The study draws from a variety of sources—including news reporting by international media, datasets, polls, and government documents—to provide a comprehensive view of Chinese activity. From there, it provides critical analysis of some of the main shortcomings of the Trump administration, whose policies were detrimental to the region, and largely failed to influence China's activities there.

The chapter begins by painting a general picture of China's activities in the region between 2017–2020, a period characterized by: (1) the region's inclusion in the Belt and Road Initiative (BRI), (2) the resumption of competition between China and Taiwan, (3) the arrival of Chinese technology firms, (4) a shift in China's investment patterns in the region, (5) a decrease in state-led development finance, and (6) a rapid response to the outbreak of COVID-19. This is followed by a critical appraisal of the Trump administration's main shortcomings in the region, which included: (1) ineffective rhetoric, (2) the erosion of regional norms, and (3) the creation of a permissive environment for diplomatic realignment. It concludes with some recommendations on how to improve the United States' policy toward LAC in a way that benefits the region.

## CHINA–LAC RELATIONS UNDER THE TRUMP ADMINISTRATION

China's position in LAC relative to the United States improved significantly under the Trump administration. Though largely a continuation of Beijing's existing approach to the region, the period is notable for China's more assertive foreign policy, which was visible in the region's inclusion in several high-profile initiatives, e.g., the BRI. These four years were also notable for the resurgence of China's drive to isolate Taiwan diplomatically, as well as the rapid rise of Chinese technology firms, which have become a focal point of the growing rivalry between the U.S. and China globally. The expansion of these high-profile diplomatic and technological endeavors somewhat eclipsed the traditional pillars of investment and state-led development finance, which fell to near-historic lows by 2019. The coexistence of these two trends—an increase in the number of LAC countries participating in the BRI and a decrease in finance and investment flows to the region—are helpful in dispelling one of the myths of the time, namely, that inclusion in the BRI is necessarily conducive to greater Chinese economic activity. China's dynamic response to the outbreak of COVID-19 was also a significant component of China's activities in the region toward the end of the Trump administration, whose slow response stood in stark contrast to Beijing's rapid, if flawed, measures.

### The Region's Inclusion in the Belt and Road Initiative

The inclusion of LAC in China's BRI was perhaps the single most scrutinized—if not necessarily the most significant—event that occurred in China–LAC relations during the Trump administration. Originally laid out in Kazakhstan in 2013, it seemed like a foregone conclusion among Asia specialists that the Silk Road Economic Belt (and the accompanying 21st Century Maritime Silk Road) would encompass only the territory of Eurasia, through which stretched its namesake historic trade routes.

This was not the case. As of January 2021, LAC countries account for 19 of the BRI's 146 participants.[3] Though LAC's participation in the Initiative seems inevitable in retrospect, the process of its inclusion—which occurred piecemeal via bilateral memorandums of understanding, as opposed to the blanket approach China initially adopted toward the countries of Eurasia—was an uncertain one, suggesting that the region's inclusion was not part of China's original vision. This possibility is supported by early documents outlining the Initiative, per instance the "Vision and Actions on Jointly Building Belt and Road," issued by the State Council's National Development and Reform Commission in March 2015, which did not explicitly mention LAC, even as it included Africa within the BRI framework.[4]

---

[3] "Geguo Gaikuang 各国概况" [Country Profiles], *Belt and Road Portal*, 2021, https://www.yidaiyilu.gov.cn/info/iList.jsp?cat_id=10037.

[4] "Tuidong gongjian sichou zhi lu jingji dai he ershiyi shiji haishang sichou zhi lu de yuanjing yu xingdong 推动共建丝绸之路经济带和21世纪海上丝绸之路的愿景与行动"

It is likely that China's addition of LAC to the Initiative was influenced by the public debate among academics and foreign policy commentators that took place in both sides of the Pacific between 2014 and the region's ultimate entry in 2017—thereby hinting at China's growing ability to more effectively adapt its foreign policy.[5] The speculation about whether LAC was "in" or "out" of the Initiative became more significant as material resources, such as the Silk Road Fund (2014), were mobilized by China in support of participating countries. In the face of such speculation, Chinese leaders embraced ambiguity and long resisted clarifying what part, if any, the region played in the Initiative. President Xi Jinping himself referred to LAC as a "natural extension of the 21st Century Maritime Silk Road," without clarification, as late as May 2017.[6] The matter was finally settled with Panama's signature of a Belt and Road memorandum in November 2017, marking the ascension of the first LAC country to the Initiative, and paving the way for other LAC countries to follow suit.[7]

Despite the majority of LAC joining the BRI, the region's largest economies (i.e., Argentina, Brazil, Colombia, and Mexico) had not signed on by January 2021. Argentina publicly stated its intention to join following the inauguration of President Alberto Fernandez in December

[Vision and Actions on Jointly Building Belt and Road], *Belt and Road Forum for International Cooperation*, 2017, https://www.beltandroadforum.org/n100/2017/0407/c27-22.html.

[5] For an example arguing that LAC was not a part of the BRI, see: Margaret Myers and Ricardo Barrios, "LAC's Not Part of the Belt and Road, but Does That Matter?," *The Inter-American Dialogue*, January 26, 2018, https://www.thedialogue.org/blogs/2018/01/lacs-not-part-of-the-belt-and-road-but-does-that-matter. For an example arguing the contrary, see: "Yi dai yi lu zhuli zhongguo tong lamei hezuo 一带一路'助力中国同拉美合作," [The Belt and Road Initiative Helps China Cooperate with Latin America], *Xinhua News Agency*, May 9, 2017, https://www.xinhuanet.com//silkroad/2017-05/09/c_129596470.htm.

[6] "Xi Jinping tong agenting zongtong makeli juxing huitan liang guo yuanshou yizhi tongyi tuidong zhong a quanmian zhanlve huoban guanxi dedao geng da fazhan 习近平同阿根廷总统马克里举行会谈 两国元首一致同意推动中阿全面战略伙伴关系得到更大发展," [Xi Jingping Holds Talks with President of Argentina Macri, Two Heads of State Agreed to Promote Greater Development of China-Argentina Comprehensive Strategic Partnership], *Xinhua News Agency*, May 17, 2017, http://www.xinhuanet.com/politics/2017-05/17/c_1120990249.htm.

[7] "Zhe shi yid ai yi lu jianshi! 这就是 '一带一路'简史!," [This is a Brief History of the Belt and Road!], *Xinhua News Agency*, April 26, 2019, http://www.xinhuanet.com/world/2019-04/26/c_1124418156.htm.

2019.[8] However, it is unclear how seriously the remaining three countries are considering joining. The fact that these countries continued to receive large portions of China's finance and investment in the region between 2017–2020, all while remaining outside the BRI, calls into question the need to join it at all.

### A Renewed Campaign to Isolate Taiwan

Another notable development in the diplomatic realm was the resumption of the struggle for recognition between China and Taiwan. Ma Ying-jeou's presidency (2008–2016) was marked by a pause in the "Checkbook Diplomacy" that had come to characterize Beijing–Taipei relations. However, since the election of President Tsai Ing-wen in 2016, Beijing has renewed its efforts to eliminate official recognition of Taipei overseas.

Over the past four years, Beijing's renewed pressure campaign against Taipei resulted in the poaching of three key allies in Central America and the Caribbean, i.e., Panama (2017), the Dominican Republic (2018), and El Salvador (2018), thereby reducing the number of countries that maintain full diplomatic relations with Taiwan to 17. At the time of this writing, over half of the 15 countries that maintain diplomatic ties to Taiwan today are found in Central America and the Caribbean.[9]

### The Arrival of Chinese Technology Firms

The Trump administration coincided with an increase in the activity of Chinese technology firms in LAC, which were drawn by the region's "tech boom." Whether selling consumer electronics, such as Xiaomi, or funding local start-ups, as was the case with Baidu, a large number of Chinese technology companies expanded their business in the region,

---

[8] Michael Zarate, "'Argentina Will Join the Belt and Road Initiative'—Interview with the Argentine Ambassador to China Luis Maria Kreckler," *China Today*, November 3, 2020, http://www.chinatoday.com.cn/ctenglish/2018/ii/202011/t20201103_800225649.html.

[9] These are Belize, Guatemala, Haiti, Honduras. Nicaragua, St. Kitts and Nevis, St. Lucia, and St. Vincent & the Grenadines. Taiwan also maintains one diplomatic partner in South America: Paraguay.

and particularly in the large markets South America.[10] This was not only done through traditional channels, such as their own subsidiaries, but also in new ways, e.g., investment in local start-ups (such as Brazil's Peixe Urbano) that could more effectively tap their home markets.[11]

This increased penetration in LAC's technological ecosystems occurred simultaneously with several high-profile attempts by Chinese technology firms (e.g., Huawei and ZTE) to further integrate themselves into the region's telecommunications systems, with an eye to competing in the wave of upcoming auctions for fifth-generation (5G) telecommunications infrastructure. This interest was most clear with regard to submarine fiber-optic cables, as demonstrated by Huawei's completion of a submarine cable between Brazil and Cameroon, as well its bid for Chile's first trans-Pacific fiber-optic cable.[12] The latter project was ultimately secured by Tokyo-based NEC Corporation, reportedly following increased pressure from United States' officials who voiced opposition to Chinese players' presence in this critical sector.[13]

Huawei's price advantage made the company an attractive choice among LAC countries, many of which do not price-in the time it takes to address the security risks posed by the company's networks.[14] While stories published recently—such as ZTE's role in the establishment of Venezuela's "Fatherland Card" monitoring system[15] and the abuse of a similar system in Ecuador by the government under President Rafael

[10] Ramon Vardin, "Xiaomi se consolida como el cuarto vendedor de telefonos celulares en Mexico," *Mitrabajo*, November 10, 2020, mitrabajo.news/noticias/Xiaomi-se-consolida-como-el-cuarto-vendedor-de-telefonos-celulares-en-Mexico-20201110-0004.html.

[11] Daniela Guzman, "China's Billions Are Powering Latin America's Tech Boom," *Bloomberg*, January 8, 2019, bloomberg.com/news/articles/2019-01-08/guess-who-s-behind-latin-america-s-tech-boom-china-of-course.

[12] "South Atlantic Inter Link Connecting Cameroon to Brazil Fully Connected," *Huawei*, September 6, 2018, huawei.com/us/news/2018/9/south-atlantic-inter-link.

[13] Sarah Zheng, "China's Huawei Loses out to Japan's NEC on Chile-Asia trans-Pacific cable project," *South China Morning Post*, July 30, 2020, scmp.com/news/china/diplomacy/article/3095367/chinas-huawei-loses-out-japans-nec-chile-asia-trans-pacific.

[14] Margaret Myers and Guillermo Garcia Montenegro, "Latin America and 5G: Five Things to Know," *The Inter-American Dialogue*, December 14, 2019, https://www.thedialogue.org/analysis/latin-america-and-5%C2%A0g-five-things-to-know.

[15] Angus Berwick, "How ZTE Helps Venezuela Create China-Style Social Control," *Reuters*, November 14, 2018, https://www.reuters.com/investigates/special-report/venezuela-zte.

Correa[16]—have led to increased worries of the encroachment of technology and surveillance in LAC countries, they have had only a minor effect in dissuading the region from partnering with Chinese technology firms.

### A Qualitative Shift in Foreign Investment

Foreign investment, or the establishment of a direct ownership stake in a business overseas, represents a more involved form of economic activity than development finance, which does not imply an ownership stake. Even prior to the Belt and Road brand, non-bond investment by Chinese entities was a significant part of China's toolkit in LAC countries starting in the mid-2000s.

Although the annual value of these foreign investment flows decreased over the past four years, it still fell within historical bounds. According to data compiled by the American Enterprise Institute and Heritage Foundation's China Global Investment Tracker (CGIT), between 2017 and 2020, South America—which accounts for upwards of 95% of Chinese investment in LAC—received roughly $41.6 billion (**See Fig. 4.2**) in investment from Chinese entities, equal to roughly 10% of China's global $413.7 billion during that period.[17] By way of comparison, between 2005 and 2020, Chinese investment in South America totaled $129.2 billion, also equal to 10.8%, of approximately $1.2 trillion in China's global total. In South America, this investment has been highly concentrated in a handful of countries—i.e., Brazil (50%), Chile (21.2%), and Peru (11.5%)—and sectors—i.e., energy (58%) and metals (27%). To put this within a regional context, Chinese overseas foreign direct investments (OFDI) accounted for 7.57% of the region's total foreign direct investment (FDI) flows in 2019 according to data published by Red Academica de America Latina y el Caribe sobre China (Red ALC-China).[18]

---

[16] Charles Rollet, "Ecuador's All-Seeing Eye Is Made in China," *Foreign Policy*, August 9, 2018, https://www.foreignpolicy.com/2018/08/09/ecuadors-all-seeing-eye-is-made-in-china.

[17] "China Global Investment Tracker," *American Enterprise Institute and Heritage Foundation*, January 2021, https://www.aei.org/china-global-investment-tracker.

[18] Enrique Dussel Peters, "Monitor of Chinese OFDI in Latin America and the Caribbean 2020," *Red ALC-China*, March 23, 2020, https://www.redalc-china.org/monitor/images/pdfs/menuprincipal/DusselPeters_MonitorOFDI_2020_Eng.pdf.

Chinese Investment to South America by Year, 2005-2020 (USD Millions)

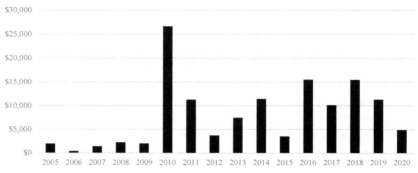

**Fig. 4.1** Chinese investment to South America by year, 2005–2020 (U.S.D. Millions) (*Source* "China Global Investment Tracker," *American Enterprise Institute and Heritage Foundation*, January 2021, https://www.aei.org/china-global-investment-tracker)

In recent years, Chinese investment in LAC has experienced a notable growth in the value of Chinese greenfield investments, or ground-level investments which involve the establishment of new facilities overseas. The increase in this type of transaction took place at the same time as annual Chinese investment in the region decreased, resulting in the resurgence of greenfield investments as a proportion of China's total investment in South America, from roughly 2.84% in 2017 to 24.18% in 2020. In light of that, Chinese activity in the region now reflects a trend evident in BRI countries—many of them developing countries where greenfield investment activity is higher due to fewer assets ready for acquisition (Fig. 4.1).[19]

[19] Cecilia Joy-Perez, "The Belt and Road Initiative Adds More Partners, But Beijing Has Fewer Dollars to Spend," *The Jamestown Foundation*, September 26, 2019, jamestown.org/program/the-belt-and-road-initiative-adds-more-partners-but-beijing-has-fewer-dollars-to-spend.

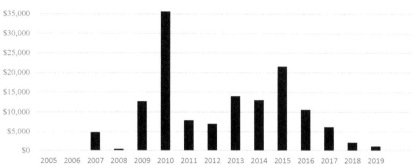

**Fig. 4.2** Chinese finance to Latin America by year, 2005–2019 (U.S.D. Millions) (*Source* Kevin P. Gallagher and Margaret Myers, "China-Latin America Finance Database," *The Inter-American Dialogue*, 2020, https://www.thedia logue.org/map_list)

### The Continued Decline of State-Led Development Finance

Similarly, Chinese state-led development finance also experienced a significant decline under the Trump administration. This was likely due to a series of factors, including fewer state resources to draw from, lack of interest from Chinese entities in financing projects that are not economically viable, and a reduced demand from regional borrowers.[20]

According to the Inter-American Dialogue (IAD) and Boston University's (BU's) China–Latin America Finance Database, between 2017 and 2019, China's two main outward-facing policy banks, China Development Bank (CDB) and the Import-Export Bank of China (CHEXIM), loaned $9.4 billion (**See Fig. 4.2**) to LAC countries.[21] The majority of this sum ($6.2 billion) was issued in 2017, making 2018 and 2019 among the lowest years on record in terms of lending. Most of the funds during this period went to Brazil (56.3%), Argentina (19.3%), and Ecuador

---

[20] Margaret Myers, "China's Financial Calculus in Latin America: Before and After COVID-19," *Global Americans*, April 2, 2020, theglobalamericans.org/2020/04/chinas-financial-calculus-in-latin-america-before-and-after-covid-19.

[21] Kevin P. Gallagher, and Margaret Myers "China-Latin America Finance Database," *The Inter-American Dialogue*, 2020, https://www.thedialogue.org/map_list.

(10.29%), which together with Venezuela and Trinidad and Tobago rank as the top five recipients of Chinese loans since 2005.

Though still noteworthy, the reduction in Chinese lending is hardly surprising. Between 2005 and 2019, CDB and CHEXIM loaned a combined $137 billion to LAC countries. After peaking at $35.6 billion in 2010, Chinese lending to the region dropped considerably, with most years failing to surpass the $15 billion mark. This largely mirrored trends captured by BU's Geolocated Dataset of Chinese Overseas Development Finance, which shows a moderate decrease in lending from these institutions at a global scale following 2009, and a much more significant drop following 2016.[22]

### Forming an Active Response to COVID-19

Lastly, China's coordinated response to the outbreak of COVID-19 in LAC was also a significant component of its foreign policy toward the region.[23] Chinese entities' initial response came in the form of swiftly delivered medical supplies and equipment—the so-called "mask diplomacy"—to the many countries of the region, including countries that maintain diplomatic relations with Taiwan, e.g., Guatemala.[24] It is difficult to place a value on the total flows of aid that China delivered to the region as part of this program, particularly as aid flows were often reported alongside sales of medical equipment to the region.

Toward the end of 2020, China shifted its pandemic-related initiatives toward a model based on the development of a treatment for the virus. China's "vaccine diplomacy" deployed in several major countries, including Argentina, Brazil, Mexico, and Peru, all four of which participated in clinical trials of Chinese-made vaccines. This program took place

---

[22] Rebecca Ray, Kevin P. Gallagher, William Kring, Joshua Pitts, and B. Alexander Simmons, "Geolocated Dataset of Chinese Overseas Development Finance," *Global Development Policy Center, Boston University*, https://www.bu.edu/gdp/chinas-overseas-development-finance.

[23] Margaret Myers and Ricardo Barrios, "China's Medical Outreach in LAC: Facts and Features," *The Inter-American Dialogue*, May 22, 2020, thedialogue.org/blogs/2020/05/chinas-medical-outreach-in-lac-facts-and-features.

[24] Eder Juarez, "Gobierno Usara Solucion de Huawei para la Rapida Deteccion de COVID-19," *La Hora*, March 18, 2020, lahora.gt/gobierno-usara-solucion-de-huawei-para-la-rapida-deteccion-de-covid-19.

largely in a vacuum, as vaccines developed by the United States were initially directed to meet domestic needs.[25]

Reactions to these programs were mixed. State actors were typically thankful for the assistance, as voiced by Mexico's Foreign Minister Marcelo Ebrard, which publicly demonstrated his gratitude toward China.[26] Nonetheless, in Brazil, China's efforts were met with disdain from President Bolsonaro, which claimed success on social media when trials of the vaccine were suspended following a "severe adverse event" with a participant.[27] Although quality concerns tarnished the image of some of these efforts, they nonetheless provided a form of visible support to the region—one which contrasted significantly with the United States' limited and poorly publicized response under President Donald Trump.[28]

## The Trump Administration's Response

The extent of China's relative gains in LAC would not have been possible if not for the Trump administration's ineffective policy, which weakened Washington's standing through the elimination of foreign aid to Central America as well as the eroding of regional institutions such as the Inter-American Development Bank (IDB). Although intended to curb China's attractiveness to the countries of the region, the United States' reliance on "us-or-them" framing and emphasis on U.S. primacy alienated many in the region who saw a clear contrast between statements from American officials and China's rhetorical emphasis on communication and multilateralism. The administration's lack of coordination among its domestic and

---

[25] Ryan Dube and Luciana Magalhaes, "For Covid-19 Vaccines, Latin America Turns to China and Russia," *The Wall Street Journal*, February 23, 2021, wsj.com/articles/for-covid-19-vaccines-latin-america-turns-to-china-and-russia-11614186599.

[26] Reuters Staff, "'Thank you China!!!' Mexico Grateful for Coronavirus Medical Supplies," *Reuters*, April 1, 2020, reuters.com/article/us-health-coronavirus-mexico-china/thank-you-china-mexico-grateful-for-coronavirus-medical-supplies-idU.S.KBN21J6U5.

[27] Eduardo Simões and Roxanne Liu, "Brazil's Bolsonaro Claims Victory as Sinovac COVID-19 Trial Halted," *Reuters*, November 10, 2020, reuters.com/article/uk-health-coronavirus-brazil-sinovac/brazils-bolsonaro-claims-victory-as-sinovac-covid-19-trial-halted-idUKKBN27Q1BO.

[28] Mac Margolis, "China Laps the U.S. in Latin America with Covid Diplomacy," *Bloomberg Opinion*, June 24, 2020, bloomberg.com/opinion/articles/2020-06-24/china-laps-u-s-in-latin-america-with-covid-19-diplomacy.

foreign policies was also at the heart of this ineffectiveness, as is visible in the case of El Salvador, where Washington's actions contributed to San Salvador's decision to ultimately break off relations with Taiwan.

### Ineffective Rhetoric

Candidate Trump's rhetoric toward the region and its people is responsible for considerable damage to U.S.–LAC relations even before the beginning of the Trump administration in January 2017. Candidate Trump's xenophobic remarks against Latinos and his continued insistence that Mexico pay for a border wall between the two countries were detrimental to the United States' image in the eyes of Latin Americans.[29] Between 2016 and 2017 alone, the Latinobarometro Survey reported that favorable responses among Latin Americans toward the United States dropped from 74 to 67%.[30] The decline was most significant in Mexico, where favorable responses dropped from 77% to roughly 47%. Although a 2020 Gallup Poll indicated that the image of U.S. leadership improved in the Americas between 2017 and 2019, median approval at the time of its publishing hovered at around 34%, one of the lowest years on record, and still below the 49% of 2016.[31]

Though arguably less detrimental to the region than candidate Trump's remarks, the Trump administration's rhetoric toward LAC was ineffective in dissuading countries of the region from engaging with China. Part of its ineffectiveness lay in the fact that the rhetoric emphasized China over the region, thereby highlighting the real concern at the heart of the administration's policy toward the Western Hemisphere. In remarks made at the Council of the Americas on April 29, 2019, for example, Assistant Secretary of State for Western Hemisphere Affairs Kimberly Breier referenced "China" or "Chinese" 74 times.[32] By way

[29] "'Drug dealers, criminals, rapists': What Trump Thinks of Mexicans," *BBC News*, August 31, 2016, bbc.com/news/av/world-us-canada-37230916.

[30] "La Era de Trump: Imagen de Estados Unidos en America Latina," *Latinobarometro*, 2017, latinobarometro.org/LATDocs/LA_ERA_DE_TRUMP.pdf.

[31] Julie Ray, "U.S. Leadership Remains Unpopular Worldwide," *Gallup*, July 27, 2020, news.gallup.com/poll/316133/leadership-remains-unpopular-worldwide.aspx.

[32] Kimberly Brier, "Remarks: Assistant Secretary of State for Western Hemisphere Affairs Kimberly Breier," *Council of the Americas*, April 29, 2019, as-coa.org/articles/remarks-assistant-secretary-state-western-hemisphere-affairs-kimberly-breier.

of contrast, references to "Latin America," "South America," "Western Hemisphere," and even "partners" together tally up to a total of only 31. This rhetorical approach, which often featured China (or U.S.–China competition) as the protagonist in the foreign policy narrative barely featured the region at all. Put differently, even in the United States' policy toward the Western Hemisphere, the administration's rhetoric reduced LAC countries to passive scenery, without addressing their own concerns.

This tendency was also evident in the lecturing tone the administration frequently utilized to warn the region of some Chinese entities' questionable practices. In February 1, 2018, Secretary of State Rex Tillerson stated, "China's offer always come at a price," adding that Beijing was "using economic statecraft to pull the region into its orbit."[33] In October 18, 2018, his successor Mike Pompeo similarly "[reminded] the entire region, that when China comes calling it's not always to the good of your citizens," before concluding that "when [China shows] up with deals that seem to be too good to be true it's often the case that they, in fact, are."[34]

Occasionally, Washington's recurring warnings were not merely ineffective, but counterproductive, drawing public rebukes from LAC leaders. Such was the case of Peru, whose Minister of Trade Eduardo Ferreyros told foreign media on February 6, 2018 that, while he "appreciates the advice," Peru is "careful with all of our trade relations," and "China is a good trade partner."[35]

## Breaking Norms and Reversing Commitments

The administration's rhetoric revealed contempt toward the normative power of institutions, which the administration frequently subverted through decisions and policies aimed at entrenching more direct forms of American power. Ironically, the administration's unrestrained pursuit

[33] Rex Tillerson, "Secretary Tillerson Delivers Address on U.S. Engagement in the Western Hemisphere," *U.S. Mission to the Organization of American States*, February 1, 2018, https://usoas.usmission.gov/secretary-tillerson-delivers-address-u-s-engagement-western-hemisphere.

[34] Michael R. Pompeo, "Remarks to Traveling Press," *U.S. Embassy and Consulates in Mexico*, October 19, 2018, https://mx.usembassy.gov/secretary-of-state-michael-r-pompeo-to-traveling-press.

[35] Marco Aquino, "Peru Defends China as Good Trade Partner after U.S. Warnings," *Reuters*, February 6, 2018, reuters.com/article/us-peru-usa-tillerson-china/peru-defends-china-as-good-trade-partner-after-u-s-warnings-idU.S.KBN1FQ36P.

of direct influence pit it against many long-standing institutions in the region which not only undermined arrangements favorable to the United States, but also eroded its credibility in the process.

One of the most visible examples of this was the politicization of the Inter-American Development Bank (IDB), as part of the administration's attempts to reduce China's influence.[36] The region's leading source of development finance, the IDB was presided by a candidate from the region since its founding in 1959, as per a norm observed throughout its six-decade history. This norm was broken by the administration, which sought (successfully) to promote an American candidate, Mauricio Claver-Carone, then head of Western Hemisphere affairs at the National Security Council, for the presidency of the IDB. Although Treasury Secretary Steven Mnuchin framed it as demonstrating Trump's "strong commitment to U.S. leadership in important regional institutions," many of the region's main economies, including Argentina and Chile, saw it as an expansion of American power at their expense and actively lobbied against it.[37] Others still saw it as a way of extending the Trump administration's agenda in the region for the position's decade-long tenure.[38]

Ironically, the unpopular decision to nominate Claver-Carone was informed at least partially by the administration's desire to directly challenge China, who also contributed to the bank's politicization. In March 2019, the IDB canceled its annual meeting, originally planned to take place in China for the first time in its history, following Beijing's refusal to allow entry by Ricardo Hausmann, Venezuelan leader Juan Guaido's representative to the Bank.[39] Regardless of who is to be ultimately blamed

---

[36] Isabel Bernhard, "Will the IDB's Politicization Pull China and Latin America Closer?," *The Diplomat*, November 5, 2020, thediplomat.com/2020/11/will-the-idbs-politicization-pull-china-and-latin-america-closer.

[37] Tracy Wilkinson, "Latin American Governments Move to Scuttle Trump's Pick for International Development Bank," *Los Angeles Times*, August 10, 2020, latimes.com/pol itics/story/2020-08-10/latin-american-governments-rally-to-scuttle-trumps-nominee-to-development-bank.

[38] Natalie Kitroeff, "Trump Ally Wants to Be First American to Head Latin American Aid Bank," *The New York Times*, August 25, 2020, nytimes.com/2020/08/25/world/americas/Claver-Carone-bank-Latin-America.html.

[39] Lesley Wroughton and Roberta Rampton, "Exclusive: IADB Cancels China Meeting after Beijing Bars Venezuela Representative," *Reuters*, March 22, 2019, reuters.com/article/us-venezuela-politics-china-iadb-exclusi/exclusive-iadb-cancels-china-meeting-after-beijing-bars-venezuela-representative-idU.S.KCN1R32NU.

for the cancelation of the meeting, the politicization of the IDB—and other regional arrangements such as the North American Free Trade Agreement (NAFTA)—during the Trump administration will likely be one of its most significant legacies, given the damage it has done to norms and institutions decades in the making.

### Creating a Permissive Environment for Diplomatic Realignments

It would be erroneous to attribute China's pursuit of Taiwan's diplomatic allies to the Trump administration. Nonetheless, it would also be erroneous to assert that the Trump administration's decisions did not contribute to that result. In the case of El Salvador, events suggest that the United States' lack of policy coordination contributed to President Nayib Bukele's decision to maintain ties with Beijing after his predecessor, Salvador Sanchez Ceren of the opposition Farabundo Marti National Liberation Front (FMLN) party broke off ties with Taipei.

Up until the early days of his presidency, President Bukele was a vocal critic of Beijing. As candidate in November 2018, President Bukele criticized his predecessor's decision to break off ties with Taiwan and publicly stated his intention to review the decision to establish ties with China.[40] He maintained this position through February 2019, when a member of his team stated to the press that "We were not consulted, nor did they give us the reasons (for establishing) relations with China. Now we have to investigate in detail."[41] One month later, in March 2019, President-Elect Bukele visited Washington, where he again publicly criticized China, stating,

> China does not play by the rules; they do not respect the rules... They develop projects that are not feasible, leaving countries with huge debt that cannot be paid back and use that as financial leverage.[42]

[40] Redaccion UH, "Bukele Anuncia que Revisara el Proceso de Apertura Diplomatica con China Continental," *Ultima Hora*, November 8, 2018, https://ultimahora.sv/bukele-anuncia-que-revisara-el-proceso-de-apertura-diplomatica-con-china-continental.

[41] Reuters Staff, "Salvadoran President-Elect to Assess Relationship with China: Aide," *Reuters*, February 7, 2019, reuters.com/article/us-el-salvador-politics/salvadoran-president-elect-to-assess-relationship-with-china-aide-idU.S.KCN1PX06J.

[42] Nelson Renteria, "Responding to El Salvador President-Elect, China Denies it Meddles," *Reuters*, March 14, 2019, reuters.com/article/us-el-salvador-diplomacy-china/responding-to-el-salvador-president-elect-china-denies-it-meddles-idU.S.KCN1QV3AI.

Nonetheless, ten days following the June 17, 2019 announcement by the State Department that it was cutting off aid to El Salvador, President Bukele's tone changed drastically.[43] That day, the president publicly stated that El Salvador had "diplomatic relations with China that are complete, that are established," marking the most significant change in position since his candidacy.[44] While not indicative of causation, this chain of events does suggest that lack of U.S. economic support was influential in San Salvador's decision to maintain ties with Beijing.

## CONCLUSIONS AND RECOMMENDATIONS

The administration of President Joseph R. Biden faces the daunting task of redirecting U.S. foreign policy after four consequential years. The end of the Trump administration will not undo the administration's legacy. It will also not address some of the root causes preventing the United States from responding effectively to China in LAC: the erosion of American soft power, the increasing sophistication of Chinese foreign policy, and the two countries' approaching economic parity. To the extent that the past four years' policy toward LAC has been the result of domestic factors in the United States, a focus on domestic policy—on issues including economic inequality, social justice, and better regulation of information technology—would significantly improve the U.S.' foreign policy over the long term.

But what is the United States to do in the short term? *America Crece* and the U.S. International Development Finance Corporation created toward the end of the Trump administration have generally been seen as the first steps toward a coherent response to China's growing presence in the region. The United States must craft an adequate policy that organizes material resources effectively within a suitable policy framework. This framework should be based on the interests and needs of the region, not on directly countering China's every advance. As suggested by Gerard

---

[43] Stef W. Kight, "U.S. to Permanently End Foreign Aid for Guatemala, Honduras, El Salvador," *Axios*, June 17, 2019, axios.com/immigration-state-department-foreign-aid-guatemala-honduras-el-salvador-a15aeabc-76bd-4586-9362-fd3db210ec50.html.

[44] Nelson Renteria, "El Salvador President Says China Relations Fully Established," *Reuters*, June 27, 2019, reuters.com/article/us-el-salvador-politics-china/el-salvador-president-says-china-relations-fully-established-idU.S.KCN1TS39O.

Johnson, the former general manager of the IDB's Caribbean Country Department,

> Reallocating a fraction of current programs to support priorities of LAC governments and private firms would boost growth and strengthen good governance, while also reversing the self-absorbed image of U.S. intervention. This is smarter than a superpower squabble where canny LAC interests play one side off against the other and suboptimal decisions are rewarded.[45]

President Biden's administration should also acknowledge that in some areas, cooperation with China may still be beneficial, and even necessary. Climate change is an imperative that must be addressed by the United States, as well as China, if only for the simple reason that it poses an existential threat to all. To that end, the two countries should commit to the principle of cooperating in addressing this global challenge, and not devalue their commitment by conditioning it with other policies. Peaceful coexistence is in the interest of all parties.

In light of the above, I offer the following recommendations to the administration of President Biden:

1. **Execute a rhetorical shift to reconcile with the region, as part of a more assertive and coordinated messaging strategy.** In 2013, Secretary of State John Kerry stated, "The era of the Monroe Doctrine is over."[46] It is against this bar that the United States should measure itself as it tries to develop a compelling narrative that provides a clear and feasible future for the hemisphere, while also acknowledging the damage caused over the past four years. To give credence to Secretary of State Kerry's assertion, this vision should consider LAC countries on their own terms. To promote this vision, the United States should design a more coordinated messaging strategy that focuses on broadcasting the tangible ways it contributes to the region. Focusing on simplistic narratives (e.g., debt-trap diplomacy) that spread a caricature of China provide no

---

[45] Gerard Johnson, E-mail correspondence to author, March 14, 2021.

[46] John Kerry, "Remarks on U.S. Policy in the Western Hemisphere," *U.S. Department of State*, November 18, 2013, https://2009-2017.state.gov/secretary/remarks/2013/11/217680.htm.

value to the region, and do the United States a disservice by not accurately depicting the challenges, thus making them harder to address.

2. **Appeal to LAC countries' interests.** Several of the Trump administration's failures in LAC can be attributed to a focus on issues the region does not recognize as problematic, such as countries' participation in the BRI and their use of Huawei telecommunications equipment. Without commenting on the individual merit of these positions, the stances adopted by the administration failed to appeal to the other party's own interest and were thus largely ineffective. LAC countries have real interests in terms of infrastructure, security, and environmental protection. Only by understanding, and appealing, to those interests can the United States avoid the sort of disconnect between the United States and LAC that was visible under the Trump administration.

3. **Provide long-term support for LAC's recovery from COVID-19 and rebalance economic relations in a way that supports countries' economic recovery.** First and foremost, the United States should focus on supporting LAC countries' recovery from COVID-19, including ensuring access to vaccines against the pandemic. With a recovery plan in place, the United States should support countries' efforts to manage their sovereign debts, while also providing new credit to foster new economic activity.

4. **Focus on setting standards and norms and seek support for them.** As part of its economic rebalance, the United States should collaborate with the region to set rules and standards (e.g., environmental standards, labor standards) and support countries' efforts to promote their adherence. These standards should be applied equally to all firms alike. Although the United States should be prepared to openly condemn any Chinese actions that threaten democratic governance and the economic and social well-being in LAC countries, it should not oppose China's overall engagement in the region.

5. **Aid the region's efforts to understand China by supporting the development of home-grown China specialists that can be arbiters of their countries' interests vis-à-vis China.** Nobody will advocate for LAC countries with greater conviction than their own people. In order to support individual countries' responses to China, the United States should support the region's efforts to produce

local experts that have a solid grasp on Chinese practices (including the invisible costs of Chinese state-finance) and can advocate for their country's best interest.

6. **Bring in allies, e.g., Japan and Korea, from outside the region.** As part of its efforts, the United States should seek to promote partners' engagement with the countries of LAC, and coordinate policies in such a way that they multiply each other's impact. It should continue initiatives such as the Japan–U.S.–Brazil Exchange (JUSBE) and the Global Cooperation and Training Framework (GCTF), with an eye to promoting the region's well-being and exchange with other partners.

CHAPTER 5

# U.S. Strategy Vis-À-Vis China's Presence in the African Continent: Description and Prescription

*Winslow Robertson and Owakhela Kankhwende*

**Abstract** For the Biden Administration to break new ground in U.S.–Africa relations while curbing China's growing influence, reversing Trump's actions is insufficient if it means simply returning to the pre-Trump status quo. Instead, for the benefit of both the U.S. and African countries, a bold new partnership framework is essential. China's growing presence on the continent, which shows no signs of stopping, results from a fundamental respect of the power of African markets and resources, if not necessarily African people or African governments. The United

---

The views and *opinions expressed* in this chapter are those of the author and do not reflect the official policy or position of any organizations with which the author is affiliated.

---

W. Robertson (✉)
IESE Business School, Barcelona, Spain

O. Kankhwende
Fordham University Gabelli School of Business, Brooklyn, NY, USA

© The Author(s), under exclusive license to Springer Nature
Singapore Pte Ltd. 2021
E. Carr Jr. (ed.), *From Trump to Biden and Beyond*,
https://doi.org/10.1007/978-981-16-4297-5_5

States should differentiate itself by playing up its comparative advantages in engagement, innovation, and norm-setting. Engagement involves initiatives such as significantly increasing high-level visits to the African continent and vice versa, as well as expanding U.S. immigration paths for African students in the U.S. Innovation should be built around two pillars: rhetoric and certification. The U.S. should refrain from referring to Chinese financial flows as "investment" when not meeting equity requirements, while also providing assistance on certification systems for African infrastructure. Finally, in terms of norm-setting, the United States can once serve a global leadership role in pressing issues such as promoting COVID vaccination supply and supporting debt relief, actions which will reverberate beyond simply countering China.

**Keywords** Africa · Foreign Direct Investment · Infrastructure · EXIM (Export & Import) · COVAX (Covid-19 Vaccines Global Access) · AfCFTA (African Continental Free Trade Area) · AGOA · African Growth Opportunity Act · Debt · SDR · Special Drawing Rights · IMF · International Monetary Fund · OPT · Optional Practical Training

## INTRODUCTION

Joseph Biden winning the U.S. presidency marks an inflection point for U.S. relations towards China, but how does that relate towards the African continent?[1] The previous administration's attitudes towards

---

[1] This chapter is not attempting to summarize Chinese relations with African countries, as there are too many specific issues to do the topic justice. For background information, see: Howard W. French, "China's Second Continent: How a Million Migrants Are Building a New Empire in Africa" (New York: Knopf, 2014); Li Anshan, "African Studies in China in the Twentieth Century: A Historiographical Survey," *African Studies Review* 48, no. 1 (2005): 59–87, https://doi.org/10.1353/dem.2005.0002; Luke Patey, *The New Kings of Crude: China, India, and the Global Struggle for Oil in Sudan and South Sudan* (London: Hurst and Company, 2014); David H. Shinn, "China and Africa—Bibliography," last modified August 6, 2020, https://doi.org/10.1353/dem.2005.0002; Shinn and Joshua Eisenman, *China and Africa A Century of Engagement* (Philadelphia; University of Pennsylvania Press, 2012); Tu Huynh, T. and Yoon Jung Park, "'Chineseness' through Unexplored Lenses: Identity-Making in China–Africa Engagements in the 21st Century," *Asian and Pacific Migration Journal* 27, no. 1 (2018): 3–8, https://www.scribd.com/document/471608883/China-and-Africa-Bibliography; Bob

the continent bordered on disrespectful.[2] President Biden's policy plans explicitly aim to reverse the previous administration's isolationist leanings. Yet, what does that mean specifically? In terms of China's presence on the African continent, both the Obama and Bush administrations' policies did not curb China's growing influence. Therefore, just reversing Trump's actions is insufficient if it will result in a pre-Trump status quo of American policy towards African nations. Instead, for the benefit of both the U.S. and African nations,[3] a bold new partnership framework is essential.[4] China's growing presence on the continent, which shows no signs of abating,[5] results from a fundamental respect of the power of African markets and resources, if not necessarily African people or African governments. The Trump administration's approach to Africa was often framed as part of a larger goal of confronting China instead of valuing African partners for their own sake. The Biden administration should not appear to continue with the framing of decidedly treating African partners as bystanders of an ongoing struggle between the U.S. and China.[6] Valuing African countries on their own terms will be the best way for the Biden administration to effectively counter Chinese influence on the continent since, by focusing narrowly on Chinese influence alone, that also means the U.S. might not work with China to support broader African goals, such as responding to COVID-19, UN peacekeeping missions, and more.

Wekesa, "New Directions in the Study of Africa–China Media and Communications Engagements," *Journal of African Cultural Studies* 29, no. 1 (2017): 11–24, https://doi.org/10.1080/13696815.2016.1270197.

[2] Darlene Superville, "Trump: Some African Nations are 'Very Tough Places to Live'," *Associated Press*, May 1, 2018, https://apnews.com/article/4f605f0a3da642b5902c4302b4486743.

[3] Brahima Sangafowa Coulibaly, "Looking Forward: US-Africa Relations," *Brookings Institution*, March 27, 2019, https://www.brookings.edu/testimonies/looking-forward-us-africa-relations/.

[4] Aubrey Hruby, "It's Time for an Africa Policy Upgrade," *Foreign Policy*, November 30, 2020, https://foreignpolicy.com/2020/11/30/united-states-africa-policy-biden/.

[5] Earl Carr and Owakhela Daniel Finlay Kankhwende, "The US versus Chinese Investment in Africa," *Forbes*, September 4, 2020, https://www.forbes.com/sites/earlcarr/2020/09/04/the-us-versus-chinese-investment-in-africa/?sh=263032ad65d4.

[6] Marcus Hicks, Kyle Atwell, and Dan Collini, "Great-Power Competition Is Coming to Africa," *Foreign Affairs*, March 4, 2021, https://www.foreignaffairs.com/articles/africa/2021-03-04/great-power-competition-coming-africa.

African nations do not want to decide between partnering with the U.S. and China, as they want to maintain strong relations with both.

President Biden has indicated a greater willingness to compete with China's global presence. In 2019, he spoke on the importance of "building a united front of friends and partners to challenge China."[7] This "united front of friends and partners" is predicated on respecting African markets and citizens of African countries, which President Biden emphasized as necessary in his February 5th remarks to the African Union:

> The United States stands ready to be your partner, in solidarity, support, and mutual respect. We believe in the nations of Africa. In the continent-wide spirit of entrepreneurship and innovation. And though the challenges are great, there is no doubt that our nations, our people, and the African Union are up to this task.[8]

These sentiments mean the U.S. should play up its comparative advantages in engagement, innovation, and norm-setting. This chapter will weave both description and prescription in the text in order to more persuasively make its points, since many of the weaknesses relating to the U.S.-Africa relationship predate the Trump administration.[9]

---

[7] Bob Davis and Lingling Wei, "Biden Plans to Build a Grand Alliance to Counter China. It Won't Be Easy," *The Wall Street Journal*, January 6, 2021, https://www.wsj.com/articles/biden-trump-xi-china-economic-trade-strategy-policy-11609945027.

[8] "President Biden's Message to African Union Summit Participants," *The White House*, February 5, 2021, video, https://www.youtube.com/watch?v=CE3X77YBSN8.

[9] This extends to the analysis of the Belt and Road Initiative (BRI), which is generally misunderstood on part of policymakers. It is not so much a discrete policy which causes and explains Chinese actions, so much as a reframing existing Chinese goals promoting Chinese goods and services. It is not an infrastructure initiative or an investment initiative, since many of these projects or their initial planning predate the announcement of BRI itself in 2013. BRI allows local stakeholders to engage with Chinese stakeholders to access finance through the invocation of the idea BRI itself. That means African stakeholders, who wish to access Chinese credit lines, will find this language useful in lieu of access to competing lines of credit. For more analysis, see: Min Ye, *The Belt Road and Beyond: State-Mobilized Globalization in China: 1998–2018* (New York: Cambridge University Press, 2020); Eyck Freymann, *One Belt One Road: Chinese Power Meets the World* (Boston: Harvard University Press, 2020); Angela Tritto and Alvin Camba, "The Belt and Road: The Good, the Bad, and the Mixed,' *The Diplomat*, April 15, 2019, https://thediplomat.com/2019/04/the-belt-and-road-the-good-the-bad-and-the-mixed/; Erik Myxter-Iino, "10: Is the Belt and Road Initiative a 'Grand Strategy'? with Dr. Lee Jones," *The*

## ENGAGEMENT

Beyond the damage done to U.S.-Africa relations due to the actions of the Trump administration,[10] these relations never merited a sustained U.S. response to China even before Trump's presidency. While there is still considerable debate about the nature of Africa-China relations before the first Forum on China-Africa Cooperation (FOCAC) in 2000,[11] the current trajectory and velocity of these relations can be traced to that event.[12] China has been adept in developing relationships with various African countries by emphasizing reciprocity and mutual respect. Even if that respect is performative and transactional, it is appreciated. An African head of state visiting China is treated as such, as are ministers. The Biden administration should emphasize that senior government officials treat African partners as partners on par with how European counterparts are treated. Engagement begins with reciprocity and mutual respect, and China should not have a monopoly on either.

### *Visits*

In order to further engagement, the Biden administration should commit to cabinet-level trips to African nations within the first two years in office. There are realistic limitations for the U.S. President, but sending Vice President Harris would be a highly effective demonstration of U.S. commitment if President Biden himself cannot travel there. It is imperative to engage with regional powers such as South Africa, Nigeria, Egypt, Morocco, Kenya, and Ethiopia, as well as countries of more modest strategic value. As a point of comparison, Chinese foreign ministers have been making African countries their first foreign visits to start the new year for over three decades.[13] Foreign Minister Wang Yi already visited

---

*Belt and Road Podcast*, podcast audio, April 23, 2013, https://podcasts.apple.com/us/podcast/the-belt-and-road-podcast/id1419143614?i=1000434046136.

[10] John Campbell, "U.S. Africa Policy Needs a Reset," *Foreign Affairs*, October 12, 2020, https://www.foreignaffairs.com/articles/africa/2020-10-12/us-africa-policy-needs-reset.

[11] Deborah Brautigam, *The Dragon's Gift: The Real Story of China in Africa* (New York: Oxford University Press, 2011).

[12] Chris Alden, *China in Africa* (London: Zed Books, 2007).

[13] "Wang Yi Briefs on the Chinese Foreign Minister's Tradition of Choosing Africa as First Destination of a Year and the 'Four Staunch Supports' Conveyed during His Visit,"

Nigeria, the Democratic Republic of the Congo, Botswana, Tanzania, and Seychelles in early January of 2021. Successful engagement requires Americans to act as guests as well as receive them.

China already has a robust engagement presence on the African continent with its existing diplomatic strategy. The United States will need to use every comparative advantage it has to compete in this area, such as the African diaspora. Even in situations of tricky domestic politics of African countries, the Biden administration should strongly consider bringing in more members of the African diaspora to assist in formulating and implementing Africa policies. Granted, caution is needed in these engagements since African governments do not consider all African diasporas representative of their constituents. Still, this population can be essential partners in furthering both American and African country goals. Beyond partnering with organizations like the International Career Advancement Program (ICAP) and Congressional Black Caucus Foundation, hiring and promoting African diaspora staff is crucial for these efforts. Stakeholders in African countries need to understand that Americans welcome foreigners, including those of African origin. China, as of yet, cannot compete in this area.

## Education

One area that both promotes engagement and demonstrates a positive articulation of U.S. support is education. There are currently around 80,000 Africans studying in China,[14] while roughly half of that number is studying in the U.S.[15] Furthermore, China offers up to 10,000 scholarships a year to many of these African students, often for one year of language training and four years of undergraduate education. While providing scholarships to African students might not be possible, what the U.S. can provide is a bold alternative in offering all African students,

---

*Ministry of Foreign Affairs of the People's Republic of China,* January 6, 2021, https://www.fmprc.gov.cn/mfa_eng/zxxx_662805/t1844910.shtm.

[14] "School's Out: Covid-19 Disrupts China's Rise as a Destination for Foreign Students," *The Economist,* January 30, 2021, https://www.economist.com/china/2021/01/30/covid-19-disrupts-chinas-rise-as-a-destination-for-foreign-students.

[15] Institute of International Education, "All Places of Origin," *Open Doors 2020 Report on International Educational Exchange,* 2020, https://opendoorsdata.org/data/international-students/all-places-of-origin/.

regardless of major, an expedited path towards Permanent Residence status upon applying for Optional Practical Training (OPT) for F-1 students. These Green Cards would be specially designated for these students, capped to at least 10,000 a year, and could be applied retroactively. If necessary, they could be declared in honor of Barack Obama Sr., a student of African descent whose presence changed the course of American history. China can offer better funding, but the U.S. can offer a better future. This Green Card program would require expanded State Department capacity, which could also be used to more quickly and courteously process visas for African citizens. African passports do not get much respect when African citizens travel abroad, and these citizens would highly appreciate that the U.S. has a better and more welcoming visa system for them. It would go a long way towards furthering engagement and highlighting Chinese bureaucracy's difficulties.

One incentive for promising African students to choose the United States over China would be for the Biden administration to build back the Fulbright Program.. That means not just restoring the budget amount cut during the Trump administration but increasing that funding to attract more students. Related to these efforts, the Biden administration should protect the Obama administration's Young African Leaders Initiative by offering more secure funding processes or assisting in securing partners. Engagement requires ongoing efforts, not quick fixes.

Governments of African countries, like all governments, value mutual respect, which is something that China well understands. The U.S. should be cognizant of these efforts and learn from them when appropriate and improve on them when possible. This action will begin the process of repairing the severely fractured relationships left by the Trump administration and change the narrative of U.S. engagement from a distant partner to an engaged one.

## INNOVATION

Along with engagement, the United States should focus on innovation. Since the turn of the century, Beijing has offered loans, often through two Chinese policy banks, China Development Bank (CDB) and the Import-Export Bank of China (Eximbank), for Chinese contractors to build infrastructure. It should be noted that this practice is not an "investment" in the usual sense, as the Chinese state-financed these projects to promote Chinese goods and services rather than the bankability of the projects themselves. These projects are rarely owned or managed by Chinese entities, so essentially, Chinese contractors get paid with Chinese money while taking on none of the risks of managing these projects long-term. This trend is a product of Chinese financial innovation. This phenomenon resulted from specific decisions and bold policymaking on China's part to harness its existing party-state capitalism capabilities to support and protect their domestic industries.[16] The U.S. does not have a corresponding state capitalism system, but there is space for the United States to compete with Chinese financial flows through innovation.

### *FDI Rhetoric*

First, though, innovation requires a clear understanding of core ideas, and there is a lack of knowledge around Chinese financial flows. As a rhetorical innovation, the U.S. should refrain from calling Chinese financial flows "investment" since most of these flows do not meet the equity requirements to count as FDI. This distinction is crucial in practice[17] since most countries wish to attract investors, and the U.S. should want other countries to invest in African states, sChina included.[18] Chinese loans made through a state-owned policy bank for the sake of Chinese contract work must be distinguished from other financial flows. This rhetorical innovation means that, while China is the African continent's largest trading partner, it is not yet the largest investor. Though FDI figures can be unreliable, and Chinese official statistics are almost certainly undercounting FDI, China has a limited FDI portfolio in Africa.[19]

[16] Harry Sanderson and Michael Forsythe, *China's Superbank: Debt, Oil and Influence—How China Development Bank is Rewriting the Rules of Finance* (Singapore: Wiley, 2013).

[17] Marvelous Ngundu and Nicholas Ngepah, "Comparative Effects of Foreign Direct Investment from China and Other Sources on Africa's Economic Growth," *AidData* Working Paper #93, January, 2020, https://www.aiddata.org/publications/comparative-effects-of-foreign-direct-investment-from-china-and-other-sources-on-africas-economic-growth.

[18] Irene Sun, *The Next Factory of the World: How Chinese Investment Is Reshaping Africa* (Boston: Harvard Business Review Press, 2017).

[19] Deborah Brautigam, Xinshen Diao, Margaret McMillan, and Jed Silver, "Chinese Investment in Africa: How Much Do We Know?," *PEDL Synthesis Series* No. 2, December 2017, https://pedl.cepr.org/sites/default/files/PEDL_Synthesis_Papers_Piece_No._2.pdf.

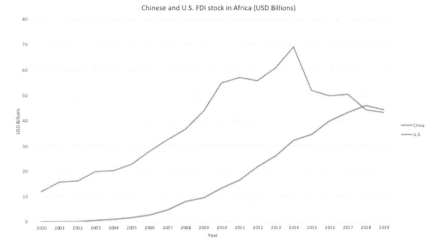

**Fig. 5.1** Chinese and U.S. FDI stock in Africa, 2000–2019 (USD Billions, unadjusted) (*Source* "Data: Chinese Investment in Africa," *Johns Hopkins University, China Africa Research Initiative, School of Advanced International Studie,* 2021, http://www.sais-cari.org/chinese-investment-in-africa)

Many actors mistakenly conflate FDI with Chinese policy bank loans to Chinese contractors. For example, in terms of FDI stock, China only recently became a comparable investor to the United States on the African continent (Fig. 5.1).

Even in terms of FDI flows, the numbers were quite comparable until 2014, and that is because the U.S. had negative flows rather than an unstoppable increase of Chinese investment itself.[20] While again, these numbers do not reflect Chinese policy bank loans, they indicate that both American and Chinese investors, not creditors, are not too far apart in terms of assessing opportunities in Africa (Fig. 5.2).

Furthermore, Chinese investors do not consider Africa, as compared to other parts of the world, a desirable Chinese capital destination. This notion is an essential point to highlight since, when Chinese policy banks

---

[20] Lina Benabdallah and Winslow Robertson, "Xi Jinping Pledged $60 Billion for Africa. Where Will the Money Go?," *Washington Post*, September 17, 2018, https:// www.washingtonpost.com/news/monkey-cage/wp/2018/09/17/xi-jinping-pledged-60-billion-for-africa-where-will-the-money-go/.

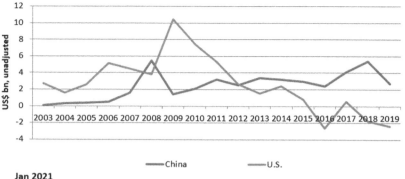

**Fig. 5.2** Chinese and U.S. FDI to Africa, Flow USD Billions, unadjusted) (*Source* "Data: Chinese Investment in Africa," *Johns Hopkins University, China Africa Research Initiative, School of Advanced International Studie*, 2021, http://www.sais-cari.org/chinese-investment-in-africa)

do not back Chinese actors, these actors rarely view African markets as a better opportunity than other parts of the world. According to Brautigam et al.'s 2017 *Private Enterprise Development in Low-Income Countries study of Chinese investment in Africa*, "… China only accounted for around 5% of global FDI into Africa in 2015." China is the African continent's fourth-largest investor in terms of stock as of 2018 (Fig. 5.3).[21]

**Key Points**

- American investors can and do compete with Chinese investors.
- When using their own money, Chinese investors are not nearly as willing to build infrastructure.

[21] Thierry Pairault, "Guest Post—Investment in Africa: China vs "Traditional Partners"—Part 1," *China in Africa: The Real Story*, July 31, 2020, http://www.chinaafricarealstory.com/2020/07/guest-post-investment-in-africa-china.html.

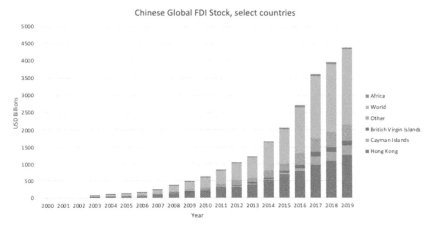

**Fig. 5.3** Global Destinations of Chinese FDI, 2000–2019 (USD Billions, unadjusted) (*Source* "Data: Chinese Investment in Africa," *Johns Hopkins University, China Africa Research Initiative, School of Advanced International Studie*, 2021, http://www.sais-cari.org/chinese-investment-in-africa)

- However, American investors think they are competing against Chinese contractors backed by Chinese policy banks, which is not the case.
- If the Biden administration continues to call Chinese economic engagement "investment," actual investors will understandably think they cannot compete with or innovate against billions of dollars from Beijing.

Actual American investment in Africa has dropped. Unfortunately, promoting U.S. private sector investment, while laudable, is not something the U.S. has the tools to appropriately promote. It is important to note China itself cannot even get private investors to use their own capital despite the broader array of financial tools at its disposal, as demonstrated by the China-Africa Development Fund (CAD Fund), China's first and largest equity investment fund focusing on Africa. This Fund, announced in 2006 and created in 2007, is backed by CDB and has invested $4.6

billion through 2018.[22] While an impressive number, over the Fund's life cycle, it actually reflects a difficulty in finding projects. This insight is reflected by a CAD Fund informant in a 2019 interview with Hangwei Li:

> The Fund would love to work more closely with African companies, especially the private sector. But often, it is not feasible commercially. First, the Fund is different from loans or aid. The Fund has an expectation on profits. Second, if using the 'investment + loan' model, the company not only needs to have borrowing capacity but also repayment ability, which many African companies lack.[23]

If a $10 billion equity investment fund promoted by the highest levels of the Chinese government has these problems, it is unclear whether the U.S. can respond with a similar action. Furthermore, the record of various African government policy tools towards attracting long-term private investment has proven quite mixed. Asking an American specifically to invest in Kenya over Kentucky is incredibly challenging. However, the Biden administration can use strategic innovation to promote and protect the Export–Import Bank of the United States (EXIM) from domestic political criticism. EXIM is a very successful organization, but the organization's uncertain political future severely limited its ability to function.[24] Rather than let EXIM stay an obscure executive agency, the administration should make it the centerpiece for dealing with China in Africa since export credit agencies are necessary to promote goods and services. Tie the desire to counter China to the promotion of EXIM. Protecting EXIM means that reauthorization is never in doubt, that no change in administration will result in a change in existing operations, and that it is one of the most critical tools for competing with China globally.

This notion does not mean that the U.S. should treat EXIM as a policy bank to compete with China at every level. A significant reason that African governments agree to Chinese loans is that they do not

---

[22] Hangwei Li, "From Politics to Business: How a State-Led Fund is Investing in Africa? The Case of the China-Africa Development Fund," *Boston University*, GCI Working Paper 010, February 2020, https://www.bu.edu/gdp/files/2020/02/WP10-Hangwei-1-1.pdf.

[23] Ibid., 11.

[24] Nicholas Norbrook, "US EXIM: 'We Have a New Mandate to Take China on Around the World'," *The Africa Report*, June 11, 2020, https://www.theafricareport.com/29796/us-exim-we-have-a-new-mandate-to-take-china-on-around-the-world/.

have many financing options for infrastructure. EXIM cannot necessarily help in these issues. Crucially, as China takes the lead on infrastructure financing and contracting, it is not prudent for the U.S. to center its foreign policy aims on criticizing and countering Chinese loans with nothing tangible to offer as an alternative. Chinese financial flows offer African countries choices they otherwise would not have, and American innovation must be similarly focused on providing African partners with appropriate options. The U.S., also as a matter of rhetorical innovation, should find another term for these Chinese loans than "debt-trap diplomacy," as they fail to account for the agency of African leaders and the specific reasons for why a project was built in the first place.[25]

### Financing

Then, what would financial innovation that offers African partners tangible options look like? One example is the U.S. International Development Finance Corporation (DFC) recent deal to help Ecuador pay Chinese loans by coordinating private-sector financial institutions to buy Ecuador assets and raise cash for the Ecuadorian government to pay off its Chinese debt.[26]

### Infrastructure Certification

Another example would be a certification program for African infrastructure projects combined with a mechanism to finance such certified projects. Infrastructure is rarely profitable but necessary for many governments, not just African ones. Many of the infrastructure projects being financed were conceived decades ago. For example, Ethiopia wished to work with European partners to refurbish its Addis-Djibouti corridor, and in 2009 the European Commission offered 50 million euros for the project. Not only was the money insufficient, as 50 million euros

[25] Deborah Brautigam and Meg Rithmire, "The Chinese 'Debt Trap' is a Myth," *The Atlantic*, February 6, 2021, https://www.theatlantic.com/international/archive/2021/02/china-debt-trap-diplomacy/617953/.

[26] Sevastopulo, Demetri, and Gideon Long, "US Development Bank Strikes Deal to Help Ecuador Pay China.

Loans," *Financial Times*, January 14, 2021, https://www.ft.com/content/affcc432-03c4-459d-a6b8-922ca8346c14.

cannot cover these sorts of infrastructure costs, but even then, due to other difficulties in financing and with the contractor, the refurbishment was abandoned in 2011.[27] African governments often turn to Chinese loans not because they offer the best terms but because they are either the only option, or these loans are disbursed quickly. Suppose these infrastructure projects met the requirements for a proposed national development certificate. In that case, the U.S. could use its diplomatic capital in existing multilateral development banks (MDBs) to create unique programs that offset the difference in interest rates and disbursement speeds for these infrastructure projects.

To explain how this would work, first, the U.S. should understand that these projects were inevitable, as African governments often waited decades to find the financing for them. If these projects were going to be built, then the U.S. position must be that it objects to the specificity of Chinese financing, not the project itself. Since the U.S. will not finance the project, and the funding market is not in favor of these African countries, a national development certification of these projects would have MDBs cover the difference in interest rates between the proposed Chinese financing and the competitors. This action will make sure the disbursement of funds happens just as quickly as with Chinese funding. The U.S. does not offer the loan in this scenario since it is the MDB itself that funds this. The MDB is not technically paying for the infrastructure since they are merely offsetting the costs of a non-Chinese policy bank financing such a project. The certification would not stop Chinese loans from going to Africa since some African governments will take Chinese loans for reasons outside of national development. However, if such a certification was implemented, that would only help make the case that Chinese debt is not in the interest of national development since national development projects would overwhelmingly be funded without Chinese involvement.

An additional area of innovation involves regulatory innovation through prioritizing support for African-led initiatives like the African

[27] Yunnan Chen, "Laying the Tracks: The Political Economy of Railway Development in Ethiopia's Railway Sector and Implications for Technology Transfer," *China Africa Research Initiative, School of Advanced International Studies* Working Paper No. 2021/43, January 2021, https://static1.squarespace.com/static/5652847de4b033f56d 2bdc29/t/601d65dd9314e665654343bf/1612539358965/WP+43+Chen+Ethiopia+Rai lway+Tech+Transfer.pdf.

Continental Free Trade Area agreement (AfCFTA), which will create the largest free trade area in the world by the number of countries participating. The deal connects 1.3 billion people across 55 countries with a combined GDP valued at $3.4 trillion.[28] This area offers fantastic opportunities for expanding American businesses, contributing to job creation both in the U.S. and in African markets. AfCFTA will create substantial demand for U.S. goods and services and harmonize relevant policies and regulations. U.S. exports of agricultural products to sub-Saharan Africa totaled $2.6 billion in 2013, which will only grow as African country populations continue to grow. It will result in the same rules being implemented at the continental level, reducing transaction costs. These regulations have historically been a concern for U.S. businesses, and thus it is imperative for the Biden administration to support these agreements.

Engaging more with AfCFTA would also complement existing U.S. initiatives such as the African Growth and Opportunity Act (AGOA), a program initiated by the Clinton administration in 2000 that provided unilateral duty-free exports for 6,500 products from Africa to the United States.[29] Free trade harmonization could also promote African goods entering the U.S. market. This opportunity is particularly relevant for agribusiness products, as farming remains the primary employment source for 65% of Africa's population.[30] With an emphasis on regulatory innovation, U.S. entities could promote these African goods to meet American regulatory requirements, which would help these goods export to both the United States and other foreign markets. China is slowly but consistently opening up its market to new African agricultural products. Meeting Chinese requirements is quite complicated. If African countries can put a dent in their trade deficits with China through AfCFTA and AGOA, that helps American political and commercial goals.

[28] "The African Continental Free Trade Area," *World Bank Group*, July 27, 2020, https://www.worldbank.org/en/topic/trade/publication/the-african-continental-free-trade-area#:~:text=The%20African%20Continental%20Free%20Trade%20Area%20(AfCFTA)%20agreement%20will%20create,valued%20at%20US%243.4%20trillion.

[29] Gracelin Baskaran, "US-Africa Trade Relations: Why is AGOA Better than a Bilateral Free Trade Agreement?," *Brookings Institution*, September 24, 2020, https://www.brookings.edu/blog/future-development/2020/09/24/us-africa-trade-relations-why-is-agoa-better-than-a-bilateral-free-trade-agreement/.

[30] Steven Radelet, "Africa's Rise-Interrupted?" *International Monetary Fund*, FINANCE & DEVELOPMENT 53, no. 2, June 2016, https://www.imf.org/external/pubs/ft/fandd/2016/06/radelet.htm.

Africa is open for business, and there is enough space for both American and Chinese presence on the continent. As Naunihal Singh, Josephine Appiah-Nyamekye Sanny, and E. Gyimah-Boadi explain in the Washington Post using Afrobarometer data:

> Importantly, it appears that for many Africans, U.S.-China "competition" may not be an either-or proposition but a win-win. Those who are positive about the influence of China are more likely to feel positively about U.S. influence as well — the two views are strongly and positively correlated, instead of moving in opposite directions (where one increases as the other decreases), which we would expect if Africans perceived this to be purely a competition.[31]

The U.S. must demonstrate that it is an innovative partner to various African stakeholders. A partnership that leads to mutual economic benefit is more attractive than a distant relationship centered around lectures on the dangers of China's presence on the continent.

## NORM-SETTING

The U.S. is still a global leader that sets international norms. As President Biden considers which areas require immediate U.S. leadership in setting these norms, COVID-19 and Africa's debt crisis stand out. The U.S. understands first-hand the difficulties in national vaccine rollouts, and African countries have not secured vaccines despite the COVID-19 Vaccines Global Access (COVAX) agreement. Furthermore, many African economies, large and small, are feeling the brunt of unsustainable debt loads, compounded by COVID-19.

### *Vaccines*

For COVID-19, the United States should lead every wealthy country by setting aside its vaccine supply purchases for African nations and using diplomatic means to get U.S. allies to do the same. This is an important

---

[31] Naunihal Singh, Josephine Appiah-Nyamekye Sanny, and E. Gyimah-Boadi, "U.S.-China Competition May be a Win–Win for Africa," *Washington Post*, November 20, 2020, https://www.washingtonpost.com/politics/2020/11/20/us-china-competition-may-be-win-win-africa/.

enough topic that, even without specific implementation recommendations, the Biden administration must be seen as valuing African lives and attempting to use political capital to help. Regardless of storage, infrastructure, or intellectual property difficulties, the Biden administration needs to secure vaccine supply, rather than funding, for citizens of African countries. Vaccine nationalism is regrettable but understandable, as almost no country can navigate the domestic political difficulties of sharing vaccines.[32] However, the only country in the world that has the power to lead in this area is the United States. Vaccine nationalism does not work with a global pandemic, as a strain in another country can disrupt even a well-vaccinated society. Thus, as a matter of national security, the Biden administration must focus on international vaccination efforts in parallel with the domestic vaccination policies, and not have the former come at the expense of the latter. China is attempting to offer vaccine options to African nations[33] and COVAX itself.[34] The U.S. must set the norms for wealthy countries by not letting vaccine nationalism prolong COVID-19 and also not letting governments renege on the spirit of their COVAX commitments. If China is better equipped to manufacture and distribute vaccines, the U.S. should assist in those efforts. If the U.S. can improve on those efforts, then the U.S. should do so. The U.S. has the power to set global norms here and can save millions, perhaps even billions, of lives in the process.

## Debt

As for debt, this issue has exposed the degree to which the U.S. has failed to create alternatives to China's innovative financing model. Even before

---

[32] Peel, Michael, David Pilling, and Donato Mancini, "Can Covax Deliver the Vaccines Much of the World Needs?," *Financial Times*, February 12, 2021, https://www.ft.com/content/fffe8e68-238a-4a4b-bcad-47417882e0ed.

[33] Nwachukwu Egbunike, "COVID-19 Vaccine in Africa: Caught Between China's Soft-Power Diplomacy and the West's Vaccine Nationalism, Part I," *Global Voices*, February 1, 2021, https://globalvoices.org/2021/02/01/covid-19-vaccine-in-africa-caught-between-chinas-soft-power-diplomacy-and-the-wests-vaccine-nationalism-part-i/.

[34] Reuters Staff, "China to Provide 10 Million Vaccine Doses to COVAX Initiative," *Reuters*, February 3, 2021, https://www.reuters.com/article/health-coronavirus-vaccine-china/update-1-china-to-provide-10-million-vaccine-doses-to-covax-initiative-idUSL1N2K90HS.

the pandemic hit, many African nations had enormous debt burdens,[35] which grew heavier as their currencies' value fell relative to the foreign currencies in which the debt was denominated. As this happened, the income necessary to make regular interest payments on the debt dried up. The initiative that came out of last spring's G-20 meeting—the Debt Service Suspension Initiative (DSSI), covered only bilateral deficits, only to the end of 2020, and only for the poorest African countries, even though this issue goes beyond them alone. A proposal to grant the IMF Special Drawing Rights (SDRs), which would have given these countries access to additional financing, also failed. The United States blocked the measure since the SDRs would have been available to all countries—benefiting collaborators and competitors alike.

Efforts are underway to improve DSSI to include the private sector and increase Chinese transparency and full participation.[36] Should that fail, the U.S. could lead the way to appeal that decision and amplify pressure to stress more accountability from bilateral lenders, such as China. Biden could also reverse Trump's SDR veto and unlock a significant source of relief to debt-imperiled countries, weakening the bargaining position of other debt holders such as China. They should work with Paris Club lenders and other relevant players to promote transparency by publishing all African loan data, including terms and interest rates, in an easily accessible database. America's own EXIM bank must be more transparent in the data it provides. For legal issues regarding revealing of contract terms, the Biden Administration should work with international law experts in the United States to put together a continent-wide framework for loan transparency. Setting the norms for global transparency requires leading by example.

---

[35] Theodore Murphy, "Biden's Priority in Africa Should Be Debt Relief," *Foreign Policy*, November 12, 2020, https://foreignpolicy.com/2020/11/12/debt-relief-africa-financing-china-sdr/.

[36] Kevin Acker, Deborah Brautigam, and Yufan Huang, "Debt Relief with Chinese Characteristics," *China Africa Research Initiative, School of Advanced International Studies* Working Paper No. 2020/39, June 2020, https://static1.squarespace.com/static/5652847de4b033f56d2bdc29/t/5efe942ba09c523cbf9440a9/1593742380749/WP+39+-+Acker%2C+Brautigam%2C+Huang+-+Debt+Relief.pdf.

That extends to the U.S. leading the effort to provide African finance ministries[37] with liquidity and debt relief where reasonable, especially in such a way that does not harm their credit ratings. This is crucial because these countries will not accept any form of debt relief that impairs their ability to take on more debt in the future.[38] If the U.S. wants to argue that Chinese loans are predatory, it should set the norm for what non-predatory financing looks like and support these countries' efforts in getting out of these unfair debt burdens.

This notion is especially pertinent in terms of how China behaves as a rising power and the Chinese government's role in commercial activities. Arguably, Beijing views advancing its global footprint as more valuable than immediate debt repayment. This crisis is an area where the U.S. can and should take steps to counteract China's interests more directly through elevating global lending norms in a way that benefits African partners and U.S. citizens.

## American Renewal

President Biden's election victory signals that the United States has the resolve necessary to thrive as a global leader, significantly improving the scope and capacity of its commercial and diplomatic activities on the African continent. African markets are growing along with the African population. At the same time, the U.S. must account for Chinese actions on the African continent in formulating strategy.

The U.S. should learn from Chinese successes while charting its path in repairing connections and deepening ties as it increases its commercial presence on the continent. U.S. foreign policy directives should be centered around engagement, innovation, and norm-setting, which will benefit U.S. citizens, American national security interests, and African partners, all while counteracting the most egregious Chinese actions on the continent.

---

[37] Hannah Ryder, "What African Countries Should be Fighting for in Negotiations with China," *Quartz Africa*, February 11, 2021, https://qz.com/africa/1971145/how-china-can-help-africas-economy-recover-from-covid-19/.

[38] Gyude Moore, "Chinese Influence is Assured—How Should Africa Respond?," *African Business*, November 16, 2020, https://african.business/2020/11/trade-investment/chinese-influence-is-assured-how-should-africa-respond/.

# CHAPTER 6

# Rethinking Strategic Alignment with the Gulf States

*Yaser Faheem and Asad Hussaini*

**Abstract** "This chapter analyzes how China has actively engaged countries in the Gulf Cooperation Council (GCC), in particular the UAE and Saudi Arabia. As the GCC powerhouses Saudi Arabia and the UAE seek to diversify their economies and attract more foreign investment, enhancing and bolstering trade and economic relations with other regional powers have become core priorities. However, given the Gulf's inherent reliance on the security umbrella of the United States to establish an effective deterrent against Iran, the GCC states may inevitably find themselves

---

---

Y. Faheem (✉)
Graduate, NYU Center for Global Affairs, New York, NY, USA
e-mail: myf221@nyu.edu

A. Hussaini
Managing Partner, ZAFCOMM, Dubai, UAE
e-mail: asad@zafcomm.ae

© The Author(s), under exclusive license to Springer Nature Singapore Pte Ltd. 2021
E. Carr Jr. (ed.), *From Trump to Biden and Beyond*,
https://doi.org/10.1007/978-981-16-4297-5_6

engaged in a balancing act due to increasing animosity between their primary security and commercial benefactors as well as the United States' growing disinterest in the region."

**Keywords** China · UAE · United Arab Emirates · Saudi Arabia · Iran · United States · Middle East · GCC · Economy · Belt and Road · BRI

## Introduction

The departure of Donald Trump from office is being felt deeply across the Gulf States as the Biden administration is moving quickly to reverse the U.S. policy on Iran under Trump, readdress the United States' engagement in Yemen, and prioritize Saudi Arabia's growing human rights concerns. Former President Trump, whose first foreign trip in office was to Riyadh, was well received in the region for his maximum pressure campaign against Iran, support for Saudi Arabia's position in the Yemen war and defense of the Saudis in the aftermath of the killing of Washington Post journalist Jamal Khashoggi. However, there is a new sheriff in town now. A renewed relationship and a strategic shift in the U.S.–Gulf alliance already seemed to be in the works during the first few weeks of the Biden Presidency. As President Joe Biden and his team worked aggressively to undo many of former President Trump's legacies during their first weeks, the new administration has also halted billions of dollars in weapons sale to Saudi Arabia and the United Arab Emirates—in line with President Biden's campaign rhetoric as well as a growing bipartisan consensus to bring about accountability and review the role of the Gulf countries in Yemen as well as the Kingdom's human rights record.

## Backdrop

Fracking—a term eponymous with a new era in American history and world at large. Perhaps most affected by this tectonic shift in the dynamics of global energy markets were the oil rich states of the Arabian Gulf. In the aftermath of the Cold War, the United States had moved aggressively to consolidate a broader international coalition against the Soviet Union. Access to reliable energy was a critical part of this infrastructure. On the back of this indispensability, the once backward States of the Gulf quickly ascended to prominence awash with wealth and suddenly became a central pillar in the global economic system.

This significance afforded them a special relationship with the United States as stability in the oil rich parts of the Middle East was essential to the United States' mandate to keep the global economic order in check, and thereby the Gulf region was functionally a protectorate of the United States. A sizable naval, air and ground force contingent was established to help quell any domestic or regional security threats within the region. In the decades that ensued, the countries and governments of the Gulf came to rely on this guarantee as an essential part of their security strategy and were acutely aware of the threat posed by the Iranian regime and their relatively limited capabilities to deal with them.

Nonetheless, as long as the United States was willing to stand guard for the Gulf region and asked very little for providing that security, the status quo held. However, in more recent years, this security understanding has begun to fade and the footprint of American forces in the region has dwindled and has been on a demonstrable downward trajectory with few exceptions throughout the past several years consistent across both republican and democratic administrations.

## BIDEN ADMINISTRATION

While President Joe Biden is vastly familiar with the Middle East, the Middle East region he knew as Vice President is not the one he has inherited as the 46th President of the United States. Washington's relationships with some of its closest Middle East allies—Israel, Saudi Arabia, and the United Arab Emirates—were drastically renewed under President Trump, who emboldened their leadership while muzzling U.S. criticism over a number of their human rights concerns. As has been made clear by his foreign policy approaches during his first months in office, President Joe Biden is more interested in bringing back Iran to the table through a renewed version of the JCPOA and less keen on offering any peace plans for the Israeli–Palestinian conflict—unlike his predecessor who managed to broker a peace deal between Israel and the United Arab Emirates.[1]

---

[1] Anne Gearan, "Trump Emboldened Israel and Saudi Arabia; Now Biden Will Try to Rein Them in a Little," *Washington Post*, January 6, 2021, https://www.washingtonpost.com/politics/2020/12/09/biden-israel-saudi-arabia-middle-east/.

Additionally, Biden has plans on keeping the Gulf hegemon Saudi Arabia at arm's length and their de facto leader—Crown Prince Mohamed Bin Salman—in check. During his first weeks in office, Biden already punished the Saudi Crown Prince by declassifying the U.S. intelligence report that directly implicates him in the murder of Jamal Khashoggi. He has also halted a weapon's sale to Saudi Arabia and UAE—in line with his promises to pivot the United States away from the conflict in Yemen. Furthermore, Biden who called Saudi Arabia a "pariah" during the presidential campaign and vowed to confront the kingdom over its human rights record is expected to yank the backing of the White House for the Saudi-led war in Yemen and may also sign on to the congressional reprimands of Saudi Arabia over the humanitarian cost of the war. All of these factors coupled with Biden's promise on reducing American military presence overseas and America's growing energy interdependence will likely define the Biden era policy towards the Gulf States and the larger Middle East region.[2]

## China Filling the Gap

With the new Biden administration taking reins of the U.S. government—and with Democratic control of both the House and the Senate—ties between the United States and the Gulf countries are likely to deteriorate. The United States' growing energy independence as well as an increasing bipartisan consensus to punish the Kingdom for its role in Yemen, as well as Crown Prince Mohammed bin Salman's involvement in the murder of the Washington Post Journalist Jamal Khashoggi are likely to create lasting ripples in the U.S.–Gulf relationship during President Biden's tenure. As the United States grows weary of its relationship with its Gulf allies, China has used this growing incompatibility to its advantage. China has recently adopted an active engagement approach with the countries in the Gulf Cooperation Council (GCC) and in particular the United Arab Emirates and the Kingdom of Saudi Arabia. Both countries have found an eager participant in China, which has sought new economic cooperation under its Belt and Road Initiative (BRI). However, a growing fondness for China and a reemergence of the U.S. foreign policy under the new Biden administration could very well put the GCC States in the

---

[2] "American Leadership: Joe Biden," *Joe Biden for President: Official Campaign Website,* July 29, 2020, https://joebiden.com/americanleadership/.

crosshairs of U.S.–China rivalry making it very tricky for them to balance their economic partnership with China and their national security allyship with the United States.

## THE GROWING ENERGY INTERDEPENDENCE BETWEEN CHINA & GULF STATES

The Growing cooperation between the Kingdom's national oil company, Saudi Aramco, and Chinese state-owned energy companies epitomizes the coordinated effort being made by both governments to strengthen their commercial ties. In 2016, President Xi of China and the Saudi King Salman also oversaw the inauguration of a giant $10bn refinery at the Saudi port city of Yanbu, a strategic location along the Maritime Silk Road. China's significant domestic energy imports from the region are also evidence of a growing interdependence with the GCC to fuel its insatiable economic growth, especially in light of Covid-19. During 2019 leading into 2020, OPEC constituted the majority of supply (55%) of China's crude oil imports. China imported its highest-ever volume of crude oil in May last year where imports from the world's top oil exporter, Saudi Arabia, nearly doubled to the highest on record. The decision to improve and strengthen economic relations with the Kingdom was clearly a strategy to hedge and diversify economic ties as a result of the Trump led U.S.–China Trade War, which continued despite Trump's touted "great" relationship with Chinese President Xi.

In 2017 and 2018, China and the UAE also further enhanced their energy ties as State oil companies from both sides signed a multitude of agreements. During the same time, the Chinese National Petroleum Corporation also sought $3bn stake in Abu Dhabi oilfields, and received the largest onshore-offshore seismic survey contract from Abu Dhabi National Oil Company, worth $1.6bn.[3]

---

[3] Earl Carr, "The U.S., Gulf States & China: Oil, Power, and Geo-Strategic Influence," *Forbes*, December 14, 2020, https://www.forbes.com/sites/earlcarr/2020/09/25/the-us-gulf-states-and-china-oil-power--geo-strategic-influence/?sh=1cf5fe2b70d5.

## How Chinese Capital is Changing
## the Geopolitical Landscape in the Gulf Region

Another noteworthy investment trend has been the surge in the influx of Chinese capital in the infrastructure projects across the Gulf countries drawn by the region's investment-friendly environment and geostrategic location as an increasingly indispensable artery of global commerce. Accordingly, Chinese firms have committed hundreds of millions of dollars to these projects. For their hosts, Chinese investment can act as the catalyst that kick-starts diversification and leads to a plethora of local construction activity. This investment is a welcome development at a time when governments are seeking austerity. According to the Heritage Foundation, Chinese companies tendered an estimated $30bn worth of contracts in the Gulf countries between 2005 and 2014 (Fig. 6.1).

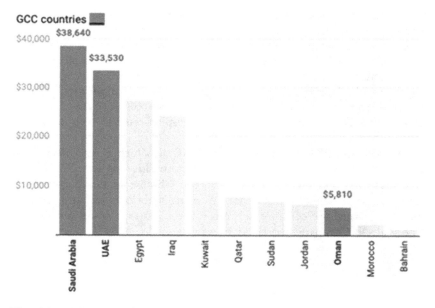

**Fig. 6.1**   GCC States have been the biggest recipients of Chinese investments over the last two decades (*Source* "China Global Investment Tracker," American Enterprise Institute and Heritage Foundation, accessed September 15, 2020, https://www.aei.org/china-global-investment-tracker/)

In Saudi Arabia, a grand speed railway project connecting the city of Jeddah to the holy sites of Mecca and Medina has been undertaken in cooperation with Chinese firms. In Dubai, a Chinese-Saudi bid secured the contract to construct the extension of the Mohammed bin Rashid Al Maktoum Solar Park. In Oman, a grandiose 11-hectare "Chinese-Omani Park" is being built in Duqm, 550 km south of the capital city of Muscat. Amongst these projects, Duqm stands out as the primary Gulf port not in the Strait of Hormuz region, which would make itself a primary transit point in the event of any disputes with Iran. Unsurprisingly, it is also China's primary point of focus in Oman.

## REIMAGINING THE CHINESE RENMINBI AS A GLOBAL RESERVE CURRENCY

Analysts at Morgan Stanley predicted in a report in 2020 that sustained foreign investment into Chinese markets could elevate the adoption of the Chinese Yuan and push it to become the third largest reserve currency in the world—only behind the U.S. dollar and the Euro. In addition to energy and infrastructure cooperation projects, China and the GCC State have also worked on vastly improving their trade and commercial ties. Chinese financial establishments have grown in presence in the Gulf region, facilitating the exchange of local currencies with Chinese Yuan and also expanding Yuan financing options. The United Arab Emirates has been the hallmark for such activity since the signing of an MoU in 2015 for the establishment of a Yuan clearing center in the Gulf country. Furthermore, the central banks of the two countries also renewed a three-year $5.2bn agreement to reduce the cost of currency exchange by avoiding the need to convert local currency into dollars. While China is a long way away from being able to effectively de-Dollarize its financial engagements with the Gulf country, the groundwork is being laid for establishing a Yuan centric payment system which would be a notably practical step given the United States' recent moves to limit Hong Kong's access to the Dollar.

## United States Versus China: American Policy Moving Forward

Beyond economic partnerships, the Middle East region as a whole is quickly becoming an increasingly contested space for regional powers to exert and expand their sphere of influence. Previously uncontested American supremacy is now being challenged by the likes of China and Russia. The growing uncertainty of American policy toward the region has encouraged American partners like the Saudis and the Emiratis to hedge and cultivate other power-wielding relationships besides Washington. In line with that, China continues to establish comprehensive strategic partnerships with both the Gulf countries. The diplomatic hedging by the Saudis and Emiratis is also reflective of the uncertainty of the United States commitment to the region. While the United States is no longer an energy importer, it must not downplay the fact that it still remains tied to the region and its security through its partners. The energy market is a global one, so any fluctuation in oil prices due to a security misadventure in one place will have consequences elsewhere—a risk the United States cannot afford.

The presence of the United States military in the region has been vital for the Asian countries, whether or not they are U.S. allies. Over the last couple of decades, the United States has provided a security umbrella under which the growth in Gulf-Asian connectivity has thrived. But that does not necessarily mean that the Asian powers are fully in agreement with the U.S. foreign policy approach toward the region. Few were comfortable with the American decision to withdraw from the nuclear deal with Iran in 2018, since it meant the re-imposition of sanctions on the country and any other third-party that does business with it. With the new Biden administration in office and a U.S. reversal on its Iran policy under Trump, Asian countries—especially those in direct confrontation with Iran, i.e., the GCC nations—are growing wary of the uniformity and dependability of U.S. foreign policy toward the region. This air of confusion has allowed China to pivot itself in a leadership role for the region. A rapid expansion of BRI projects in the Gulf region signifies the growing Chinese relevance and influence in the Arabian Peninsula. As both Saudi Arabia and United Arab Emirates seek to diversify their economy and attract more foreign investment, enhancing and bolstering trade and economic relations with China has become a core priority. A rising Chinese engagement and soft power influence in the region capitalizes on the United States' growing disinterest in the region stemming from an overreach and effective energy independence. As a comprehensive package of foreign direct investment, the Belt and Road Initiative by China represents a captivating alternative to American financial assistance, even if it will fundamentally fail to replace the American security umbrella. Whether China can sustain and build on this newly found relationship will determine how long Chinese officials maintain their allegiance with the sheikhdoms of the GCC.[4]

For the Gulf States, it is becoming overwhelmingly clear that the United States is making a concerted effort to draw down its presence in the region and is no longer interested in occupying the role of the grand arbiter in this part of the world. That being said, the manner in which the American drawdown takes place and the structures that replace it will be critical in determining what level of residual influence the United States maintains in this part of the world. The authors of this chapter firmly believe that it is still in the U.S. interest to maintain a level of influence in the region and maintain some dominance there vis-a-vis the Chinese whose subsequent activities and engagement in the region have substantially ramped up over the past few years. In accordance with the aforementioned objective, a framework of regional integration could be proposed that ensures that the United States withdraws from the region without greatly compromising its stability and jeopardizing their deep structural integration with the West.[5]

While the Arab Gulf states have traditionally had very weak militaries that largely relied on the United States to function as their security guarantor, these countries in the past two decades built up sizable defense capabilities consistently ranking amongst the highest spenders globally on the purchase of defensive systems. Today, they boast state of the art American and Western fighter aircrafts, air defense systems, as well as early warning and radar detection capabilities. However, despite the advent of this equipment, integration between these regional allies remains loose

[4] Guy Burton, "The Growing Connectivity Between the Gulf and East Asia," *The Diplomat*, March 4, 2020, https://thediplomat.com/2020/03/the-growing-connectivity-between-the-gulf-and-east-asia/.

[5] Sanam Vakil, "The GCC in 2021: Outlook and Key Challenges," *Chatham House, Royal Institute of International Affairs*, January 29, 2021, https://www.chathamhouse.org/2021/01/gcc-2021-outlook-and-key-challenges.

and haphazard. It would be in the interest of the United States to encourage these allies to work together to increase training and coordination capabilities amongst themselves in order to bolster a stronger and more cohesive deterrent to the Iranian threat. Additionally, closer defense cooperation with Israel must be a central part of the strategy. While the United Arab Emirates & Bahrain have led the way in normalizing relations with Israel, these engagements have largely remained economic in nature. By encouraging more Arab nations to normalize relations with Israel and forcing additional defense cooperation amongst these allies, this policy can become a bedrock for American security policy in the region. Finally, there could also be credence in suggesting that the countries of the Gulf Cooperation Council and Israel move to sign a mutual defense pact making American security guarantees contingent upon some level of defense integration between the GCC block and Israel.[6]

For the Biden administration, it must ensure that America's growing disengagement from the region doesn't result in a vacuum that is quickly and entirely filled up by China. A hasty shift in priorities could end up putting the United States at a strategic security disadvantage in the region. The Biden administration must remain privy to the growing Chinese engagement with the Gulf States and must ensure that the U.S. directly or indirectly continues to maintain their strategic and foreign policy dominance in the Gulf region.

---

[6] Austin Bodetti, "The Gulf's Balance between the US and China," *Gulf State Analytics*, June 28, 2019, https://gulfstateanalytics.com/the-gulfs-balance-between-the-us-and-china/.

# CHAPTER 7

# Reshaping U.S.–South Korea–Japan Trilateral Relations

*Jeeho Bae*

**Abstract** When the U.S. government developed its "America First" philosophy during the last four years, the position of global leadership was left vacant. Since Joe Biden entered the White House as 46th President of the United States, he announced, "diplomacy is back at the center of foreign policy." While that may be the case, significant challenges remain. Regaining global leadership, reassuring alliances, and reestablishing credibility are the most urgent American foreign policy objectives. Particularly, repairing key U.S. allies in the East Asia region is urgent to rebalance the power between the United States and China—the region considered most critical with respect to global security and economic growth. The United States needs to cooperate with key allies such as South Korea and Japan to avoid repeating mistakes made by its predecessor and to confront

---

The views and opinions expressed in this chapter are those of the author and do not reflect the official policy or position of any organizations with which the author is affiliated.

---

J. Bae (✉)
Senior Research Analyst, Pivotal Advisors, New York, NY, USA

E. Carr Jr. (ed.), *From Trump to Biden and Beyond*,
https://doi.org/10.1007/978-981-16-4297-5_7

the challenge of China's expanding influence. China's strategic diplomacy has been bold and sophisticated, so the United States should rethink its strategies to face the geopolitical prowess of China and realign its relations with regional partners to reinforce regional security and influence in East Asia. To that end, Washington should proceed in building high technology and economy-focused trilateral relationships and secure the foundation of regional alliances.

**Keywords** South Korea · Japan · Technology cooperation · The U.S. foreign policy · East Asia · China · 5G Competition · Dual Circulation · ROK-Japan relations

When the U.S. government aimed its *"America First"* philosophy for the last four years, the position of global leadership was left vacant. Since Joe Biden entered the White House as 46th President of the United States, he announced, "diplomacy is back at the center of foreign policy.[1]" While that may be the case, significant challenges remain. In the post-initial lockdown COVID-19 era, fighting the pandemic and getting the domestic economy back on track should be the Biden Administration's top priority. However, at the same time, regaining global leadership, reassuring alliances, and reestablishing credibility are the most urgent American foreign policy objectives. Particularly, repairing the key U.S. allies in the East Asia region is urgent to rebalance the power between the United States and China—the region considered most critical with respect to global security and economic growth.

As stated by President Joe Biden, the United States needs to cooperate with key allies such as South Korea and Japan to avoid repeating mistakes made by his predecessor and to confront the challenge of China's expanding influence. To reaffirm the U.S.' influence in the East Asia region and to secure the balance of power against the expanding hegemony of China, cooperation with U.S. allies is essential. However, although the United States and its allies share the challenge of the

---

[1] "Remarks by President Biden on America's Place in the World," *The White House*, February 4, 2021, https://www.whitehouse.gov/briefing-room/speeches-remarks/2021/02/04/remarks-by-president-biden-on-americas-place-in-the-world/.

growing regional hegemony of Beijing, the previous U.S. administration's coercive behavior and inconsistent foreign policies did not produce tangible results nor enhanced regional cooperation. For the last years, Beijing has exploited its economic interdependence to expand China's dominance over the region. As a result, America's staunchest allies South Korea and Japan face a growing dilemma on how best to balance relying on the United States for military protection while at the same time needing China for trade and investment. China's strategic diplomacy has been bold and sophisticated, so the United States should rethink its strategies to face the geopolitical prowess of China and realign its relations with regional partners to reinforce regional security and influence in East Asia. To that end, Washington should proceed in building high technology and economy-focused trilateral relationships and secure the foundation of regional alliances.

## INTRODUCTION

In his first foreign policy speech, on February 4th, President Joe Biden declared that "America is Back."[2] Clearly differentiating the new administration from his predecessor, he also clarified China as the most serious competitor to the United States.[3] As many challenges are ahead, cooperation with partners that share common values is critical to achieve U.S. foreign policy objectives.

South Korea, officially known as the Republic of Korea (ROK), and Japan, the strongest U.S. allies, have played significant roles as regional partners for decades with respect to East Asian security and trade. Despite their importance, the coercive treatment of the Trump administration renegotiating for U.S. troops stationed in ally territories and their respective Free Trade Agreements weakened ties to these allies and left them questioning Washington's resolve to the region.[4]

To recalibrate these relationships, Washington's approach should not be based on a forced anti-China alliance but on a respectful partnership that works together to build win–win cooperation as a coalition

---

[2] Ibid.

[3] Ibid.

[4] Lara Seligman and Robbie Gramer, "Trump Presses Japan to Pay Up for U.S. Troops," *Foreign Policy*, November 18, 2019, https://foreignpolicy.com/2019/11/18/trump-japan-south-korea-pay-united-states-troops-billions-asia-pacific/.

of democracies. China's enhanced economic and military prowess has impacted geopolitical issues that favor China's interests. As the COVID-19 pandemic impacted global supply chains in 2020, for many countries, this only intensified their economic dependence on China—the first major global economy that managed a V-shape recovery.[5]

Regional partners will find it hard to stand against China from a geopolitical perspective due to their economic reliance on China. As a result, U.S. policy should aim to reinforce alliances with ROK and Japan and compete with China from a position of collective strength. It should also focus more on recovering credibility and building economic-technology cooperation, rather than military capacity as short and mid-term strategies.

## INTERCONNECTED REGIONAL RELATIONS

### The U.S., ROK, Japan, and China

As one of the most dynamic regions where the confluence of global security and trade intersect, East Asia involves several key stakeholders. In the case of South Korea and Japan, the two countries have maintained strong relations with the United States as indispensable allies since the end of Korean War. However, during the Trump administration era, the United States mistreated its allies by renegotiating U.S.–South Korea, U.S.–Japan free trade agreements (KORUS, USJTA) and threatened to withdraw all U.S. forces unless the two countries would raise the cost of U.S. troops' presence on their soil.

While political ties with Washington have been strained, the economic cooperation of ROK and Japan with China has advanced in recent years. Having been the two countries' largest trading partner, China has also been in Free Trade Agreement negotiations with ROK since 2012. Moreover, since the establishment of the China-led Regional Comprehensive Economic Partnership (RCEP) in November of 2020, China accelerated talks for a trilateral free trade agreement between China–South Korea–Japan, connecting the major economic powers in the region.

---

[5] Lily Kuo, "China becomes first major economy to recover from Covid-19 pandemic," *Guardian*, October 19, 2020, https://www.theguardian.com/business/2020/oct/19/china-becomes-first-major-economy-to-recover-from-covid-19-pandemic.

Even though economic interdependence has been accelerated in the region, conflict in the ROK–Japan bilateral relations—caused by historically unresolved disputes regarding wartime forced labor and forced sexual slavery issues—resulted in the worst relations between the two countries ever since the Korean War. As a result, the ROK–Japan trade war has substantially impacted on the semiconductor production in ROK and influenced global supply chains in the region.[6] Although former U.S. President Trump offered to help ease tensions, it did not yield any practical solutions.[7] The redefined definition of Japan in the recently released South Korean 2020 Defense White Paper as "a close neighbor" from "a regional partner" demonstrates how the bilateral relations have been exacerbated.[8]

### The Weakened U.S. Trilateral Alliance

A fractured ROK–Japan bilateral relationship ostensibly weakens the U.S. alliance in East Asia and has implications for U.S. trilateral defense cooperation.[9]

In August 2019, South Korea announced not to renew, but withdraw from the General Security of Military Information Agreement (GSOMIA), an intelligence-sharing pact between ROK and Japan—one of the crucial regional defense systems in East Asia. Even though Seoul withdrew the decision and decided to maintain the GSOMIA three

---

[6] Samuel M. Goodman, Dan Kim, and John VerWey, "The South Korea-Japan Trade Dispute in Context: Semiconductor Manufacturing, Chemicals, and Concentrated Supply Chains," *Office of Industries of the U.S. International Trade Commission*, October 2019, https://usitc.gov/publications/332/working_papers/the_south_korea-japan_trade_dispute_in_context_semiconductor_manufacturing_chemicals_and_concentrated_supply_chains.pdf.

[7] Reuters Staff, "Trump offers to help ease tension in Japan-South Korea dispute," *Reuters*, July 19, 2019, https://www.reuters.com/article/us-southkorea-japan-laborers-trump/trump-offers-to-help-ease-tension-in-japan-south-korea-dispute-idUSKCN1U E248.

[8] Ministry of National Defense, Republic of Korea, *2020 Nyeon gugbangbaegseo* 2020년 국방백서 [2020 Defense White Paper] (Seoul: Ministry of National Defense, Republic of Korea, December 2020), https://www.mnd.go.kr/user/mnd/upload/pblictn/PBLICT NEBOOK_202102040549325290.pdf.

[9] Sung-mi Ahn, "Seoul-Tokyo ties still mired 1 year after GSOMIA row," *The Korea Herald*, November 22, 2020, https://www.koreaherald.com/view.php?ud=202011220 0194.

months later, maintenance of the regional intelligence sharing agreement in the future is still unclear since it depends on relations between Seoul and Tokyo, and how Washington will intervene given heightened tensions.

It is critical that the Biden Administration exercises leadership and works to improve relations between ROK and Japan as a way to collectively engage China in the region. However, because of the magnified economic and trade interdependence on Beijing, imposing the allies with a binary choice between China and the United States is not an ideal means to rebuild and sustain an alliance, rather it could also result in putting additional strain and or pressure on U.S. allies in the region. This was particularly the case of South Korea that experienced economic retaliation from China due to the deployment of the Terminal High Altitude Area Defense (THAAD), the U.S. missile defense system in the country in 2017. Becoming a member of the U.S.-led defense alliance, such as the Quadrilateral Security Dialogue (Quad), could prompt China to boycott goods from Seoul as a response.

## China's Alternative Strategy

Taking a more assertive foreign policy strategy, Beijing announced "Made in China 2025" in 2015, which was designed to make China the world's most competitive economy based on high-tech industries. The initiative aimed to increase its domestic production of core components in high-tech fields up to 40 percent by 2020 and 70 percent by 2025. During the 19th Party Congress in October 2017, Chinese President Xi Jinping stated that China would be a global leader of power and global influence by 2049[10] and would build a "stable international order" in which China's "national rejuvenation" could be fully achieved.[11] The statement of the country's leader was clear, asserting that China would place shaping the future global order as a key policy priority (Fig. 7.1).

---

[10] The Policy Planning Staff, *The Elements of the China Challenge* (Office of the Secretary of State, November 2020), https://www.state.gov/wp-content/uploads/2020/11/20-02832-Elements-of-China-Challenge-508.pdf.

[11] Hal Brands, "What Does China Really Want? To Dominate the World," *Bloomberg*, May 20, 2020, https://www.bloomberg.com/opinion/articles/2020-05-20/xi-jinping-makes-clear-that-china-s-goal-is-to-dominate-the-world.

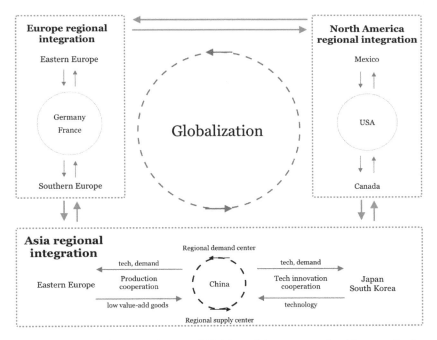

**Fig. 7.1** Globalization in a "Multi-modal structure" (*Source* Evelyn Cheng, "How China is preparing its economy for a future where the U.S. isn't the center of global demand," *CNBC*, August 31, 2020, https://www.cnbc.com/2020/09/01/dual-circulation-how-china-is-pre paring-for-a-new-role-in-international-trade.html)

However, due to the drastic change of external circumstances, responding to the intensified restrictions on high-tech industries from the U.S. and global economic uncertainty amid the COVID-19 pandemic, Beijing announced a new initiative, the Dual Circulation Strategy (DCS) as a pivot of national economic policy.[12] The vague concept of DCS was introduced for the first time during China's Politburo in May 2020,[13] and

---

[12] Jude Blanchette and Andrew Polk, "Dual Circulation and China's New Hedged Integration Strategy," *Center for Strategic & International Studies*, August 24, 2020, https://www.csis.org/analysis/dual-circulation-and-chinas-new-hedged-integration-strategy.

[13] Chang Xuemei 常雪梅 and Wang Keyuan 王珂园, "Zhonggong zhongyang zhengzhi ju changwu weiyuanhui zhaokai huiyi zhonggong zhongyang zong shuji xijinping

later, it was included in China's 14th Five-Year Plan.[14] The basic concept of the economic policy started from the idea that the shifted external circumstances around China would be unsustainable for the country to last relying on demand abroad and keep its enormous manufacturing gears running.[15] Hence, the key point of the initiative is to reinforce its domestic market by pursuing supply-side structural reform[16] (domestic circulation) while maintaining its contact with the global value chain (international circulation).

Beijing promotes the Dual Circulation strategy as its major economic policy and as one of the objectives of the 14th Five-Year Plan that prioritizes the central role of innovation and the increase of technological strength.[17] It is the first time that China's Five-Year Plan positions high-technology independence and self-reliance as core strategies for the country's national development.[18] Given that, it manifests that the domestic innovation aiming at high-technology development and less reliance on overseas is one of the key economic development priorities of the Chinese Communist Party (CCP).

Yet, China experts and economists point out the challenges of implementing the concept of Dual Circulation. To consolidate China's

zhuchi huiyi" 中共中央政治局常务委员会召开会议 中共中央总书记习近平主持会议 [The Standing Committee of the Political Bureau of the CPC Central Committee held a meeting, Xi Jinping, General Secretary of the CPC Central Committee, presided over the meeting], *Renmin Wang*人民网, May 15, 2020, http://cpc.people.com.cn/n1/2020/0515/c64094-31709627.html?mc_cid=28966ada58&mc_eid=902fe70bde.

[14] "China's 14th Five-Year Plan: A First Look," *Congressional Research Service*, January 5, 2021, https://crsreports.congress.gov/product/pdf/IF/IF11684.

[15] Frank Tang, "What is China's dual circulation economic strategy and why is it important?," *South China Morning Post*, November 19, 2020, https://www.scmp.com/economy/china-economy/article/3110184/what-chinas-dual-circulation-economic-strategy-and-why-it.

[16] Ouyang Shijia and Zhou Lanxu, "Supply-side reform gets greater boost," *China Daily*, January 6, 2021, https://www.chinadaily.com.cn/a/202101/06/WS5ff4f35ca31024ad0baa0ac2.html.

[17] Anna Holzmann and Caroline Meinhardt, "MERICS China Industries Briefing - October 2020," *Mercator Institute for China Studies*, November 3, 2020, https://www.merics.org/en/briefing/merics-china-industries-briefing-october-2020.

[18] Zhan Jing 詹婧, "Jianchi chuangxin zai xiandaihua jianshe quanju zhong de hexin diwei" 坚持创新在现代化建设全局中的核心地位 [Insist on the core position of innovation in the overall situation of modernization], *Xinhua News Agency*, October 30, 2020, http://www.xinhuanet.com/politics/2020-10/30/c_1126677682.htm.

domestic consumer market for the urgent needs of sustainable domestic demand, could in fact undermine overseas export competitiveness because it requires raising the labor cost to raise domestic consumption.[19] However, considering what Beijing perceives as a global hostile environment around China, especially related to China accessing the global 5G and semiconductor supply chains which are the core pillars of high-technology infrastructure development, Beijing already has more than enough reasons to develop and proceed with the Dual Circulation as the core economic strategy.

Since June 2020, the value of the Chinese Yuan has risen against the U.S. dollar. Economists point out that a stronger Yuan would support the shift of China to a consumption-driven economy and help China to import commodities and semiconductors at cheaper prices.[20] Considering China's persistence on domestic development for cutting-edge technology such as 5G, artificial intelligence, quantum technology, and advanced semiconductors, Chinese policymakers will likely support any plans related to high-tech infrastructure development and supply chain through policies and trade deals. While China has already experienced heavy constraints from Washington and anticipates continuous tech and innovation decoupling with the United States, Beijing has secured alternative markets in South East Asia. With the RCEP, which includes South Korea, Japan, and Australia, China is close to securing an alternative solution for its supply chain. Additionally, on 30 December 2020, an investment deal between China and the European Union (EU) was announced by the European Commission, the executive arm of the EU, after seven years of negotiation.[21] The Comprehensive Agreement on Investment (CAI) indicates that China will be able to achieve building its high-tech supply chain infrastructure to a certain degree by bypassing the U.S. market. Of course, concerns on intellectual property

---

[19] Michael Pettis, "The problems with China's 'Dual Circulation' economic model," *Financial Times*, August 25, 2020, https://www.ft.com/content/a9572b58-6e01-42c1-9771-2a36063a0036.

[20] Stella Yifan Xie, "China Lets Yuan Rise Steadily, Pressuring Exporters," *The Wall Street Journal*, February 25, 2021, https://www.wsj.com/articles/china-lets-yuan-rise-steadily-pressuring-exporters-11614261708?mod=markets_minor_pos1.

[21] "EU and China reach agreement in principle on investment," *European Commission*, December 30, 2020, https://ec.europa.eu/commission/presscorner/detail/en/ip_20_2541.

rights (IPR) and any form of potential damage to U.S.–EU relations still require approval from the European Parliament. However, given economic concerns especially after the COVID-19 pandemic hit, making a trade deal with the world's largest economy is an option that should hardly be abandoned given the current global trading environment. Thus, the EU-China deal will accelerate the international circulation of the DCS and give China momentum to be less reliant on the United States and keep sharpening its competitiveness as a potent cutting-edge technology hub.

As a result of promoting the economic benefits of joining dual circulation, cooperation to deal with the COVID-19 pandemic, and the trilateral Free Trade Agreement between South Korea, Japan, and China, Beijing has accelerated talks with Seoul and Tokyo.[22] One of the concerns of this proposed cooperation is that the success of China's domestic market reinforcement driven by its economic strategies will likely have severe impacts on South Korea and Japan where high-tech industries contribute a large share to the industrial output.[23] Moreover, a Anti-China sentiment among the U.S. allies has grown significantly. According to a survey from Pew Research Center, the most advanced economic countries including South Korea, Japan, Germany, and Australia have negative views on China. 75 percent of South Korean respondents had negative views on China, and Japan showed 86 percent, while 73 percent of the U.S. respondents had a negative impression of China.[24]

Given the current competitive regional environment, allies positively responded to the new U.S. administration's intention to reinforce their

[22] Hyonhee Shin, "Chinese foreign minister arrives in South Korea amid talk about Xi visit," *Reuters*, November 25, 2020, https://www.reuters.com/article/us-southkorea-china/chinese-foreign-minister-arrives-in-south-korea-amid-talk-about-xi-visit-idUSKBN28 50LI.

[23] Jost Wübbeke, Mirjam Meissner, Max J. Zenglein, Jaqueline Ives, and Björn Conrad, "MADE IN CHINA 2025: The making of a high-tech superpower and consequences for industrial countries," *Mercator Institute for China Studies,* December 2016, https://merics.org/sites/default/files/2020-04/Made%20in%20China%202025.pdf.

[24] Laura Silver, Kat Devlin, and Christine Huang, "Unfavorable Views of China Reach Historic Highs in Many Countries," *Pew Research Center,* October 6, 2020, https://www.pewresearch.org/global/2020/10/06/unfavorable-views-of-china-reach-historic-highs-in-many-countries/.

alliance and strengthen cooperation on a number of issues in the region.[25] However, despite the fact that ROK and Japan present intentions to cooperate with the United States, Washington needs to provide more tangible and practical economic and political incentives to compete with their economic ties with Beijing, which could have impact on the U.S. trilateral partnership. Economic and high-tech cooperation with ROK and Japan led by Beijing can support China's technology and supply shortages caused by the U.S.' strict export control and the U.S.–China decoupling, and also utilize it as a lever to break the US–ROK–Japan trilateral alliance.

## STRATEGIC PILLARS OF THE U.S. EAST ASIA POLICY

Unlike China, the United States loosened its ties with its strong allies under the Trump administration. Considering U.S. regional diplomacy for the last four years and the Biden administration's intention to boost domestic competitiveness in the global market, U.S. allies doubt whether the new administration will be a trustworthy partner or just another coercive power player for its own interests. To reinforce the trilateral relations as like-minded partners, and reduce the allies' economic reliance on China, developing technology-focused economic partnerships and building mutually cooperating economic ties in a form of a coalition of democracies should be the center of these strategies. Also, it is crucial to give credibility to offset the nations' concerns for the new administration's domestic policy focusing on the "Make in America and Buy in America" philosophy.[26] The Biden administration should be able to give certainty to its allies that the new U.S. administration is willing to build a mechanism of mutually cooperative economic partnerships, not just to strengthen the value chain of U.S. domestic industries and their market competitiveness. To do that, Washington should: (1) revert back to multilateral trade blocs, (2) ensure high-technology-focused cooperation, and (3) take an active role in mediating conflicts between ROK and Japan.

---

[25] Sangmi Cha, "South Korea's Moon pledges to upgrade alliance with U.S. in call with Biden," *Reuters,* February 3, 2021, https://www.reuters.com/article/us-southkorea-usa-idUSKBN2A4028.

[26] Mireya Solis, "Great Power Competition and Asia's Economic Architecture: An Agenda for US-ROK Cooperation," *East Asia Institute*, December 7, 2020, https://www.eai.or.kr/new/en/pub/view.asp?intSeq=20218&board=eng_issuebriefing%27,%27eng_workingpaper%27,%27eng_special%27,%27eng_multimedia&keyword_option=&keyword=&more=.

## *Back to Plurilateral Trade Blocs*

First, by joining in multinational economic trade agreements with ROK and Japan and lifting the tariffs on the two parties, the United States can rebuild the credibility of cooperation among the three countries. ROK and Japan are already members of RCEP with China which eliminates around 90 percent of tariffs on imports among the member countries. Even though the United States made bilateral free trade agreements with ROK (KORUS) and Japan (USJTA) respectively, they are not in any multilateral economic bloc together yet. Taking the United States back to the Comprehensive and Progressive Agreement for Trans-Pacific Partnership (CPTPP) is the most ideal option, unless they want to create a new form of partnership. Having hesitated to join the mega-regional trade agreement, ROK officially announced that the country was actively interested in joining the pact.[27] As Japan is already a member country of the CPTPP, if the United States rejoins the Asia–Pacific regional trade agreement, Washington will be closer to building the trilateral economic ties with Seoul and Tokyo while ensuring the center of the economic bloc. Moreover, a more mutually beneficial trade agreement can be utilized as an effective channel to strengthen U.S.–ROK–Japan relations while addressing concerns of Beijing's economic reprisals.

Given historical precedents it is difficult for Joe Biden's administration to preclude the domestic opposition from Congress concerning the impact of trade liberalization. Yet, considering China's consistent interest in joining the CPTPP[28] and the implicit sway in the region due to the U.S.–China trade war, joining the regional multilateral trade bloc is required for the U.S. Besides, if China joins the CPTPP, the United States will be able to lead building a rule-based multilateral trading system agreed by China and other member countries including South Korea and Japan, and also ensure fair trading practice between the parties related to

---

[27] Soo-yeon Kim, "S. Korea to 'actively' consider joining CPTPP this year," *Yonhap News Agency,* January 11, 2021, https://en.yna.co.kr/view/AEN20210111003900320.

[28] Kinling Lo, "China shows renewed interest in joining trade pact Trump left in 2017," *South China Morning Post,* January 15, 2021, https://www.scmp.com/news/china/politics/article/3117944/china-shows-renewed-interest-joining-trade-pact-trump-left-2017.

modern trade issues such as intellectual property rights (IPR) protection and cross-border data flows.[29]

### High-Technology-Focused Cooperation

Second, in the post COVID-19 pandemic era, high-technology development cooperation is one of the critical tools to enhance cooperation and reinforce the effort of building a tech value chain system in the region. In the case of the United States and South Korea, the two countries have made progressive cooperation for science and technology development.[30] In recent years, the United States and Japan have also engaged in about 160 joint projects in the various fields under the Japan–U.S. Science and Technology Agreement.[31]

To expand the bilateral cooperation to a trilateral level and build value chains via science and technology cooperation with advanced industrial partners, the strategies need to be based on a concept of mutually benefiting partnership. The main risk of building a direct trilateral high-tech cooperation alliance is that since the CCP regards these kinds of activities as a direct U.S.-led strategic coalition to compete with China, it highly likely to prompt Beijing's economic retaliation as was evident with South Korea for its decision on the THAAD missile defense system.

In the case of the Clean Network, an initiative introduced by the Trump administration in 2020 to exclude Chinese firms from the global telecommunication network, South Korea and Japan did not present positive signs even though other like-minded countries from regions such as Latin America and Europe presented their support for the anti-China

[29] Mireya Solís, "Is America back? The high politics of trade in the Indo-Pacific," *Brookings Institution*, January 4, 2021, https://www.brookings.edu/blog/order-from-chaos/2021/01/04/is-america-back-the-high-politics-of-trade-in-the-indo-pacific/.

[30] "News Release: U.S., Republic of Korea to Partner in Science, Technology, and Information Communication Technology," U.S. Department of Homeland Security, October 24, 2019, https://www.dhs.gov/science-and-technology/news/2019/10/24/news-release-us-rok-partner-science-technology-rd#:~:text=Seoul%2C%20South%20Korea%20%E2%80%93%20Today%2C,safety%20such%20as%20security%20and.

[31] "Japan-US Science and Technology Cooperation," Ministry of Foreign Affairs of Japan, accessed February 27, 2021, https://www.mofa.go.jp/region/n-america/us/q&a/science/Science.html.

initiative.[32] Tokyo expressed that the country would not join the initiative,[33] and Seoul also did not present a positive response to Washington's call for joining in.[34] Beijing, regarding this issue, pushed the countries not to cooperate with the United States but, instead, with China on the 5G network development.[35]

Likewise, the Trump Administration's Economic Prosperity Network (EPN), which was another strategic anti-China initiative to build a technology value chain infrastructure with like-minded partners to reduce their reliance on China,[36] confronted allies' strong economic ties with China. In 2000, the potential EPN member countries'—Australia, India, Japan, New Zealand, South Korea, and Vietnam—global value chain (GVC) trade with the United States was three times greater than GVC trade with China.[37] However, by 2017, the GVC trade of the countries with China accounted for 3.7 percent of world GVC trade and had increased so much that it exceeded their GVC trade with the United States, which accounted for 2.6 percent of world GVC trade in 2017. Moreover, from 2000 to 2017 the participation in global value-added supply chains of the United States and Japan had declined relative to China's share.[38]

---

[32] "The Clean Network," U.S. Department of State, accessed February 27, 2021, https://2017-2021.state.gov/the-clean-network/index.html.

[33] Reuters Staff, "Japan will not join U.S. plan to bar China from telecoms networks: Yomiuri," *Reuters*, October 15, 2020, https://www.reuters.com/article/us-japan-usa-china/japan-will-not-join-u-s-plan-to-bar-china-from-telecoms-networks-yomiuri-idUSKB N271003.

[34] Seung-yeon Kim, "U.S. renews calls on S. Korea to join economic security campaign against China," *Yonhap News Agency*, October 14, 2020, https://en.yna.co.kr/view/AEN 20201014008400325.

[35] Ji-eun Kim, "Chinese ambassador to S. Korea asks for 'increased cooperation' on 5G networks," *The Hankyoreh*, November 19, 2020, https://english.hani.co.kr/arti/eng lish_edition/e_international/970690.html.

[36] Humeyra Pamuk and Andrea Shalal, "Trump administration pushing to rip global supply chains from China: officials," *Reuters*, May 4, 2020, https://www.reuters.com/article/us-health-coronavirus-usa-china/trump-administration-pushing-to-rip-global-sup ply-chains-from-china-officials-idUSKBN22G0BZ.

[37] Guy Erb and Scott Sommers, "Asian Supply Chains, Reshoring, and the TPP," *Washington International Trade Association*, May 26, 2020, https://www.wita.org/blogs/asian-supply-chains-reshoring-and-the-tpp/.

[38] Ibid.

If the United States, ROK, and Japan can be in the same strategic group to overcome fundamental concerns and augment mutual trust, this can help protect Seoul and Tokyo from Beijing's condemnation and possible economic reprisals.

The U.K. prime minister Boris Johnson expressed his ambition to expand the Group of Seven (G7) to Democratic 10 countries (D10) as a coalition of democratic global partners by including South Korea, India, and Australia.[39] By forming the D10 club, the U.K. aims to reduce reliance on China for 5G technology development and prevent its dominance in high-tech infrastructure in the future. With respect to the new form of group, some of the G7 member countries expressed concerns that it might be considered an anti-China coalition and even questioned this new form would be permanent.[40] Even so, forming the new institution of 10 countries, including the three leading democracies in the Asia Pacific region, will give Washington another strategic solution to work with Asian allies for a more substantial strategic cooperation on 5G technology development.

While joining multinational blocs together, connecting technology cooperation to strategic policies toward Southeast Asia and the Indo-Pacific region also can add momentum on recovering trilateral technology development partnerships. For South Korea, President Moon Jae-In's administration has developed strategic ties with Southeast Asian countries and built capacity in the regions via the New Southern Policy (NSP) while the United States and Japan work together on implementing the Free and Open Indo-Pacific Strategy (FOIPS). Since ROK and the United States agreed to put forth harmonious cooperation between ROK's NSP and the U.S.' Indo-Pacific Strategy,[41] the two countries have been working

[39] Lucy Fisher, "Downing Street plans new 5G club of democracies," *The Times*, May 29, 2020, https://www.thetimes.co.uk/article/downing-street-plans-new-5g-club-of-democracies-bfnd5wj57.

[40] Patrick Wintour, "UK plans early G7 virtual meeting and presses ahead with switch to D10," *The Guardian*, January 15, 2021, https://www.theguardian.com/world/2021/jan/15/uk-plans-early-g7-virtual-meeting-and-presses-ahead-with-switch-to-d10.

[41] Ministry of Foreign Affairs, Republic of South Korea, *Opening Remarks by President Moon Jae-in at Joint Press Conference Following Korea-U.S. Summit*, (Seoul: Ministry of Foreign Affairs, Republic of South Korea, June 30, 2019), https://www.mofa.go.kr/eng/brd/m_5674/view.do?seq=319902&srchFr=&srchTo=&srchWord=&srchTp=&multi_itm_seq=0&itm_seq_1=0&itm_seq_2=0&company_cd=&company_nm=.

together to promote international collaboration for enhancing 5G security.[42] However, it should be reminded that, even though the respective bilateral cooperation of the United States to ROK and the United States to Japan are progressive, the shared interests among the three countries in economic growth and regional prosperity is essential. Hence, the convergence of the two initiatives is ultimately imperative, not only to reinforce the trilateral cooperation, but also to reinforce regional rules-based order.[43]

## *Mediating the Bilateral Conflict*

Third, considering the strategic blueprints toward the region, the United States needs to be intentional about mediating deep-rooted ROK–Japan disputes to ensure a constructive trilateral coalition. The strife between the two key U.S. allies only weakens the democratic coalition and regional security. Even though Washington's bilateral relations with Seoul and Tokyo are likely to recover shortly, the escalated tensions between the two countries are likely to not thaw anytime soon. Conflict between the two countries ultimately will act as an impediment to the implementation of the other two strategic actions proposed earlier. In January 2021, Japan strongly objected to Britain's proposal to invite the three Asian countries of ROK, India, and Australia to G7 as potential D10 members, and part of the reason was due to tension with South Korea.[44] If this situation persists, it is difficult to expect practical cooperation between

---

[42] U.S. Department of State, "The United States of America and The Republic of Korea on Working Together to Promote Cooperation between the Indo-Pacific Strategy and the New Southern Policy," U.S. Department of State, November 13, 2020, https://2017-2021.state.gov/the-united-states-of-america-and-the-republic-of-korea-on-working-together-to-promote-cooperation-between-the-indo-pacific-strategy-and-the-new-southern-policy/index.html.

[43] Tomoo Kikuchi, Jaehyon Lee, Sandip Kumar Mishra, Chu Minh Thao, Scott A. Snyder, Duyeon Kim, and Gordon Flake, "Embracing the Indo-Pacific? South Korea's progress towards a regional strategy," *Perth USAsia Centre*, December 3, 2020, https://perthusasia.edu.au/getattachment/Our-Work/Embracing-the-Indo-Pacific-South-Korea%E2%80%99s-progress/PU-164-Korea-Book-WEB.pdf.aspx?lang=en-AU.

[44] Alberto Nardelli and Isabel Reynolds, "Japan Pushes Back Against U.K. Plan to Boost G-7 Asia Reach," *Bloomberg*, January 27, 2021, https://www.bloomberg.com/news/articles/2021-01-27/japan-pushes-back-against-u-k-plan-to-boost-g-7-reach-in-asia.

the three parties in the region. The Biden administration needs to under-score dividing the cooperative agenda from the competitive agenda in the middle of the two allies. Globally challenged issues such as climate change, human rights, the COVID-19 pandemic, and science and technology cooperation are crucial subjects that need to be handled through proper cooperation, along with the issue of North Korea. To emphasize cooperation on these agendas in the short-term, Washington will need to intervene in those dialogues and endeavor to expand the scope of the partnership in both the short and long-term.

## CONCLUSION

For the very first cabinet-level overseas travel, the U.S. Secretary of State Antony Blinken and Defense Secretary Lloyd J. Austin III visited South Korea and Japan in the third week of March 2021. During the visits, the two most U.S. senior envoys presented that the Biden administration prioritizes rebuilding the East Asian alliances to confront China. With warning China against using "coercion and aggression,"[45] Mr. Blinken said that

> *It's no accident that we chose the Republic of Korea for the first Cabinet-level overseas travel of the Biden-Harris administration, along with Japan. This alliance between us is, as we've said, the linchpin for peace, for security and prosperity, not just for our two nations but for the Indo-Pacific region and, indeed, for the world. The alliance is unwavering, it's ironclad, and it's rooted in friendship, in mutual trust, and in shared values.*[46]

While demonstrating the conviction of strong alliances toward the two countries, Washington must secure practical short-term strategies to

---

[45] Humeyra Pamuk, Kiyoshi Takenaka, and Ju-min Park, "Blinken warns China against 'coercion and aggression' on first Asia trip," *Reuters*, March 15, 2021, https://www.reuters.com/article/us-usa-asia-blinken-japan/blinken-warns-china-against-coercion-and-aggression-on-first-asia-trip-idUSKBN2B71C9.

[46] "Secretary Antony J. Blinken and Republic of Korea Foreign Minister Chung Eui-yong Before Their Meeting," U.S. Department of State, March 17, 2021, https://www.state.gov/secretary-antony-j-blinken-and-republic-of-korea-foreign-minister-chung-eui-yong-before-their-meeting/.

strengthen the alliances rather than mid- and long-term ones.[47] Since the Joe Biden administration aims to return to multilateralism with rebuilding alliances, the question should not be about simply rejoining the CPTPP, but about when the United States will come back to the regional multi-lateral trade bloc and how to maximize its influence. In addition, to rebalance South Korea's and Japan's economic reliance on China and recover the trilateral relationship, Washington should build a technology-focused economic partnership with the two U.S. allies. To that end, high-technology development-focused cooperation with the two democ-racies via multilateral democratic coalitions such as Britain's D10 alliance of democracies is a goal that Washington needs to achieve as one of its short-term strategies.

For China, due to the strict control of the United States, in short and mid-term perspectives, it seems very difficult to achieve its goals such as self-reliance on high technologies, develop supply chain infras-tructure, and be a leader in cutting-edge tech industries in the near future. However, in a long-term perspective, Beijing's strategic policy to strengthen the domestic market and high-technology industries, and to expand economic technological cooperation with industry leaders such as ROK and Japan will act as an accelerator to reach its goals. Moreover, the China-led high-tech focused economic nexus would not only undermine the U.S.' strategies to strengthen the trilateral alliance between Wash-ington, Seoul, and Tokyo, but also weaken solidarity of the democratic coalition.

South Korea and Japan's cooperation plays a pivotal role in anchoring the United States to the economic/trade center in the region. Primarily, the Seoul-Tokyo dispute needs to be solved in the short term to secure the strategic trilateral relations. To that end, the United States should work on dividing the cooperative agenda from the competitive agenda in order to rebuild credibility among the two parties. Of course, Washington alone will not be able to completely mend the complicated dispute between ROK and Japan. However, by leading the direct cooperation of two key

---

[47] Kuyoun Chung, Saeme Kim, Bo Ram Kwon, Jessica J. Lee, Sara Bjerg Moller, Masashi Murano, Junya Nishino, Ankit Panda, Andrew I. Park, and Ayumi Teraoka, "Reinvesting in U.S.-Japan-Republic of Korea Strategic Relations: A Prac-tical Trilateral Agenda," *The National Committee on American Foreign Policy*, January 2021, https://www.ncafp.org/2016/wp-content/uploads/2021/01/NCAFP_Trilateral_Final-Draft_2021.pdf.

allies on shared issues essential to opening a constructive dialogue, the United States may be able to mitigate tension between the two countries and reinforce the trilateral strategic alliance in East Asia.

# CHAPTER 8

# Pathways for U.S.–China Climate Cooperation Under the Biden Administration

## *Jackson Ewing*

**Abstract** The Biden administration should extend US–China climate change cooperation, and pursue opportunities for virtuous competition that can accelerate global climate mitigation. Obama-era efforts saw the United States and China develop a tangible climate partnership that was fundamental to the construction and enactment of the Paris Agreement. Following rollbacks from President Trump, Biden has the chance to reinvigorate and evolve the former partnership for the current state of both the climate challenge and the wider US–China relationship. This chapter offers eight recommendations for how: (1) return to regular climate dialogue that [re]builds trust and familiarity; (2) develop adjacent bilateral

---

---

J. Ewing (✉)
Senior Fellow, Duke University Nicholas Institute for Environmental Policy Solutions, Durham, NC, USA
e-mail: jackson.ewing@duke.edu

E. Carr Jr. (ed.), *From Trump to Biden and Beyond*,
https://doi.org/10.1007/978-981-16-4297-5_8

climate goals that create mutual accountability and signal ambition to the rest of the world; (3) negotiate to buttress climate finance and roll back coal investment through major international venues; (4) drive virtuous competition with China through strategic infrastructure and R&D investments; (5) mainstream climate issues in bilateral trade relations, at the WTO, and through the potential deployment of carbon border adjustment tools; (6) expand and support track- II, subnational, and sectoral dialogue to find areas of pragmatic climate cooperation; (7) help find mutually acceptable solutions to outstanding barriers to Paris Agreement implementation, particularly the exchange of mitigation outcomes across borders; and (8) insulate climate change from spoilers rooted in other avenues of the US–China relationship.

**Keywords** Climate change · Diplomacy · UNFCCC · Energy · Trade

## INTRODUCTION

President Biden's incoming administration should rekindle and extend U.S.–China climate change cooperation. The last time Biden worked in the West Wing the US and China forged a climate partnership that reversed decades of animus and fundamentally shifted the parameters of international climate diplomacy. Presidents Barack Obama and Xi Jinping announcing and pursuing climate goals in concert, and developing tangible partnership agreements at national and subnational levels to help achieve them, was crucial for success at the UN climate summit in Paris and for the rapid ratification of the ensuing Paris Agreement.

President Trump ended this brief but impactful period of national climate cooperation between the world's two largest emitters, rolling back climate regulations at home and largely ignoring climate developments abroad. While the opportunity costs for these shortsighted actions are massive and lasting, the fundamentals for revitalizing and deepening climate cooperation between the United States and China persist. This provides opportunities for President Biden, Special Presidential Climate Envoy John Kerry, and the broader U.S. climate apparatus.

The United States and China remain the two indispensable countries for addressing climate change. Together they account for nearly 40 percent of global GHG emissions, not counting the emissions impacts of their international investment or the embedded emission of their imports.[1] Vulnerable countries see United States and Chinese climate policies as the strongest national forces shaping the future climate with which they must contend. Major economies look to the United States and China as signposts for the level of global climate action that will be possible. Businesses and markets watch the two countries' individual and collective actions to assess risks and search for opportunities.

Both governments are voicing future net-zero emissions ambitions, and both face uncertainties and political challenges—albeit of vastly different varieties—for how to get there. The Biden Administration is quickly rolling back many of President Trump's domestic climate policies, and signaling America's return to the international climate arena in earnest.[2] President Xi enhanced China's climate change ambitions on the international stage during the 2020 United Nations General Assembly, speeding up China's timeframe for peaking emissions to before 2030 and committing to carbon neutrality by 2060.[3] Biden seeks to set a durable foundation for the future of U.S. climate policies domestically and internationally, even if his primary tools prove to come from overarching executive branch powers that are vulnerable to the dictates of his successor. Xi's China meanwhile continues to grapple balancing emissions reductions with economic recovery and development, and faces strong headwinds from fossil fuel-driven modes of production that refuse to go quietly.

The Paris-system of voluntary emissions reduction policies for all countries—with less bifurcation between developed and developing—suits both countries in unique ways and provides space for cooperative actions. Such actions range from the sort of *quid pro quo* target setting and joint messaging that defined the second Obama term, to new forms of cooperation and virtuous competition suited for the nascent Biden era. This

---

[1] "Global Emissions," *Center for Climate and Energy Solutions*, data reflect recorded numbers from 2019, https://www.c2es.org/content/international-emissions.

[2] Coral Davenport, "Restoring Environmental Rules Rolled Back by Trump Could Take Years," *New York Times*, January 22, 2021, https://www.nytimes.com/2021/01/22/climate/biden-environment.html.

[3] Echo Xie, "Climate change: Xi Jinping makes bold pledge for China to be carbon neutral by 2060," *South China Morning Post*, September 23, 2020, https://www.scmp.com/news/china/diplomacy/article/3102761/climate-change-xi-jinping-makes-bold-pledge-china-be-carbon.

chapter provides background and context on U.S.–China climate relations, and a set of recommendations for how the Biden Administration can advance U.S. domestic and global climate goals through cooperating and competing with China.

## LOGGERHEADS, COOPERATION, AND A VACUUM

Climate change long existed as an avenue for strategic posturing between the world's two largest emitters, with China clinging to its status as a developing country with little culpability for the problem, and the United States justifying its inflexibility through China's inaction. The failure of the United States to ratify the 1997 Kyoto Protocol—the most impactful pre-Paris agreement—stemmed from arguments that cutting emissions while developing, non-Annex I, countries did not put the United States at a competitive disadvantage while leaving the global climate at risk.[4] Congressional opposition to the international climate commitments was bipartisan and often overwhelming,[5] and singled out China as a large and rapidly growing emitter that had to be brought into any commitment regime for it to be fair or effective. China meanwhile emphasized "common but differentiated responsibilities" for addressing climate change and was content to operate in a system that placed no emissions restrictions on it. These positions defined the George W. Bush (2000–2007) and Hu Jintao (2002–2012) administrations, limiting international progress significantly.

The United States and China remained at climate loggerheads into the Obama administration. The 2009 UN Framework Convention on Climate Change summit in Copenhagen had long been circled as the Conference of Parties (COP) that would usher in a new generation of international climate policy. It did not go well. The entrenched distance between United States and Chinese positions, and animosity built up over years of diplomatic friction were on full display. Premier Wen Jiabao snubbed a proposed meeting with President Obama early in the conference, and denounced industrialized countries for failing to live up to

---

[4] Carli Coon, "Why President Bush Is Right to Abandon the Kyoto Protocol," *Heritage Foundation*, 2001, https://www.heritage.org/environment/report/why-president-bush-right-abandon-the-kyoto-protocol.

[5] The Kyoto Protocol was voted down in the U.S. Senate through the Byrd–Hagel Resolution by a vote of 95–0.

the promises made in the Kyoto Protocol. Chinese officials singled out the United States for "moving backwards" on issues of funding and technology, and continued to emphasize the poverty challenges and development needs of it and other G77 countries as an argument for modest actions and for continuing to avoid emissions reduction commitments. Obama arrived in Copenhagen having just received word from a group of Senators that any agreement giving China a "free ride" would be a non-starter.[6] While Obama's rhetoric supported action commensurate with the global climate challenge, his administration's lack of room to maneuver on the issue and the history of U.S. intransigence eroded his diplomatic capital and saw his statements fall largely on deaf ears. Late in the conference Obama inserted an uninvited United States into private talks between Chinese, Indian, and Brazilian negotiators—which along with South Africa found a lowest common denominator agreement at Copenhagen that left few satisfied.[7]

These fractures persisted. Negotiations in 2010 saw renewed vigour over binding versus non-binding targets for Annex I countries, and on levels of transparency on emissions reducing actions. In 2013 China and the rest of the G77 walked out of a negotiation session because of disputes over how the developed states were and were not filling the climate finance coffers of the Green Climate Fund. Diplomatic tension fed creative language in which Chinese delegates began referring to the United States not by name but as the "developed country that is not part of the Kyoto Protocol," while the United States lamented the absence or failings of "important players" on issues such as monitoring, reporting and verification (MRV) where they could not get the Chinese policy movement they sought. At one point a Chinese negotiator responded to criticisms from U.S. climate to envoy Todd Stern by likening him to a "pig admiring itself in the mirror."[8]

These examples illustrate a larger and more fundamental dynamic that was *the* major sticking point in pre-Paris climate change diplomacy: the

[6] Meredith Shiner, "Sens. outline climate approach," *Politico*, December 10, 2009, https://www.politico.com/story/2009/12/sens-outline-climate-approach-030470.

[7] Lisa Lerer, "Obama's dramatic climate meet," *Politico*, December 18, 2009, https://www.politico.com/story/2009/12/obamas-dramatic-climate-meet-030801.

[8] Lisa Friedman, "U.S. and China maintain polite disagreement as climate talks reach final days," *EENews*, December 8, 2010, https://www.eenews.net/special_reports/cancun/stories/1059942913.

United States and China disagreed on their respective responsibilities to address global climate change, and on the appropriate mechanisms for national and collective action. The countries grew closer on both fronts during the Obama administration's second term.

With domestic climate legislation unlikely, Obama began aggressively deploying the power of the executive branch. Domestically this yielded executive orders that undergirded America's international climate commitments, most notably the Clean Power Plan,[9] vehicle emissions standards,[10] lowering the government's own greenhouse gas emissions (GHG),[11] and the investment in renewable energy[12] among other measures. Internationally, the Obama Administration entered into substantive climate talks with China that would yield three bilateral agreements and place global climate negotiations on a new, more productive, pathway.

Obama's climate overtures came at an opportune time for Beijing. By the mid-2010s, addressing conventional air pollution (by some measurements leading to 1.6 million deaths in China per year)[13] had become a strategic imperative. President Xi called poor air quality Beijing's "most

[9] "FACT SHEET: Overview of the Clean Power Plan," *U.S. Environmental Protection Agency*, accessed April 1, 2021, https://archive.epa.gov/epa/cleanpowerplan/fact-sheet-overview-clean-power-plan.html.

[10] "Obama Administration Finalizes Historic 54.5 MPG Fuel Efficiency Standards," The *White House*, August 28, 2012, https://obamawhitehouse.archives.gov/the-press-office/2012/08/28/obama-administration-finalizes-historic-545-mpg-fuel-efficiency-standard.

[11] Council on Environmental Quality, Federal Leadership on Climate Change and Environmental Sustainability - EXECUTIVE ORDER 13,693, https://obamawhitehouse.arc hives.gov/administration/eop/ceq/initiatives/sustainability.

[12] "FACT SHEET: Obama Administration Announces Clean Energy Savings for All Americans Initiative," *The White House*, July 19, 2016, https://obamawhitehouse. archives.gov/the-press-office/2016/07/19/fact-sheet-obama-administration-announces-clean-energy-savings-all; Robert M. Simon and Davik J. Hayes, "America's Clean Energy Success, by the Numbers," *Center for American Progress*, June 29, 2017, https://www. americanprogress.org/issues/green/reports/2017/06/29/435281/americas-clean-ene rgy-success-numbers/.

[13] Robert A. Rohde and Richard A. Muller, "Air Pollution in China: Mapping of Concentrations and Sources," *Berkeley Earth* (2015): 1–15, http://berkeleyearth.org/wp-content/uploads/2015/08/China-Air-Quality-Paper-July-2015.pdf.

prominent" challenge in 2014,[14] and accelerated efforts to measure and respond to—through both reward and censure—the environmental performance of local governors.[15] China passed a raft of domestic regulations in the 2013–2014 period, including the National Climate Change Plan, Air Pollution Prevention and Control Plan, and Energy Development Strategic Action Plan, each of which sought to abate pollution and enhance Chinese leadership in emerging energy sectors. These efforts dovetailed with Chinese ambitions to move away from the dominance of heavy industry and relatively low-value exports as pillars of its economy, and move into more service and high-tech sectors which would be both cleaner and more economically resilient. This period saw China's energy intensity decrease alongside the share of heavy industry in the overall economy, services exceed manufacturing in overall output, and a 73 percent growth in non-fossil energy generation from 2010 to 2014.[16]

Such measures have the corollary effect of reducing GHG emissions, which changed the ways that Chinese leadership viewed its options in the international climate arena and created an opening for U.S. bilateral overtures. For China, outside pressures to reduce GHGs long seen as anathema to the country's development needs, and a distraction from its core business of wealth generation and societal development, became opportunities for gaining partnerships, technical support and finance to help China transition toward a cleaner energy future. The United States was the ideal partner. For the United States, engaging China on climate through both cooperative measures and *quid pro quo* climate mitigation commitments could bring China into a new international climate regime that called on it to substantially address its own GHG footprint.

Secretary of State John Kerry and leading climate official Todd Stern pursued this opportunity assertively. Stern began to meet regularly with leading Chinese climate negotiator Xie Zhenhua, to whom

---

[14] Bloomberg News,"Xi Jinping Calls Pollution Beijing's Biggest Challenge," *Bloomberg*, February 27, 2014, https://www.bloomberg.com/news/articles/2014-02-26/xi-calls-pollution-beijing-s-biggest-challenge-as-smog-eases.

[15] Michelle Ker and Kate Logan, "New environmental law targets China's local officials," *China Dialogue*, April 28, 2014, https://chinadialogue.net/en/pollution/6939-new-environmental-law-targets-china-s-local-officials/.

[16] Fergus Green and Nicholas Stern, "China's changing economy: implications for its carbon dioxide emissions," *Climate Policy* (2017), 17:4: 423–442, https://doi.org/10.1080/14693062.2016.1156515.

he had suggested in 2009 to make climate change a success story in the difficult U.S.–China relationship. Presidents Obama and Xi met in Southern California's Sunnylands Estate in 2013 to discuss climate partnership in earnest.[17] These efforts yielded the late-2014 U.S.–China Joint Announcement on Climate Change that jointly affirmed the importance of a successful outcome to Paris climate negotiations slated for the following year, and—in a move almost unthinkable in prior years—bilaterally declared the core climate goals of the two countries. Paragraph 3 of the Joint Announcement would constitute the basis of the countries' respective Nationally Determined Contributions to address climate change through the UNFCCC, reading:

> *Today, the Presidents of the United States and China announced their respective post-2020 actions on climate change, recognizing that these actions are part of the longer range effort to transition to low-carbon economies, mindful of the global temperature goal of 2°C. The United States intends to achieve an economy-wide target of reducing its emissions by 26%-28% below its 2005 level in 2025 and to make best efforts to reduce its emissions by 28%. China intends to achieve the peaking of CO2 emissions around 2030 and to make best efforts to peak early and intends to increase the share of non-fossil fuels in primary energy consumption to around 20% by 2030. Both sides intend to continue to work to increase ambition over time.[18]*

The United States and China would build on this foundation in advance of the Paris climate negotiations and in their wake. In September 2015, months before the Conference, Presidents Obama and Xi released the Joint Presidential Statement on Climate Change to reaffirm their 2014 commitments, again pledge to work toward an ambitious Paris outcome, and outline substantive domestic climate policies along with bilateral and multilateral cooperation measures.[19] The two leaders released a second

---

[17] "US-China Conversation on Climate Change Moves Forward," *Sunnylands*, July 30, 2013, https://sunnylands.org/article/u-s-china-conversation-on-climate-change-moves-forward/.

[18] "U.S.-China Joint Announcement on Climate Change," *The White House*, November 11, 2014, https://obamawhitehouse.archives.gov/the-press-office/2014/11/11/us-china-joint-announcement-climate-change.

[19] "U.S.-China Joint Presidential Statement on Climate Change," *The White House*, September 25, 2015, https://obamawhitehouse.archives.gov/the-press-office/2015/09/25/us-china-joint-presidential-statement-climate-change.

Joint Presidential Statement in March 2016—roughly three months after the Paris Agreement's negotiation—declaring their intention to take the domestic steps necessary to formally ratify the agreement as early as possible that year.[20] They would do so in September 2016 in Hangzhou, China. The 2016 Presidential Statement began by stating that "[o]ver the past three years, climate change has become a pillar of the U.S.-China bilateral relationship," and concluded by claiming that "joint efforts by China and the United States on climate change will serve as an enduring legacy of the partnership between our two countries."[21]

It is difficult to overstate the importance of the 2014–2016 bilateral statements to the Paris climate regime's formation and entry into force. U.S.–China loggerheads on climate had established and reflected core camps on climate culpability and responsibility for action throughout much of the international community. With this wall eroding, it became possible to focus on details in Paris that—while contentious—did not pose the same existential diplomatic risk of climate regime failure. The agreement that emerged established the voluntary, bespoke climate commitments for all counties of their own making that continues to define the international climate landscape. It was ratified quickly by UNFCCC standards, in part because of U.S.–China bilateral commitments to do so themselves, and backchannel diplomacy by the two countries encouraging others to follow suit.

The Paris Agreement's flexibility also reduces its durability. While it appeals to preferences in Washington, Beijing, and many other capitols to avoid constrictive international regimes, it offers scant ramifications for countries that choose to backtrack on the commitments made within it. Upon entering office, and prior to moving against Paris directly, President Trump removed any mention of climate change from the executive branch agenda, and sought to dismantle the U.S. Clean Power Plan (CPP), open up federal lands to fossil fuel exploration, reduce vehicle emissions standards, and broadly defund and de-emphasize environmental regulation and enforcement. This undermined both the U.S.

[20] "U.S.-China Joint Presidential Statement on Climate Change," *The White House*, March 31, 2016, https://obamawhitehouse.archives.gov/the-press-office/2016/03/31/us-china-joint-presidential-statement-climate-change.

[21] Ibid.

Paris commitments and those contained in its bilateral agreements with China.[22]

President Trump later sought to remove the United States from the Paris Agreement entirely in mid-2017. He claimed that the agreement places disproportionate burdens on America while letting other countries—and China specifically—skate through with lesser commitments. Trump claimed the agreement would cost millions of American jobs and trillions of dollars without leading to substantial global emissions reductions.[23] These claims and justifications for withdrawing from Paris were spurious given Paris's characteristics of inclusiveness and self-determined commitments, and they called upon economic and environmental policy analyses with dubious interest-driven origins.[24] Withdrawing from Paris was also deliberately designed to be a multiyear affair in the design of the agreement itself, leaving the Trump administration confined to voicing its intention to withdraw when it became possible near the end of his term in office. However, there was little to keep Trump from ignoring or undermining Paris and bilateral commitments with China at a federal level throughout his time in office—which his administration did.[25]

These radical differences between U.S. presidential administrations are germane to future challenges and opportunities for U.S.–China climate cooperation. But so too is the substantial subnational cooperation between the two countries that both predated and was bolstered by the actions of the Trump Administration. The 2015 U.S.–China Climate Leaders Summit in Los Angeles brought together a range of officials

[22] Jackson Ewing, "U.S.-China Climate Relations: Beyond Trump." *RealClear-World*, April 27, 2017, https://www.realclearworld.com/articles/2017/04/27/us-china_climate_relations_beyond_trump.html.

[23] Pilita Clark and Lauren Leatherby, "Trump transcript on Paris climate deal exit – annotated Analysis of the president's Rose Garden speech," *Financial Times*, June 1, 2017, https://ig.ft.com/trump-paris-agreement-speech-annotator/.

[24] Glenn Kessler and Michelle Ye Hee Lee, "Fact-checking President Trump's claims on the Paris climate change deal," *Washington Post*, June 1, 2017, https://www.washingtonpost.com/news/fact-checker/wp/2017/06/01/fact-checking-president-trumps-claims-on-the-paris-climate-change-deal/?utm_term=.134ecf55b333.

[25] Robert Stavins, "Reflecting on Trump's Record and Anticipating Biden's Performance," *An Economic View of the Environment* (blog), posted on January 5, 2021, http://www.robertstavinsblog.org/2021/01/05/reflecting-on-trumps-record-and-anticipating-bidens-performance/.

seeking local-to-local climate partnerships.[26] Then Vice President Biden and Climate Envoy Stern joined California Governor Jerry Brown and Los Angeles Mayor Eric Garcetti in attendance alongside Chinese leaders from Beijing, Shenzhen, Guangdong, and multiple other major cities and provinces. Shenzhen, Guangdong, and Los Angeles signed a memorandum of understanding (MoU) to expand best practice cooperation to reduce emissions, while a collection of institutes pledged to design and implement carbon market training programs in China, and to introduce California's zero-emission vehicle credit trading mechanism in Beijing. Los Angeles and Beijing developed a litany of cooperative measures on low-carbon urban planning and transportation, while Los Angeles and Zhenjiang became the first cities to endorse the Subnational Global Climate Leadership MoU.[27] Such connectivity is not confined to California, with President Xi reaching accords with five U.S. state governors later in 2015 to reduce transportation emissions, support clean energy technologies, and exchange ideas with their Chinese counterparts.[28]

President Trump's climate regressions contributed to additional waves of subnational and private sector action in the United States, connecting with China in direct and indirect ways. 630 American businesses signed an open letter to President Trump and the U.S. Congress advocating to remain in the Paris Agreement prior to Trump's declaration of withdrawal.[29] Technology companies like Apple and Google, large manufacturers including General Motors and General Electric, energy companies including Chevron and Exxon-Mobile, large electricity generators (PG&E and National Grid), and even coal producers (Arch Coal, Peabody

[26] "U.S.-China Climate Leaders Summit: Fact Sheet," *Office of Eric Garcetti, Mayor of Los Angeles*, accessed April 1, 2021, https://www.lamayor.org/summitfacts.

[27] Signatories to this MoU have committed to either reduce greenhouse gas emissions from 80 to 95 percent below 1990 levels by 2050 or achieve a per capita annual emissions target of less than 2 metric tons by 2050, while seeking to influence global climate negotiations through their own concrete local actions.

[28] Jackson Ewing and Juan Wei, "The US and China go local on Climate Cooperation," *The Diplomat*, September 24, 2015, https://thediplomat.com/2015/09/the-us-and-china-go-local-on-climate-cooperation/.

[29] Lydia O'Conner, "More Than 600 Companies Urge Trump Not to Renege on Climate," *Huffington Post*, January 10, 2017, https://www.huffpost.com/entry/companies-climate-change-trump-letter_n_5873ebe5e4b099cdb0fede62.

Energy) all advocated remaining in.[30] Just hours after Trump's Paris announcement, the U.S. Climate Alliance was formed as a bipartisan collection of U.S. states committed to upholding the goals of the Agreement.[31] From its outset this group had a collective population of over 100 million and a GDP approaching $7 trillion.[32] More than 1,200 governors, mayors, businesses, attorneys general, investors, and colleges and universities later declared their intention to continue pursuing the Paris Agreement goals. Meanwhile President Xi quickly noted China's intention to continue to honor its climate commitments under the bilateral agreements with the United States and those made to the UNFCCC, and China's intention to double-down on subnational cooperation with major U.S. actors. He did so most visibly by feting Governor Brown publicly in Beijing—a rare occurrence for a non-head of state—as the two discussed expanding China–California partnerships on climate and clean energy.[33]

Such subnational action now has the opportunity to converge with a national level climate reset between the two countries under a Biden Administration. China's record on climate has been mixed since the Obama–Xi bilateral breakthroughs. President Xi's 2060 carbon neutrality pledge was a landmark commitment in the Chinese context, but China also commissioned 38.4 gigawatts (GW) of new coal plants in 2020, more than three times the 11.9 GW commissioned in the rest of the world.[34] There may be more significant emissions growth in the pipeline, with China initiated 73.5 GW of new coal plant proposals in 2020—more than

[30] Robert Stavins, "Trump's Paris Withdrawal: The Nail in the Coffin of U.S. Global Leadership?," *An Economic View of the Environment* (blog), posted on June 6, 2017, http://www.robertstavinsblog.org/2017/06/06/trumps-paris-withdrawal-nail-coffin-u-s-global-leadership/.

[31] "United States Climate Alliance Adds 10 New Members to Coalition Committed to Upholding the Paris Accord," *Office of Governor Andrew M. Cuomo*, June 5, 2017, https://www.governor.ny.gov/news/united-states-climate-alliance-adds-10-new-members-coalition-committed-upholding-paris-accord.

[32] Jess Shankeleman, "BoE's Carney Sees Up to $7 Trillion Invested in Renewable Energy," *Bloomberg*, July 15, 2016, https://www.bloomberg.com/news/articles/2016-07-15/boe-s-carney-sees-up-to-7-trillion-invested-in-renewable-energy.

[33] Javier C. Hernández and Adam Nagourney, "As Trump Steps Back, Jerry Brown Talks Climate Change in China," *New York Times*, June 6, 2017, https://www.nytimes.com/2017/06/06/world/asia/xi-jinping-china-jerry-brown-california-climate.html?_r=2.

[34] Global Energy Monitor, *China Dominates 2020 Coal Plant Development*. San Francisco: Global Energy Monitor, 2021, accessed April 1, 2021, https://globalenergymonitor.org/wp-content/uploads/2021/02/China-Dominates-2020-Coal-Development.pdf.

five times the capacity proposed across the rest of the world combined. Such mixed signals lead to soul searching in Beijing about the country's energy future—most directly via a cutting censure of the National Energy Administration by central environmental inspectors, and the realization that China's reorganized Ministry of Ecology and Environment will need to flex its muscles still further for China to reach its stated climate goals.[35] Meanwhile President Biden immediately brought the United States back into the Paris fray, and signed a raft of executive orders to reverse much of the Trump domestic and international climate policies.[36] Yet Biden faces the limitations of a divided legislature and populace, and there is little sign of what his intended climate sea change will mean for climate relations with China.

Biden campaigned on a strong, competitive, overall stance on China, and actions and rhetoric during the early days of his administration have born this out.[37] Such competition is not anathema to a return to productive climate relations between the two countries. While there is no prospect of a reset back to the 2016 context of cooperation, there is space for renewed engagement—both competitive and cooperative—that reflects current conditions and opportunities both within the relationship and in the global climate arena. The following section provides eight such pathways.

## Opportunities

1. **Return to regular dialogue.** During the Obama Administration, then Secretary of State John Kerry established the U.S.–China Climate Change Working Group, which drove both bilateral deal-making and collaborative work on the Paris Agreement. Climate leaders Todd Stern, Xie Zhenhua, and their teams had frequent

---

[35] Hongqiao Liu, "Q&A: Could an environmental inspector's criticisms accelerate China's climate policies?," *Carbon Brief*, February 5, 2021, https://www.carbonbrief.org/qa-could-an-environmental-inspectors-criticisms-accelerate-chinas-climate-policies.

[36] Coral Davenport, "Restoring Environmental Rules Rolled Back by Trump Could Take Years," *New York Times*, January 22, 2021, https://www.nytimes.com/2021/01/22/climate/biden-environment.html.

[37] Casey McDonald, "Biden says U.S. won't lift sanctions until Iran halts uranium enrichment," *CBS News*, February 7, 2021, https://www.cbsnews.com/news/biden-interview-iran-sanctions-nuclear-agreement/.

and regular interactions that bred familiarity and necessary trust. In Stern's words, the "nature of our cooperation was never easy…[b]ut the two sides came to understand, over time, that at the end of the day we would find a way to agree."[38] With Secretary Kerry now Biden's Special Presidential Envoy on Climate, and Minister Xie recently reinstalled as China's Special Envoy for climate, there is a foundation from which to build. Biden should ensure as a starting point that the U.S.–China Climate Change Working Group (or a similar body) is reinvigorated, well-resourced, and prioritized in the climate change and relevant foreign affairs apparatuses of the country, and encourage President Xi to do the same. Given the importance of the China relationship for U.S. climate policy, the working group should additionally provide policy inputs on relevant trade, economic, and energy issues adjacent to its direct purview.

2. **Develop and highlight aligned bilateral ambition.** The top-line outputs from the Obama–Xi bilateral agreements were the *quid pro quo* climate mitigation commitments. Producing these commitments together allowed the countries to address ambition alignment and competition issues privately within the parameters of the bilateral relationship, rather than only in the public multilateral spaces of the UNFCCC and elsewhere. The resulting joint declarations were a boon to international climate ambition and broadened the space for agreement across the rest of the global landscape. For these reasons the countries should again develop and release bilateral agreements on climate ambition. Such agreements can predate major UNFCCC summits, including the upcoming COP26 in Glasgow in December 2021, and contain major domestic climate commitments that enhance the countries' respective National Climate Plans (NDCs). Goals worth pursuing include codifying Biden's campaign statements on putting the United States on the path to net-zero emissions by 2050, creating a hard emissions cap in China's 14th Five Year Plan, and bilaterally agreeing to pursue the aspirational Paris Agreement target of a 1.5 degree C temperature increase over pre-industrial levels.

---

[38] Todd Stern, "Can the United States and China reboot their climate cooperation?," *Brookings Institution*, September 14, 2020, https://www.brookings.edu/articles/can-the-united-states-and-china-reboot-their-climate-cooperation/.

3. **Lead on climate and coal finance in multiple venues.** As a candidate President Biden voiced support for low-carbon approaches to overseas finance by the U.S. Export–Import Bank and the U.S. International Development Finance Corporation, including prohibiting finance for coal projects.[39] Biden likewise called for the United States to scale up alternative sources of investment for clean energy projects in Belt and Road Initiative (BRI) recipient countries. Meanwhile, growing outbound investment in renewable energy notwithstanding, China is supporting more than 100 GW of coal power expansion through development, construction, underwriting, and financing along the BRI.[40] With other major coal financiers— Japan and the Republic of Korea—set to curtail their investments, China will soon be on an island as a public outbound lender. The Biden Administration should privately pressure China to stop financing new international coal projects immediately, and phase out international coal investment completely during the period of the country's 14th Five Year Plan (2021–2025). It should use public forums such as the G-20, the Strategic and Economic Dialogue, the Major Economies Forum, and the US-led 2021 Climate Leaders Summit to call for all major economies to foreswear outbound coal investment, leveraging partnerships in East Asia and Europe to make the case.

4. **Pursue virtuous competition.** President Biden's Build Back Better stimulus plan describes China—the only foreign country mentioned—as a rival in the battle for low-carbon sector primacy.[41] China is currently leading this rivalry in terms of the scale of domestic penetration in electric vehicles, modern rail development, renewable energy, and new nuclear development—all of which are targeted by the Made in China 2025 plan as strategic sectors for

---

[39] Thom Woodroofe and Brendan Guy, "Climate Diplomacy under a New U.S. Administration," *Asia Society Policy Institute*, April 2020, https://asiasociety.org/policy-institute/climate-diplomacy-under-new-us-administration-0.

[40] David Sandalow. "China's Response to Climate Change: A Study in Contrasts and a Policy at a Crossroads," *Asia Society Policy Institute*, July 30, 2020, https://asiasociety.org/policy-institute/chinas-response-climate-change-study-contrasts-and-policy-crossroads.

[41] Battle for the Soul of the Nation, Build Back Better: Joe Biden's Jobs and Economic Recovery Plan for Working Families, accessed April 1, 2021, https://joebiden.com/build-back-better/.

public investment.[42] While the United States will not pursue the level of centralized industrial policy as does China, the Biden administration should invest substantial public money in clean energy R&D and high value production across supply chains at home. As low-carbon product lines expand in both countries, the vast market scales of their combined economies will drive down prices both in the United States and China and in their outbound low-carbon investments. The Biden Administration can make progress to this end by revitalizing the National Network of Manufacturing Innovation—jointly managed by the Department of Energy, National Institute for Science and Technology, National Science Foundation, and Department of Defense—and insisting that it fosters documentable progress to scale low-carbon technology.[43] Biden can likewise quickly create and fund aggressively the proposed Clean Energy Export and Climate Investment Initiative to promote clean energy exports and international investments.

5. **Make progress on climate-sensitive trade.** President Biden pledged as a candidate to account for climate commitments in future trade agreements and revisit existing trade arrangements with climate standards in mind. This could produce border adjustments or tariffs that account for the embedded GHGs of U.S. imports, and level the playing field for U.S. producers that face growing GHG regulations. The EU is further along in developing such a system, with the Carbon Border Adjustment Mechanism signaling to the international trade community that accounting for carbon leakage, improving low-carbon competitiveness, and reducing the footprints of international supply chains are ascendant. For U.S.–China relations, deploying such tools would require strong domestic GHG regulation in the United States, and close negotiations on the shape of border GHG adjustments at the WTO and bilaterally with

---

[42] James McBride and Andrew Chatzky, "Is 'Made in China 2025' a threat to global trade?," *Council on Foreign Relations*, May 13, 2019, https://www.cfr.org/backgroun der/made-china-2025-threat-global-trade.

[43] "National Network for Manufacturing Innovation," *Office of Energy Efficiency and Renewable Energy*, https://www.energy.gov/eere/amo/national-network-manufacturing-innovation.

China. The accounting involved is complex,[44] and could ultimately bolster monitoring, reporting, and verification efforts in China in the pursuit of wide-ranging access to the U.S. market. Such actions should be coordinated closely with European partners, and become key elements for addressing the trade friction that President Biden inherited from his predecessor.

6. **Expand support for track II, subnational, and sectoral dialogue.** The Aspen Institute, Asia Society Policy Institute, National Committee on U.S.–China Relations, and World Resources Institute are just a few significant institutions in the United States pursuing track II dialogue with Chinese counterparts on climate and energy issues. Subnational cooperation at municipal and state-province levels continues. Such efforts help build relationships, common bases for knowledge and understanding, and can advance climate cooperation during otherwise difficult periods in the overall U.S.–China relationship. Similarly, sectoral cooperation in renewable energy, storage, efficiency, transportation and the like on business-to-business levels and in the development of industry and ESG standards can create synergistic supply chains and more uniform low-carbon policies, respectively. While the Biden Administration should not attempt to manage such efforts, it can champion those with the most promise and discernable success. The Biden Administration should therefore create a U.S.–China track II climate funding mechanism within the State Department office of Secretary Kerry. This would enable those engaging most directly on track I U.S.–China climate relations to make funding decisions on how to supplement their work with track II efforts.

7. **Drive solutions to the outstanding impasse on Paris Agreement implementation.** The most important outstanding issue for implementing the Paris Agreement is finding solutions on international exchanges via an Article 6 rulebook.[45] Article 6 seeks to clarify how "mitigation outcomes"—essentially GHG reduction credits—can be transferred from one country to another and accounted

---

[44] Michael A. Mehling, Harro van Asselt, Kasturi Das, Susanne Droege, and Cleo Verkuijl, "Designing Border Carbon Adjustments for Enhanced Climate Action," *American Journal of International Law* 113, no. 3 (2019): 433–81, http://doi.org/10.1017/ajil.2019.22.

[45] Jackson Ewing , "Net-zero Commitments make Madrid carbon market letdown

for national climate commitments. To function effectively these exchanges need rules to ensure that emissions reductions are real and are only counted once. Negotiations must also determine what to do with a previous generation Clean Development Mechanism (CDM) credits, of which China is the largest holder.[46] Together, these and adjacent Article 6 issues have derailed two successive UNFCCC climate summits. The most likely and apt outcome here is a bargain in which some increased transparency and monitoring practices are agreed upon alongside a percentage of older CDM credits carrying over to the new carbon market landscape. The United States and China should reach some bilateral consensus on their preferences on this issue prior to COP26 in December 2021. While other players will rightly pursue their own, counter, positions, U.S.–China alignment would give this round of Article 6 negotiations a greater chance for success.

8. **Insulate climate change from spoilers.** While it is not possible or preferable to isolate climate change considerations from bilateral trade and competitiveness issues, they should be insulated from potential spoilers where possible. The Biden Administration should make clear that issues around Hong Kong's self-determination, territorial claims and force deployments in the South China Sea, human rights and plight of minority groups, and freedom of speech and information are important, but will not be conflated with bilateral climate change issues. It should in turn insist that China likewise does not condition movement on climate change to external geopolitical and geo-economic issues.

more critical," *World Bank CPLC* (blog), January 9, 2020, https://www.carbonpricin gleadership.org/blogs/2020/1/9/net-zero-commitments-make-madrid-carbon-market-letdown-more-critical.

[46] "State and Trends of Carbon Pricing 2019," *World Bank Group,* June, 2019, https://openknowledge.worldbank.org/handle/10986/31755.

## CONCLUSION

Pursuing these measures guarantees nothing but would put the United States and China back onto a productive climate path. Through regular dialogue new difficulties and new opportunities not envisioned here or by current climate leaders in either capitol will undoubtedly emerge. However it is the effort as much as the outcomes on behalf of the world's two largest emitters that can bolster international climate progress. Experiences from the Obama-Xi rapprochement show the galvanizing power of the two countries coming together with a degree of shared vision— regardless of its particulars. For this reason along with the material impacts that it would make possible, the Biden Administration should make bilateral diplomacy with China the most urgent, and most well-resourced issue in its international climate change agenda and thus reimagine U.S.–China relations.

# CHAPTER 9

# The U.S. and Unresolved Cross-Strait Relations: From Trump to Biden

*Kwei-Bo Huang*

**Abstract** This chapter introduces contemporary cross-Strait relations from 2016 to early 2021, followed by a section that briefly discusses the highly unpredictable, or unprecedented, policies of President Donald Trump toward the two sides of the Taiwan Strait. Emphasis is also placed on President Joe Biden's policies toward the Mainland and Taiwan, with a focus on "strategic ambiguity" of the Biden administration that involves the three U.S.-PRC communiqués, the Taiwan Relations Act, as well as the "six assurances" to Taiwan. The chapter ends with two scenarios

The views and opinions expressed in this chapter are those of the author and do not reflect the official policy or position of any organizations with which the author is affiliated.

K.-B. Huang (✉)
Department of Diplomacy, Center for Global and Regional Risk Assessment, College of International Affairs, National Chengchi University, Taipei, Taiwan (ROC)
e-mail: kweibo@nccu.edu.tw

between the U.S. and the PRC that are more possible to take place in the coming four years.

**Keywords** Strategic ambiguity · Cross-Strait relations · United States (U.S.) · China, People's Republic of · Taiwan, Republic of China

Cross-Strait relations between Taiwan (officially known as the Republic of China, ROC, established in 1912) and mainland China (officially known as the People's Republic of China, PRC, founded in 1949) has become one of the lingering critical issues after the end of the World War II. The United States (U.S.) forged official ties with the ROC from 1913 to 1978, and then, under Jimmy Carter's leadership, switched recognition from the ROC to the PRC in January 1979.

Both Taiwan and mainland China are not satisfied with but do not challenge or oppose proactively the "one China policy," or a framework of "strategic ambiguity," defined and implemented by the U.S. Meanwhile, they have their own insistences on relations between the two sides of the Taiwan Strait. For the ROC, the Kuomintang (KMT) government endorsed a "one China principle" in accordance with the ROC Constitution whose content upholds the ROC as an independent sovereign country and thus invalidates the PRC's claim that Taiwan is part of the PRC, whereas the current Democratic Progressive Party (DPP) government favors a "China (PRC)-Taiwan" formulation that simply treats China and "Taiwan" as two separate sovereign countries. For the PRC under the one-party rule of the Chinese Communist Party (CCP) that has always wanted to reunite with Taiwan, it has insisted on its own "one China principle" in which the PRC represents the sole legal government of China and has stood firm against "two Chinas," "one China, one Taiwan," and "Taiwan independence."

In such a context, the ensuing section of this chapter will introduce contemporary cross-Strait relations from 2016 to the present (early 2021), and then, a section that briefly discusses the highly unpredictable, or unprecedented, policies of the Donald Trump administration toward the two sides of the Taiwan Strait will follow. The third section will touch on the Joe Biden administration's cross-Strait policies that are still developing. The last section will be an analysis based on two possible scenarios between the U.S. and the PRC in the future.

## Contemporary Cross-Taiwan Strait Relations

There have been ups and downs in cross-Strait relations since the authorized civilian representatives of both the KMT government and the CCP government met a few times in the early 1990s in Hong Kong (when Hong Kong had not been returned to the PRC) and gained a basic level of mutual trust and understanding for future exchange. To better grasp such changing relations, one can identify four dimensions of analysis covering from "one China" to four critical issue-areas.

First, the "one China" policy has been defining Taiwan and mainland China's patterns of interactions. Both constitutions are based on "one China," and the "China" referred to by each of the constitutions differs. This explains the fundamental tacit understanding—"one China"—that made possible the two sides' meetings in Hong Kong in 1992 and ensuing functional cooperation. The Cross-Straits Economic Cooperation Framework Agreement (ECFA) signed in 2010 is also a product of such a tacit understanding, sometimes described as the "1992 consensus."

The DPP in Taiwan has never recognized the existence of such a tacit understanding in 1992. Its long-standing position that Taiwan has been an independent sovereign country under the title of the Republic of China neglects the history of the country and detaches Taiwan from "China." In other words, the DPP's "one China," if any, would mean there is only one China (PRC) that has nothing to do with the government and people of Taiwan (plus Penghu, Quemoy, and Matsu). Nonetheless, the very limited cross-Strait cooperation that has remained since the inauguration of the ROC president Tsai Ing-wen, e.g., the ECFA's "early harvest" list, is still on the basis of the past tacit understanding between the two sides.

Second, two confronting values have led to the sharp differences in ways of life, and particularly political and economic development. Taiwan, suffering from incremental strangulation of democracy, is an advanced democratic polity in the global Chinese community. Mainland China, ruled by a communist regime since late 1949, endorses "socialism with Chinese characteristics" and grows under a one-party authoritarian regime. This "binary opposition"—democracy and communism/socialism—results in the high difficulty of political integration between Taiwan and mainland China.

Third, cross-Strait relations are not only a two-actor but a three-actor game. Regardless the U.S. direct or indirect interest involved in the

Taiwan Strait, it is undeniable that the destiny of "China" has been heavily influenced by the U.S. since the 1930s, and as a result of two World Wars and the civil war between the KMT and the CCP.

To put it simply, when Taiwan was separate from the Chinese mainland again in late 1949, the U.S., from hesitation to strategic determination, decided to defend Taiwan mainly due to the outbreak of the Korean War. After the severing of U.S.-ROC diplomatic ties, the U.S. has claimed that it will assist Taiwan to defend itself. Right before the end of the World War II, the U.S. government agreed that sovereignty over Taiwan belonged to China, represented by the ROC, and for the very first time after the separation of the two sides of the Taiwan Strait, the U.S. appointed its ambassador to (free) China, Karl Rankin, in 1953. The U.S. does not argue that Taiwan is part of (communist) China, and it has begun to take no position on sovereignty over Taiwan after its normalization of relations with the PRC in 1979. Although the U.S. has switched recognition from the ROC to the PRC, the U.S. intervention has maintained peace in the Taiwan Strait as a strategic priority.

Last, there are four critical issue-areas largely determining future cross-Strait relations. The first issue-area is reunification/independence and bridging the significant gap between the two societies, Taiwan and mainland China. Reunification/independence in the future is too complicated to answer in this chapter, but the distance between Taiwanese and mainland Chinese societies is widening mainly due to several factors. These include: worsened relations between the DPP and the CCP governments since mid-2016, the 2019–2020 Hong Kong "Anti-Extradition Law Amendment Bill Movement," and the "anti-China" sentiment heightened explicitly by the Trump administration. The global pandemic has also contributed to worsening relations followed by political petty moves or small tricks unhelpful for mutual understanding.

The second issue-area is related to security which includes territorial disputes. It is important to note that the arms sale packages from the U.S. to Taiwan are primarily defensive in nature. However, when it comes to defending Taiwan from a Chinese communist attack, Washington's official policy is "strategic ambiguity": The U.S. won't disclose how it would respond. With regard to the overlapped territorial claims over the South China Sea and the Diaoyu Islands (also called Diaoyudao by the PRC or the Senkaku Islands by Japan) in the East China Sea, the previous and current governments in Taiwan have never collaborated with the Beijing authorities to defend these disputed areas.

The third issue-area is economics and trade. Taiwan's asymmetric trade dependency on mainland China (and Hong Kong) has risen again since Tsai took office in May 2016—generally speaking, from 39% (2015) to 43.8% (2020). It would be fair to say that Taiwan relies on the market on mainland China, while mainland China needs Taiwan's high-tech and ICT products.[1] Yet, owing to the high percentage of Taiwan's trade export to mainland China, the Mainland Affairs Council at the ROC Executive Yuan (Branch) has contended in 2020 that it does not hope the ECFA will suspend or cease to function over political reasons and that all the agreements and memorandums of understanding signed between the two sides of the Taiwan Strait are still valid.

The fourth issue-area is diplomacy. It has not become totally hope-less when the ROC has been excluded from the mainstream international community for about forty years since it lost the "China seat" to the PRC in 1971. Yet, the ROC is able to participate in simply a few number of international governmental organizations, and it has lost a number of diplomatic allies from a high of 70 (in 1970) to only 15 (in 2020), a historic low. Furthermore, located in the Asia Pacific, the ROC is only a member of the Asian Development Bank (ADB) and of the Asia-Pacific Economic Cooperation (APEC), and it has no easy access to the recently established Regional Comprehensive Economic Partnership (RCEP) and the Comprehensive Progressive Trans-Pacific Partnership (CPTPP). Winning an obvious advantage over Taiwan but being anxious about the possible gain of the ROC/Taiwan as an independent sovereign political entity, the CCP government's very assertive approach to the ROC's external relations has created a significant hindrance to the improvement in cross-Strait relations.

---

[1] Chia-Hung Lu 呂嘉鴻, "Taiwan chukou zhongguo zhan bi pansheng yinbao jingji bici yilai huo 'tuogou'bianlun" 台灣出口中國佔比攀升 引爆經濟彼此依賴或「脫鈎」辯論 [The Rising Proportion of Taiwan's Exports to China Ignites the Debate on Economic Interdependence or "Decoupling"], *BBC News Zhongwen* 中文, January 11, 2021, https://www.bbc.com/zhongwen/trad/chinese-news-55587490.

## Donald Trump and His Cross-Strait Policies

The policies of the U.S. toward Taiwan and mainland China had a sharp divergence particularly between Trump's first two years and last two years as U.S. president.

Trump tested the bottom line of the Chinese communist authorities by tweeting about changing the "one China policy." He also maintained that the U.S. should not abide by the "one China policy" unless it secured concessions from Beijing on trade deals. After a couple of weeks, it appeared that Trump realized this was not a realistic objective and agreed to honor the "one China policy" the U.S. has defined since the 1980s.[2] In March 2017 when U.S. Secretary of State Rex Tillerson visited the PRC, he openly stated that bilateral relations between the U.S. and the PRC have been "guided by an understanding of non-conflict, non-confrontation, mutual respect, and win–win cooperation"—very similar to the "new model of great power relationship" Xi Jinping has proposed at the Sunnylands (California) summit with Barack Obama in 2013.[3]

Despite providing Taiwan with a number of oral and written support (including tweets), agreeing on eleven arms sale packages (one in 2017, one in 2018, three in 2019, and six in 2020) reaching a historical high at 18.6 billion U.S. dollars, and sending or trying to send cabinet-level or senior officials to Taiwan, Trump in his four-year term neither altered or denied the "one China policy" publicly, nor did he advance Taiwan's statehood proactively. Trump personally rarely talked about Taiwan in public, despite the fact that his administration, roughly after 2019, did not

---

[2] Nomann Merchant, Christopher Bodeen and Julie Pace, "In Shift, Trump Tells Xi He Will Honor 'One China' Policy," *Associated Press*, February 11, 2017, https://www.apnews.com/article/515798dbf6c545beb7f19711e092c1e0.

[3] Joseph S. Nye, "A New Great Power Relationship," *China Daily*, March 4, 2013, http://www.chinadaily.com.cn/opinion/2013-03/04/content_16271838.htm; Mike D. Lampton, "A New Type of Major-Power Relationship: Seeking a Durable Foundation for U.S.-China Ties," *Asia Policy* no. 16, 2013, pp. 51–68, https://doi.org/10.1353/asp.2013.0025; Cheng Li and Lucy Xu, "Chinese Enthusiasm and American Cynicism Over the 'New Type of Great Power Relations'," *China-U.S. Focus*, December 4, 2014, https://www.chinausfocus.com/foreign-policy/chinese-enthusiasm-and-american-cynicism-over-the-new-type-of-great-power-relations/; Jinghan Zeng, "Constructing a 'New Type of Great Power Relations': The State of Debate in China (1998–2014)," *The British Journal of Politics and International Relations* 18, no. 2, May 2016, 422–442, https://doi.org/10.1177/1369148115620991.

fear to mention Taiwan and its democracy and international participation (so long as that it did not involve statehood).

The Trump administration pushed the envelope during the second half of his presidency by gradually lifting the "self-imposed" restrictions in dealing with Taiwan.[4] For example, after an existing practice that the U.S. sent a cabinet-level official, Secretary of Health Alex Azar, II, to Taiwan in August 2020, the U.S. State Department's Undersecretary of State for Economic Growth, Energy, and the Environment, Keith Krach, paid a groundbreaking visit to Taiwan to tribute late ROC President Lee Teng-hui in September 2020.

Azar's visit to Taiwan both echoed the U.S.'s recognition of Taiwan's superior epidemic prevention effort and, once again, drew attention to U.S. criticism of mainland China's mishandling of the epidemic and concealing the critical information that caused a further spread of the coronavirus. Azar and his counterpart in Taiwan witnessed the signing of the memorandum for public health cooperation between the American Institute in Taiwan (AIT) and the Taiwan Council for U.S. Affairs (TCUSA). Krach's visit was highly sensitive because the State Department had never allowed an incumbent undersecretary or above to visit Taiwan after 1979. A handful of assistant secretaries of state ever visited Taiwan did not deal with political or East Asian issues. A low-profile and very short statement issued by the U.S. State Department indicates that Krach visited Taiwan to attend Lee's memorial service only, and the United States showed great respect for Lee's legacy "by continuing our strong bonds with Taiwan and its vibrant democracy through shared political and economic values."[5]

In addition to the TRA and "six assurances," Trump signed a few Taiwan-friendly bills, enacted by the Congress between February 2018 and December 2020, into domestic public laws articulating the collective will of the U.S. legislative branch to bolster bilateral political, security, and economic ties with Taiwan and safeguard Taiwan from the aggressive attempts by Beijing. These laws include the *Taiwan Travel Act*, the

---

[4] Michael R. Pompeo, "Lifting Self-Imposed Restrictions on the U.S.-Taiwan Relationship," *U.S. Department of State*, January 9, 2021, https://2017-2021.state.gov/lifting-self-imposed-restrictions-on-the-u-s-taiwan-relationship//index.html.

[5] Morgan Ortagus, "Under Secretary Keith Krach's Travel to Taiwan," *U.S. Department of State*, September 16, 2020, https://2017-2021.state.gov/under-secretary-keith-krachs-travel-to-taiwan/index.html.

*Asia Reassurance Initiative Act* of 2018, the *Taiwan Allies International Protection and Enhancement Initiative* (TAIPEI) Act of 2019, as well as the *Taiwan Assurance Act* of 2020.[6]

Before the end of Trump's presidency, it was highly significant to see the signing of the memorandums of understanding on health cooperation (August 10, 2020), the framework for infrastructure finance and market building cooperation (September 30, 2020), and establishing a U.S.–Taiwan economic prosperity partnership (EPP) dialogue (November 20, 2020). It was also unusual to see a sudden cancellation of already scheduled visits of two high-ranking U.S. officials to Taiwan: Andrew Wheeler, Administrator of the U.S. Environmental Protection Agency (scheduled for early December 2020), and Kelly Craft, U.S. Ambassador to the United Nations (scheduled for mid-January 2021). Unsurprisingly, the CCP government opposed all these.

## JOE BIDEN AND HIS CROSS-STRAIT POLICIES

Biden has had a long history of dealing with mainland Chinese leaders in a relatively friendly way and calling for a cautious approach to Taiwan. He did not consent to a provocative policy that deliberately used Taiwan as a tool for irritating Chinese communist leaders or giving them a lesson. Hence, unlike Trump who had established a personal connection to Tsai with a phone call after he won the presidential election and before he was sworn in as U.S. president, Biden and Tsai did not make any phone call before Biden took office on January 20, 2021.

Biden's record show he was opposed to the Taiwan Security Enhancement Act that was introduced by the House of the U.S. Congress in 1999, passed by the House in early 2000, viewed as a boost for the TRA by strengthening military sales and establishing direct military communication lines, but never turned into a U.S. public law.[7] As George W. Bush

---

[6] In the case of the *Asia Reassurance Initiative Act* of 2018, Trump signed it and released a "signing statement," mentioning that some provisions of this bill had to do with diplomatic and military tasks pertaining to the president. See Michael F. Martin, Ben Dolven, Susan V. Lawrence, Mark E. Manyin, and Bruce Vaughn, "The Asia Reassurance Initiative Act (ARIA) of 2018," *Congressional Research Service*, April 4, 2019, https://fas.org/sgp/crs/row/IF11148.pdf.

[7] U.S. 106th Congress, Committee on Foreign Relations, *S. 693: The Taiwan Security Enhancement Act*, S. Hrg. 106–230 (Washington, DC: The U.S. Government

agreed in an interview in spring 2001 that the United States had an obligation to defend Taiwan and would use "whatever it took to help Taiwan defend herself."[8] Biden openly expressed disapproval of G. W. Bush's change from strategic ambiguity to strategic clarity.[9] Biden contended that the response of the United States toward the Taiwan Strait "would depend upon the circumstances" (both Taiwan's and mainland China's actions) at that time.[10] In 2005, Biden joined his colleagues at the U.S. Senate to demand the Bush administration to convey concerns over the PRC's Anti-secession Act targeting Taiwan, Xinjiang, Tibet, and other places seen as part of the PRC territories.

An anonymous U.S. official once said that "across the board, there is a sense of a change in China over the last four to five years,"[11] which reflects Biden's pledge to resist "the growing ambition of China to rival the United States" in his remarks made on February 4, 2021.[12] Biden also paid a handful of official visits to mainland China in the capacity of U.S. Vice President, covering important issues ranging from strategic and economic interdependence to regional tensions involved in both governments and/or U.S. allies. He has spent a lot of time with Xi in the past. He is one of the few former U.S. vice presidents who had more experience in Chinese affairs since the end of the World War II.

Printing Office, 1999), https://www.govinfo.gov/content/pkg/CHRG-106shrg60900/html/CHRG-106shrg60900.htm.

[8] "Bush Vows Taiwan Support," *ABC News*, April 25, 2001, https://abcnews.go.com/U.S./story?id=93471&page=1.

[9] Joseph R. Biden, Jr., "Not So Deft on Taiwan," *Washington Post*, May 2, 2001, https://www.washingtonpost.com/archive/opinions/2001/05/02/not-so-deft-on-taiwan/2adf3075-ee98-4e70-9be0-5459ce1edd5d/.

[10] Generally speaking, Biden thought there should not be "any reckless moves on either side. He vowed to help maintain Taiwan's self-defense capacity if Taiwan did not seek independences, and he said Taiwan was not an independent country and nation-state. See, Joseph R. Biden, Jr., "U.S. Foreign Policy," *C-Span*, September 10, 2001, https://c-span.org/video/?165936-1/us-foreign-policy. (49'28"-52'02.").

[11] Natasha Bertrand, "Biden Confronts China's Xi in First Call," *Politico*, February 10, 2021, https://www.politico.com/news/2021/02/10/biden-xi-jinping-phone-call-468544.

[12] "Remarks by President Joe Biden on America's Place in the World," *The White House*, February 4, 2021, https://www.whitehouse.gov/briefing-room/speeches-remarks/2021/02/04/remarks-by-president-biden-on-americas-place-in-the-world/.

Biden's cross-Strait policies have shifted from the high unpredictability and apparent confrontation in the second half of Trump's presidency to a period of higher predictability and relatively less provocation. A practical observation is that Biden's cross-Strait policies in general will be positioned somewhere between those of Obama and of the second half of Trump's presidency, as signaled explicitly or implicitly not only in Biden's but also Antony Blinken's and Jake Sullivan's remarks.[13]

The current U.S. policy toward mainland China may be equipped generally with the following four elements, i.e., "A.R.M.S.": American interest first, reduction in tension, multilateralism with U.S. allies, and "strategic patience."

"American interest first" means, as Biden put in his remarks on February 4, 2021, his administration will rebuild U.S. capacity to lead and engage its adversaries and competitors diplomatically, where it's in the interest of the U.S., and advance the security of the American people by every available means; meanwhile, his administration is "ready to work with Beijing, when it's in America's interest to do so."[14] "Reduction in tension" refers to Biden's firm insistence on countering mainland China's assertive measures and his continued call for mutual cooperation in dealing with global issues. It appears that the Biden administration is aimed at holding its position while de-escalating conflicts and reestablishing negotiations which can lead possibly to a more peaceful trajectory. "Multilateralism with U.S. allies" is illustrated by Biden that U.S. alliances are the "greatest asset" and that the U.S. will work with its allies and partners and need to renew its role in international institutions. "Strategic patience," as put by the White House Press Secretary Jen Psaki, represents the Biden administration's ongoing internal and interagency reviews of its China policy on a number of dimensions, and that needs some more time to draw conclusions.

---

[13] About Antony Blinken's, see "Secretary Blinken to Deliver Remarks to the Media in the Press Briefing Room," *U.S. Department of State*, January 26, 2021, https://www.state.gov/secretary-blinken-to-deliver-remarks-to-the-media-in-the-press-briefing-room/. About Jake Sullivan's, see "Passing the Baton 2021: Securing America's Future Together," *United States Institute of Peace*, January 29, 2021, https://www.usip.org/sites/default/files/Passing-the-Baton-2021-Transcript-FINAL.pdf.

[14] Joseph R. Biden, Jr., "Remarks by President Joe Biden on America's Place in the World," *The White House*, February 4, 2021, https://www.whitehouse.gov/briefing-room/speeches-remarks/2021/02/04/remarks-by-president-biden-on-americas-place-in-the-world/.

With presumable "strategic ambiguity" toward the Taiwan Strait, the Biden administration officials have honored the three U.S.-PRC communiqués, the TRA, as well as the "six assurances," and uttered the importance of U.S. commitment to Taiwan, bolstering workable deterrence with a pledge of helping Taiwan maintain "a sufficient self-defense capability" and continuing "to support a peaceful resolution of cross-Strait issues, consistent with the wishes and best interests of the people of Taiwan."[15] Such a commitment to Taiwan, not to a full U.S.–Taiwan relationship, has been "rock-solid" and "will absolutely endure in a Biden administration," according to U.S. Secretary of State Blinken[16] and the spokespersons of U.S. State Department[17] and of National Security Council.[18]

In addition to the "rock-solid" but limited commitment to Taiwan, the Biden administration has asked the Chinese communist government to stop the over-assertive actions of the People's Liberation Army toward Taiwan in recent years, and to "engage in meaningful dialogue with Taiwan's democratically elected representatives.[19]"

It appears that Biden has recognized the complexity of Washington–Beijing–Taipei relations and has been subtle enough to manage its relations with the two sides of the Taiwan Strait. For example, when Biden was a U.S. senator at a hearing on the Taiwan Security Enhancement Act in August 1999, he agreed on a statement made by the ROC Minister of National Defense, Tang Fei, that "poor U.S.-China relations

---

[15] Ned Price, "PRC Military Pressure Against Taiwan Threatens Regional Peace and Stability," *U.S. Department of State*, January 23, 2021, https://www.state.gov/prc-military-pressure-against-taiwan-threatens-regional-peace-and-stability/.

[16] Antony Blinken, "Statement for the Record Before the United States Senate Committee on Foreign Relations," *U.S. Senate*, January 19, 2021, https://www.foreign.senate.gov/imo/media/doc/011921_Blinken_Testimony.pdf.

[17] Ned Price, "PRC Military Pressure Against Taiwan Threatens Regional Peace and Stability," *U.S. Department of State*, January 23, 2021, https://www.state.gov/prc-military-pressure-against-taiwan-threatens-regional-peace-and-stability/.

[18] Ben Blanchard, "Taiwan-Biden Ties Off to Strong Start with Invite for Top Diplomat," *Reuters*, January 21, 2021, https://www.reuters.com/article/us-usa-biden-taiwan-idU.S.KBN29Q01N.

[19] Ned Price, "PRC Military Pressure Against Taiwan Threatens Regional Peace and Stability," *U.S. Department of State*, January 23, 2021, https://www.state.gov/prc-military-pressure-against-taiwan-threatens-regional-peace-and-stability/.

are bad news for cross-Strait relations.[20]" A two-hour phone call between Biden and Xi that came just ahead of the lunar new year (February 10 night, EST) suggests further dialogue on a wide range of issues, either conflicting or cooperative in nature, by the two leaders. Biden "committed to pursuing practical, results-oriented engagements when it advanced the interests of the American people" and those of American allies,[21] while Xi "sought a resumption of various dialogue mechanisms to avoid misunderstanding and misjudgment, and requested the U.S. should respect mainland China's core interests such as Hong Kong, Xinjiang, and Taiwan and "act cautiously."[22]

On the same trilateral relations, in May 2020, Blinken has maintained that "one of the successes… between the United States and China over many years… has been how we have dealt with the challenge posed by the relationship between China and Taiwan." He has further stated that the way cross-Strait relations had been handled in the past denoted "a source of stability, not instability," and hoped that the U.S. government should reestablish the balance.[23]

The Biden administration officials have brought up the "one China policy," the three U.S.-PRC communiqués, the TRA, and the "six assurances"—and employed a three-tier (competitive, cooperative, and adversarial) policy statement to show Taiwan and mainland China their commitment. Although Biden and his officials have taken no position on the sovereignty over Taiwan and although the U.S. Department of State has expressed no change in the U.S. "one China policy," the

---

[20] U.S. 106th Congress, Committee on Foreign Relations, *S. 693: The Taiwan Security Enhancement Act*, S. Hrg. 106–230 (Washington, DC: the U.S. Government Printing Office, 1999), https://www.govinfo.gov/content/pkg/CHRG-106shrg60900/html/CHRG-106shrg60900.htm.

[21] "Readout of President Joseph R. Biden, Jr. Call with President Xi Jinping of China," *The White House*, February 10, 2021, https://www.whitehouse.gov/briefing-room/statements-releases/2021/02/10/readout-of-president-joseph-r-biden-jr-call-with-president-xi-jinping-of-china/.

[22] Anne Gearan, "In First Call with China's Xi, Biden Stresses U.S. Commitment to Allies and Human Rights," *Washington Post*, February 11, 2021, https://www.washingtonpost.com/national-security/in-first-call-with-chinas-xi-biden-stresses-us-commitment-to-allies-and-human-rights/2021/02/10/6cb6f0fa-6c01-11eb-ba56-d7e2c8defa31_story.html.

[23] "Transcript: Joe Biden Foreign Policy Adviser Antony Blinken on COVID Shortfalls, Failures in Syria," *CBS News*, May 20, 2020, https://www.cbsnews.com/news/transcript-joe-biden-foreign-policy-adviser-antony-blinken-on-covid-shortfalls-failures-in-syria/.

possible change includes: yielding more space for Washington-Taipei official engagements, speaking for Taiwan mainly from the democracy and
human rights angle, and refraining both Taipei and Beijing from obviously
provocative actions. Moreover, it seems that the Biden administration officials have tended to place the three communiqués before the component
concerning Taiwan when speaking of the "one China policy," and called
Taiwan's key decisionmakers, including the president, "democratically
elected representatives" in order to downplay the sovereign connotation
when encouraging a constructive dialogue between Taipei and Beijing.

At his very first TV town hall on February 16, 2021, Biden explained
in brief his phone conversation with Xi. He said, "I point out to him no
American president can be sustained as a president, if he doesn't reflect
the values of the United States. I am not going to speak out against what
he's doing in Hong Kong, what he's doing with the Uyghurs in the
western mountains of China, and Taiwan, trying to end the one China
policy by making it forceful. He gets it. Culturally there are different
norms that each country and that leaders are expected to follow."[24]
Biden did not mean his administration would remain silent about or
become softer on these cases. Instead, more possibly, the Biden administration officials will keep referring to or supporting Hong Kong, Xinjiang,
Taiwan, and or other issues that the U.S. has a strategic interest in.

In mid-March of 2021, the U.S., represented by Blinken and Sullivan,
invited mainland China, represented by Yang Jiechi (director of the
Central Foreign Affairs Commission Office of the Chinese Communist Party) and Wang Yi (state councilor and foreign minister), to meet
in Anchorage, Alaska. Blinken voiced "deep concerns with actions by
China, including in Xinjiang, Hong Kong, Taiwan, cyberattacks on the
United States, and economic coercion toward our allies," and saw Beijing
as a negative impact on "the rules-based order that maintains global
stability."[25] It deserves more analysis of Blinken's words that followed

---

[24] Melissa Macaya and Veronica Rocha, "CNN Town Hall with President Biden,"
*CNN*, February 17, 2021, https://edition.cnn.com/politics/live-news/joe-biden-town-
hall-02-16-21/index.html.

[25] Antony J. Blinken, "Secretary Antony J. Blinken, National Security Advisor Jake
Sullivan, Director Yang and State Councilor Wang at the Top of Their Meeting:
Remarks," Anchorage, Alaska, *U.S. Department of State*, March 18, 2021, https://
www.state.gov/secretary-antony-j-blinken-national-security-advisor-jake-sullivan-chinese-
director-of-the-office-of-the-central-commission-for-foreign-affairs-yang-jiechi-and-chinese-
state-councilor-wang-yi-at-th/.

immediately: "That's why they're not merely internal matters and why we feel an obligation to raise these issues..." Yang responded that "Xinjiang, Tibet, and Taiwan... are an inalienable part of China's territory and that "China is firmly opposed to U.S. interference in China's internal affairs... and we will take firm actions in response." Probably because the Chinese communist authorities did not want to engage in any public dialogue concerning Hong Kong, Yang replaced Hong Kong with Tibet, a name neither Blinken nor Sullivan mentioned in their respective opening remarks.[26] According to Douglas Paal, "Biden's team wants to have its cake – sounding tough on Taiwan – while eating it, too –not pushing Beijing over the edge by abandoning the one China policy."[27]

Whether Biden and his key national security officials will be able to pivot more resources and foreign policy objectives toward mainland China and Taiwan in the post-Trump era remains to be seen. The Biden administration's successful reorientation of foreign policy priorities on mainland China and cross-Strait relations will also hinge on the change in cross-Strait relations being impacted mainly by Xi's relatively tough position toward Taiwan and the strong irredentism and growing patriotism on mainland China. Tsai's strategic patience and incremental moves toward Taiwan independence, as well as the rising "Taiwan identity" after some seven decades of separation from the Chinese mainland, will be critical factors for the U.S. as well.[28]

[26] Ibid.

[27] Douglas Paal, "The Anchorage Meeting Will Buy America Needed Time," *Asia Peace Programme—Essays*, March 25, 2021, Asia Research Institute, National University of Singapore, https://ari.nus.edu.sg/app-essay-douglas-paal/.

[28] The incremental Taiwan independence can be exemplified by Tsai Ing-wen's using frequently "Republic of China Taiwan" instead of the official national title "Republic of China" and by minimizing the official national title and place "TAIWAN" in large font on national passports. As for the rising "Taiwan identity" and its political connotations, see Cody Wai-Kwok Yau, "The Meaning of 'Taiwanese': Conceptualizing the Components of Taiwanese National Identity," *Xuanju yu yanjiu* 選舉與研究 (*Journal of Electoral Studies*) 23, No. 2, 2016, 1–54, https://doi.org/10.6612tjes/2016.23.92.01-54.

## Two Scenarios That Are More Possible

After the separation between Taiwan and mainland China in late 1949, for U.S. administrations, cross-Strait relations have become consequential issues that have critical implications for peace and prosperity in the region. By and large, Taipei and Beijing have held mutually exclusive political and legal positions, and they have lacked communication, engaged in diplomatic struggles, kept military tensions, and sometimes discouraged or curbed social and economic exchange between Taiwan and mainland China. When Taipei–Beijing relations made progress, long-standing divergences resulting in political/diplomatic rivalry and military standoff still have remained. In such a context, the U.S. commitment to the ROC (Taiwan), although downgraded from official alliance to limited and conditional partnership, has helped maintain strategic balance in the Taiwan Strait and facilitate meaningful dialogue mainly between the KMT government and the CCP government in the past (the 1990s, and from May 2008 to May 2016). Throughout the history of U.S.-PRC engagement, conflict, competition, and cooperation have always co-existed.

Viewing healthy cross-Strait relations as a source of stability for U.S.–PRC relations, the Biden administration, adhering to its own "one China policy" or the policy's most essential components, will try to ease ongoing tension between Taiwan and mainland China by discouraging incendiary or rabble-rousing behavior from both parties and necessitating peace and stability in the Taiwan Strait. As noted before, the Biden administration appears to make no change in its commitment to Taiwan regarding the expansion of international space and the continuation of providing defensive articles and services; in the meantime, it makes no change, either, in diplomatic recognition of the PRC whose cooperation can benefit the U.S. in many important cases and remains vocal about and opposed to behavior of the Chinese communist regime which, as the U.S. contends, abuses human rights or infringe on U.S. and its allies' general interest.

It is more predictable that, in comparison with the era of Trump, the U.S. under the leadership of Biden will keep a closer but relatively constrained relationship with Taiwan, and a mixed but more moderate strategic interaction with mainland China. It is more predictable as well that there will be noticeably fewer two- or three-way provocations among Taiwan, mainland China, and the U.S., unlike what it was in the second half of Trump's presidency.

Once the Biden administration has sent a "no provocation" signal to the two sides of the Taiwan Strait, Taiwan under the leadership of Tsai probably would reduce to an obvious extent the frequency of criticizing or antagonizing mainland China because that would further complicate U.S. involvement in the Taiwan Strait and go against the national interest of the U.S. Why would the DPP in Taiwan care so much about the Biden administration? One of the possible answers is: Tsai has been trying to get rid of the "troublemaker" image in Washington and has been playing a more self-restrained role in the Taiwan Strait because of the DPP's deep concern about Biden's approach "more conciliatory toward China compared with the Trump administration's—and less supportive of Taiwan."[29] Yet, whether such a signal from the U.S. will work on mainland China is still in the air. With enough capacity to act and resist, mainland China may want to bargain with the U.S. if the former is willing to lessen the pressure on Taiwan, such as the frequent intrusions into Taiwan's Air Defense Identification Zone (ADIZ) since 2020.

In light of unresolved cross-Strait relations and the U.S. policy responses, two scenarios more possible to take place in the Taiwan Strait are highlighted here.

The first scenario—one set of stable relations, plus two uncertainties—depicts (1) a growing U.S. moral support for Taiwan's international status and continued provision of defensive articles and services for Taiwan's self-defense, (2) uncertain, or lukewarm, U.S.–mainland China relations with fewer clashes, and (3) uncertain interaction between Taiwan and mainland China. As analyzed earlier, the U.S. will keep its limited commitment to Taiwan shaped after 1979, and the degree of confrontation between the U.S. and mainland China should be lower than what it was during the Trump administration. In the interim, deep distrust and discontent between the DPP and CCP governments still exist, and the influence of the U.S. government on positive changes in cross-Strait relations remains minimal. For Taiwan, an acceptable policy is one that can mitigate the pressure imposed by mainland China and meet the interest of the U.S. that encourages cross-Strait dialogue. For mainland China, its

---

[29] Gerry Shih, "Taiwan Frets Over How a Biden Administration Would Deal with China," *Washington Post*, October 30, 2020, https://www.washingtonpost.com/world/asia_pacific/biden-china-election-taiwan-obama/2020/10/30/44e55488-0868-11eb-8719-0df159d14794_story.html.

relations with Taiwan may not be an urgent issue because when and how to reduce tension in the Taiwan Strait can become a bargaining chip in a game with the U.S.

The second scenario—three sets of stable bilateral relations—describes (1) a continuity of U.S.–Taiwan substantive ties as mentioned above, (2) a slow restoration of U.S.–mainland China relations to a more controllable level, as well as (3) a very limited improvement in bilateral relations between Taiwan and mainland China. In this scenario, not only do U.S.–Taiwan ties remain stable, but U.S.–mainland China relations also return to greater stability in which skirmishes and collaboration still co-exist—that is, such stability does not involve peace only, but both governments have a better way to control differences. In addition, the two sides of the Taiwan Strait would muddle through to regain certain political foundation for the resumption of talks, either with or without the "encouragement" of the U.S.

However, one should not rule out the possibility that the window of opportunity for the two scenarios to occur and achieve some beneficial outcomes would last no more than two years since Biden's inauguration in January 2021. Both of the above-mentioned scenarios will be influenced by the following internal factors of the U.S., Taiwan, and mainland China.

It makes sense to warn that such a small window of opportunity is possible. For the U.S., within the first one hundred days or the first year, the Biden administration may want to demonstrate its awareness of the growing "China challenge," insistence on democratic values, and effort to rebuild global leadership with alliances, but it may also want to show to the American public that it is able to manage and lower rising tension with the PRC in the interest of the American people. It is unsure how the development of the U.S. government's and society's general view about the PRC will impact the U.S.'s mid-term election in late 2022, but one cannot ignore the possibility that the Biden administration will slow down its relatively less hostile approach to the PRC, compared with the Trump administration's, because of an upcoming difficult mid-term election.

For Taiwan, the ruling party, DPP, may be facing an uphill battle in the local city mayors' and county magistrates' elections in late 2022. The DPP will aim to mobilize its supporters and win tough elections by drawing attention to the deep-rooted political divisions between Taiwan and mainland China. The U.S. would have more or less influence on the DPP government, depending on the difficulty in internal politics Tsai encounters and on the DPP's purposeful or forced (by party factions) decision aimed at a more assertive attitude toward mainland China.

For mainland China, the CCP just commemorated its one hundredth anniversary in July 2021. A strong counter to the "century of humiliation" and an important mark for the beginning of a revolutionary and anti-hegemony era, this anniversary has been celebrated with a number of propaganda and education programs involving patriotism and national pride. Hence, it is likely that mainland China would react strongly to any actions that promote Taiwan independence, not to mention the CCP government's time-honored pledge of reuniting with Taiwan either peacefully or by force.

## Concluding Remarks

Both international/strategic factors and domestic politics provide insight into the ongoing dynamic trilateral relations among the U.S., Taiwan, and mainland China. Putting aside the conflict in the interest of these actors, it is clear that the involvement of the U.S. in the Taiwan Strait has kept temporary peace by helping relieve the impact resulting from mainland China's aggressive action, discouraging the obvious Taiwan independence movement, and giving Taiwan greater confidence in engaging mainland China through consultations and negotiations if necessary.

In the first year of Biden's presidency, compared with the opportunity for meaningful progress in cross-Strait relations, there is a greater chance for the continuation of U.S.–Taiwan substantive ties and the slight improvement in U.S.–mainland China relations. That is, a proactive policy implementation on the U.S. side, if receiving reciprocal responses from Beijing, could lead to a condition more preferable by the U.S. and other parties concerned. Between Taiwan's need for stronger and comprehensive U.S. support and mainland China's belligerent stance over the U.S. involvement in the Chinese reunification issue, the U.S. still has policy options to shape complicated cross-Strait relations in the interest of the American people.

The Biden administration appears to be offering support for Taiwan, including, for example, the self-defense capability and international space that have nothing to do with statehood, and seeking a two-tier approach to its relations with mainland China in its first six months. It is critically important that the Biden administration be viewed by Taiwan, mainland China, and other important regional actors as a benign hegemon (善霸)—with the awareness of a variety of challenges imposed by a growing and more assertive mainland China and committed to maintaining peace and stability in the Taiwan Strait—rather than a predatory one (惡霸) that is more singularly concerned about its interests only.

If the impasse between Taiwan and mainland China remains volatile and cannot be changed in the foreseeable future, the cross-Strait policy of the U.S. that has a higher degree of predictability will better serve as a stabilizer for the western Pacific. The U.S. should encourage both sides of the Taiwan Strait to carry out a "surprise-free" policy and work with the U.S. for a win-win-win situation that will also benefit and promote trade and investment within the Indo-Pacific region. Equally important, with a clear objective as to why the Taiwan Strait should maintain peace, stability, and prosperity, the U.S.'s strategic ambiguity toward its "one China policy" and regional security may be welcomed by Taiwan and may not be vehemently opposed by mainland China.

# CHAPTER 10

# Indo-Pacific Diplomacy, the Quad and Beyond: Democratic Coalition in the Era of U.S.–China Global Competition

*Junya Ishii*

**Abstract** The rise of China and its competition with the United States are the most important geopolitical factors in the twenty-first century. No country in the world, especially in the Indo-Pacific region, can be distant from the two superpowers' competitive coexistence or avoid considering how to deal with this issue. FOIP, the Indo-Pacific, and the Quad are outcomes of this global trend. Although the United States, Japan, India, Australia, ASEAN, and Europe have their agendas and interests, there are many areas of overlap regarding China. The key to its successful coordination is the U.S.'s continued commitment in the region, which needs to be supported by each country's efforts for mutually complementary

---

The opinions expressed in this paper are the author's own and do not reflect the view of any other person or organization including one to which the author belongs.

---

J. Ishii (✉)
Sumitomo Corporation Global Research Co. Ltd., Chiyoda City, Japan

© The Author(s), under exclusive license to Springer Nature Singapore Pte Ltd. 2021
E. Carr Jr. (ed.), *From Trump to Biden and Beyond*,
https://doi.org/10.1007/978-981-16-4297-5_10

cooperation. Allies and partners of the United States are likely to form multi-layered coalitions, in which FOIP's vision and the Quad framework have a great potential to play a central role. Key issues will be military and security, technology, supply chain, governance, and economic development assistance. Japan is expected to play the leading role for this cooperation, considering its historically solid alliance with the U.S., broad and stable partnership with India, Australia and Southeast Asian countries as well as long-term experience of managing relations with China.

**Keywords** Japan · Indo-Pacific diplomacy · Quad · Democratic coalition · US–China · ASEAN · FOIP · Allies

In recent years, the term "Indo-Pacific" has become an important concept in the world of diplomacy. In Japan, the Abe administration set forth the vision of a "Free and Open Indo-Pacific" (FOIP) as a pillar of Japan's foreign policy in 2016,[1] which the current Suga administration succeeded.[2] In the United States, President Trump announced FOIP's vision at the Asia-Pacific Economic Cooperation (APEC) summit in Vietnam in 2017,[3] and the 2017 National Security Strategy (NSS) mentioned it in the context of a geopolitical competition in the Indo-Pacific region.[4] In 2018, the National Security Council (NSC) created the U.S. Strategic Framework for the Indo-Pacific ("the Framework"),

---

[1] Ministry of Foreign Affairs of Japan, "Chapter 1: International Situation and Japan's Diplomacy in 2018," *Diplomatic Bluebook 2019* (Tokyo: Ministry of Foreign Affairs of Japan, October 17, 2019), https://www.mofa.go.jp/policy/other/bluebook/2019/html/chapter1/c0102.html.

[2] Ministry of Foreign Affairs of Japan, *Address by Prime Minister Suga at the Seventy-Fifth Session of the United Nations General Assembly* (Tokyo: Ministry of Foreign Affairs of Japan, September 26, 2020), https://www.mofa.go.jp/fp/unp_a/page4e_001095.html.

[3] White House, *Remarks by President Trump at APEC CEO Summit\Danang, Vietnam,* (Washington, DC: White House, November 10, 2017), https://trumpwhitehouse.arc hives.gov/briefings-statements/remarks-president-trump-apec-ceo-summit-da-nang-vie tnam.

[4] White House, *National Security of Strategy of the United States of America* (Washington, DC: White House, December 2017), 45–46, https://trumpwhitehouse.archives. gov/wp-content/uploads/2017/12/NSS-Final-12-18-2017-0905.pdf.

which was declassified in January 2021,[5] and the U.S. Pacific Command was renamed the "Indo-Pacific Command." The Biden administration has since succeeded FOIP, establishing a new "Indo-Pacific Coordinator" in the NSC to which former Assistant Secretary of State Kurt Campbell was appointed.

Other countries than Japan and the United States in the Indo-Pacific region are also increasingly emphasizing the Indo-Pacific. In India, Prime Minister Modi shared his vision of an Indo-Pacific focus at the Shangri-La meeting in 2018,[6] and the Ministry of External Affairs established an Indo-Pacific Division in 2019.[7] Australia stated in its 2017 Foreign Policy White Paper, the first release in 14 years, that the Indo-Pacific was of primary importance to the country, determining to realize "a secure, open and prosperous Indo-Pacific."[8] In the Quad, a cooperation framework among Japan, the United States, Australia, and India that resumed in 2017, all four member states confirmed the vision of the Indo-Pacific at its first summit meeting in March 2021.[9] The Association of Southeast Asian Nations (ASEAN) adopted the "ASEAN Outlook on the Indo-Pacific" at its 2019 summit.[10]

[5] White House, *A Free and Open Indo-Pacific*, by Robert C. O'Brien (Washington, DC: White House, January 5, 2021), https://trumpwhitehouse.archives.gov/wp-content/uploads/2021/01/OBrien-Expanded-Statement.pdf; and White House, *U.S. Strategic Framework for the Indo-Pacific* (Washington, DC: White House, August 2018), https://trumpwhitehouse.archives.gov/wp-content/uploads/2021/01/IPS-Final-Declass.pdf.

[6] Ministry of External Affairs, India, *Prime Minister's Keynote Address at Shangri La Dialogue* (New Delhi: Ministry of External Affairs, India, June 1, 2018), https://www.mea.gov.in/Speeches-Statements.htm?dtl/29943/Prime+Ministers+Keynote+Address+at+Shangri+La+Dialogue+June+01+2018.

[7] Indrani Bagchi, "In a Show of Intent, External Affairs Ministry Sets Up Indo-Pacific Wing," *The Times of India*, April 15, 2019, https://timesofindia.indiatimes.com/india/in-a-show-of-intent-external-affairs-ministry-sets-up-indo-pacific-wing/articleshow/68880720.cms.

[8] Department of Foreign Affairs and Trade, Australia, *2017 Foreign Policy White Paper* (Canberra: Department of Foreign Affairs and Trade, Australia, November 2017), 3, https://www.dfat.gov.au/publications/minisite/2017-foreign-policy-white-paper/fpwhitepaper/pdf/2017-foreign-policy-white-paper.pdf.

[9] White House, *Quad Leaders' Joint Statement: "The Spirit of the Quad"* (Washington, DC: White House, March 12, 2021), https://www.whitehouse.gov/briefing-room/statements-releases/2021/03/12/quad-leaders-joint-statement-the-spirit-of-the-quad.

[10] Association of Southeast Asian Nations, *ASEAN Outlook on the Indo-Pacific* (Jakarta: Association of Southeast Asian Nations, June 23, 2019), https://asean.org/asean-outlook-indo-pacific.

The concept of the Indo-Pacific is expanding beyond the Indo-Pacific region. In Europe, France released "France and Security in the Indo-Pacific" in 2018[11]; Germany released its policy guidelines on the Indo-Pacific region in 2020[12]; and the U.K. emphasized the growing importance of the Indo-Pacific region in the "Integrated Review 2021."[13] European Union (EU) High Representative Josep Borrell emphasized that the EU needed its strategy for the Indo-Pacific in March 2021.[14]

On the other hand, while the geographical concept of the "Indo-Pacific" is generally shared among the above-mentioned countries, it is not clear if its goals or vision are commonly defined. While the United States and Japan use the phrase "FOIP," India states a "free, open and inclusive Indo-Pacific,"[15] Australia mentions a "secure, open and prosperous Indo-Pacific," and ASEAN, France, Germany, and the U.K. simply refer to the "Indo-Pacific." When then President-elect Biden used the phrase "secure and prosperous Indo-Pacific," some scholars viewed this as a signal of the change of FOIP policy, although the Biden administration clarified its adherence to FOIP after its inauguration.[16]

---

[11] Ministry of the Armed Forces, France, *France and Security in the Indo-Pacific* (Paris: Ministry of the Armed Forces, France, June 2018 updated in May 2019), https://www.defense.gouv.fr/layout/set/print/content/download/532754/9176250/version/3/file/France+and+Security+in+the+Indo-Pacific+-+2019.pdf.

[12] Federal Foreign Office, Germany, *"Germany—Europe—Asia: Shaping the Twenty-First Century Together": The German Government Adopts Policy Guidelines on the Indo-Pacific Region* (Berlin: Federal Foreign Office, Germany, January 9, 2020), https://www.auswaertiges-amt.de/en/aussenpolitik/regionaleschwerpunkte/asien/german-government-policy-guidelines-indo-pacific/2380510.

[13] U.K. Government, *Global Britain in a Competitive Age: The Integrated Review of Security, Defence, Development and Foreign Policy* (London: U.K. Government, March 16, 2021), 66–67, https://www.gov.uk/government/publications/global-britain-in-a-competitive-age-the-integrated-review-of-security-defence-development-and-foreign-policy.

[14] Josep Borrell, "The EU Needs a Strategic Approach for the Indo-Pacific," *European Union External Action Service*, March 12, 2021, https://eeas.europa.eu/headquarters/headquarters-homepage/94898/eu-needs-strategic-approach-indo-pacific_en.

[15] Ministry of External Affairs, India, *3rd India-Australia-Japan–USA Quad Ministerial Meeting* (New Delhi: Ministry of External Affairs, India, February 18, 2021), https://www.mea.gov.in/press-releases.htm?dtl/33540/3rd_IndiaAustraliaJapanUSA_Quad_Ministerial_Meeting.

[16] Sebastian Strangio, "Is Biden Preparing to Tweak the Indo-Pacific Strategy?" *The Diplomat*, November 20, 2020, https://thediplomat.com/2020/11/is-biden-preparing-to-tweak-the-indo-pacific-strategy.

In light of this situation, this paper will analyze the background, significance, and future prospects of FOIP and the Indo-Pacific. For this analysis, the paper will attach importance to the Quad as a framework embodying FOIP. The paper will also explore the possibility of the development of multi-layered cooperative frameworks among like-minded democratic nations as an extension of FOIP and the Quad and present specific policy recommendations.

## FOIP of Japan: Values, Security, and Economic Development

It was Japan's Prime Minister Abe who first proposed FOIP. While Abe formally announced FOIP in his speech at TICAD VI in 2016,[17] he stated that its roots dated back to his "Confluence of the Two Seas" speech on his visit to India in 2007[18] and the value-based diplomacy called the "Arc of Freedom and Prosperity" proposed by Foreign Minister Aso under the first Abe administration.[19] Abe also published a paper titled "Asia's Democratic Security Diamond" at the beginning of the second administration in 2012, in which he emphasized the importance of quadrilateral security cooperation between Japan, the United States, Australia, and India in the Indian and Pacific oceans, stating that FOIP

---

[17] Ministry of Foreign Affairs of Japan, *Address by Prime Minister Shinzo Abe at the Opening Session of the Sixth Tokyo International Conference on African Development (TICAD VI)* (Tokyo: Ministry of Foreign Affairs of Japan, August 27, 2016), https://www.mofa.go.jp/afr/af2/page4e_000496.html.

[18] Ministry of Foreign Affairs of Japan, *Confluence of the Two Seas: Speech by H.E. Mr. Shinzo Abe, Prime Minister of Japan at the Parliament of the Republic of India* (Tokyo: Ministry of Foreign Affairs of Japan, August 22, 2007), https://www.mofa.go.jp/region/asia-paci/pmv0708/speech-2.html.

[19] Shinzo Abe, "*Jiyu de Hirakareta Indo Taiheiyo ni Miru Senryakuteki Shiko* (Strategic Thinking in a Free and Open Indo-Pacific)," *Gaiko*, Vol. 65 (January/February 2021), 95–96, http://www.gaiko-web.jp/test/wp-content/uploads/2021/01/Vol65_p94-99_specialinterview_Shinzo_Abe.pdf.

was a more sophisticated version of this vision.[20] The Suga administration inaugurated in 2020 has inherited FOIP.[21]

The 2017 Diplomatic Blue Paper discusses Abe's 2016 TICAD VI speech, noting that: (1) The key to the stability and prosperity of the international community is the dynamism created by the synergy between two continents, Asia, which is recording remarkable growth, and Africa, which is full of potential, and two free and open seas, the Pacific and the Indian Oceans; (2) democracy, the rule of law and the market economy have already taken root in Southeast Asia and South Asia; (3) Japan intends to promote peace and prosperity in the region by improving connectivity of Asia, the Middle East, and Africa; and (4) to this end, Japan will strengthen strategic cooperation with the United States, India, Australia, and other countries.[22] Japan's Ministry of Foreign Affairs identifies the three pillars of FOIP as: (1) the promotion and solidification of rule of law, freedom of navigation, free trade, and so on; (2) the pursuit of economic prosperity through enhancing connectivity with quality infrastructure development in accordance with international standards; and (3) commitment for peace and stability to assist capacity building on maritime law enforcement, cooperation in such fields as disaster risk reduction and non-proliferation.[23]

Given its roots and contents as described above, FOIP contains three major elements: (1) emphasis on values of democracy, rule of law, and liberal economy; (2) security centered on territorial sovereignty, freedom of navigation, and non-proliferation; and (3) support for economic development through infrastructure development in the Indo-Pacific region. The first and second points both mainly aim to deal with threats from China in light of its authoritarian system and human rights issues; its state-led capitalism and unfair economic practices; and its overwhelming

[20] Shinzo Abe, "Asia's Democratic Security Diamond," *Project Syndicate*, December 27, 2012, https://www.project-syndicate.org/onpoint/a-strategic-alliance-for-japan-and-india-by-shinzo-abe?barrier=accesspaylog.

[21] Ministry of Foreign Affairs of Japan, *Address by Prime Minister Suga at the Seventy-Fifth Session of the United Nations General Assembly*.

[22] Ministry of Foreign Affairs of Japan, "Chapter 1: International Situation and Japan's Diplomacy in 2016," *Diplomatic Bluebook 2017* (Tokyo: Ministry of Foreign Affairs of Japan, September 15, 2017), https://www.mofa.go.jp/policy/other/bluebook/2017/html/chapter1/c0102.html.

[23] Ministry of Foreign Affairs of Japan, "Chapter 1: International Situation and Japan's Diplomacy in 2018," *Diplomatic Bluebook 2019*.

military power threatening the freedom of navigation and territorial sovereignty of other countries in the South and East China Seas. Japan believes that the United States, Japan, Australia, and India share this concern and thus is working with these countries to deal with challenges posed by China. As such, FOIP and the Quad are closely co-related concepts.

On the other hand, the third point is not necessarily related to competition against China. Some argue that FOIP should be regarded as a countermeasure against China's Belt and Road Initiative (BRI), given that China's infrastructure projects are frequently criticized due to their flawed governance. Abe, however, stated in 2017 that Japan could accept the BRI as long as it "adequately" incorporated "the thinking held in common by the international community regarding the openness, transparency, economic efficiency, financial soundness, and other such aspects of the infrastructure" and cooperate with China in infrastructure development.[24] On Abe's visit to China in 2018, the two countries exchanged 52 memorandums of cooperation for businesses in third countries,[25] which implied that Japan would not object to the BRI.

Regarding the first and second points mentioned above, Japan has carefully avoided clarifying implications of targeting China because it does not only pursue to compete, but to stabilize relationship with China. For instance, while Abe stated "FOIP Strategy" in his policy speech in 2018,[26] he described FOIP as a "vision" in his policy speech in 2019.[27] This change of phrase reflects Japan's deliberate consideration for relationship with China, considering in particular that Abe made an

[24] Prime Minister of Japan and His Cabinet, *Press Conference by Prime Minister Shinzo Abe Following His Attendance at the APEC Economic Leaders' Meeting, ASEAN-Related Summit Meetings, and Other Related Meetings* (Tokyo: Prime Minister of Japan and His Cabinet, November 14, 2017), https://japan.kantei.go.jp/98_abe/statement/201711/_00007.html.

[25] Ministry of Foreign Affairs of Japan, *Prime Minister Abe Visits China* (Tokyo: Ministry of Foreign Affairs of Japan, October 26, 2018), https://www.mofa.go.jp/a_o/c_m1/cn/page3e_000958.html.

[26] Prime Minister of Japan and His Cabinet, *Policy Speech by Prime Minister Shinzo Abe to the 196th Session of the Diet* (Tokyo: Prime Minister of Japan and His Cabinet, January 22, 2018), https://japan.kantei.go.jp/98_abe/statement/201801/_00002.html.

[27] Prime Minister of Japan and His Cabinet, *Policy Speech by Prime Minister Shinzo Abe to the 198th Session of the Diet* (Tokyo: Prime Minister of Japan and His Cabinet, January 28, 2019), https://japan.kantei.go.jp/98_abe/statement/201801/_00003.html.

important visit to China in October 2018 for the first time in nearly seven years. Consequently, when it comes to realization of specific policies, the first point of FOIP has not produced meaningful outcomes, while the second point is basically limited to reactive defense measures against Chinese ships entering Japan's territorial sea in the East China Sea. Only the third point has been productively advanced as shown by a variety of infrastructure projects in Asia.

## FOIP of the U.S.: Strategy for Competition Against China

In the United States, after the Trump administration was inaugurated in January 2017, Secretary of State Tillerson mentioned FOIP for the first time in his speech on India in October[28] and President Trump announced his vision of FOIP in his policy speech at APEC in Vietnam in November.[29] In December, the 2017 NSS mentioned the importance of FOIP in the chapter "Indo-Pacific" and emphasized the need to counter China's military and economic threats.[30] The Framework was then created by the NSC in February 2018.[31]

The Framework should be regarded as the most important document for analysis of FOIP because it was prepared for purely internal use for Trump administration's national strategy. This document clarifies strategic guidance with respect to FOIP. In the section entitled "National Security Challenges," it states that:

- How to maintain U.S. strategic primacy in the Indo-Pacific region and promote liberal economic order while preventing China from establishing new, illiberal spheres influence, and cultivating areas of cooperation to promote regional peace and prosperity?

---

[28] Rex Tillerson, "Defining Our Relationship with India for the Next Century," *Center for Strategic and International Studies*, October 18, 2017, https://www.csis.org/analysis/defining-our-relationship-india-next-century-address-us-secretary-state-rex-tillerson.

[29] White House, *Remarks by President Trump at APEC CEO Summit|Danang, Vietnam.*

[30] White House, *National Security of Strategy of the United States of America*, 45–46.

[31] White House, *A Free and Open Indo-Pacific*, by Robert C. O'Brien; and *U.S. Strategic Framework for the Indo-Pacific.*

In the section entitled "Assumptions," it states that:

- Strategic competition between the United States and China will persist, owing to the divergent nature and goals of our political and economic systems. China will circumvent international rules and norms to gain an advantage;
- China aims to dissolve U.S. alliances and partnerships in the region. China will exploit vacuums and opportunities created by these diminished bonds;
- Chinese economic, diplomatic, and military influence will continue to increase in the near-term and challenge the U.S. ability to achieve its national interests in the Indo-Pacific region;
- China seeks to dominate cutting-edge technologies, including artificial intelligence and bio-genetics, and harness them in the service of authoritarianism. Chinese dominance in these technologies would pose profound challenges to free societies; and
- China's proliferation of its digital surveillance, information controls, and influence operations will damage U.S. efforts to promote our values and national interests in the Indo-Pacific region and, increasingly, in the Western hemisphere and at home.

In the section entitled "Actions," it states:

- [The U.S. should] invigorate U.S. technical assistance to friendly governments to promote rule of law and civil institutions while communicating the strings attached to China's Belt and Road Initiative; and
- [The U.S. should] develop a robust public diplomacy capability, which can compete with China's information campaigns; puncture the narrative that Chinese regional domination is inevitable.

In the section entitled "China," it referred to a document called the "U.S. Strategic Framework for Countering China's Economic Aggression." At the same time, it states that "[the U.S. should] cooperate with China when beneficial to U.S. interests." However, it only states this simple sentence, no specific policy being explained.[32]

---

[32] White House, *U.S. Strategic Framework for the Indo-Pacific*, 1–4, 6–8.

In addition, the "Indo-Pacific Strategy Report" released by the Department of Defense in June 2019 elaborates challenges posed by China first in its "strategic landscape" chapter.[33] Another report, "A Free and Open Indo-Pacific: Advancing a Shared Vision," released by the Department of State in November 2019 does not directly refer to China, but states that the U.S. "is implementing a whole-of-government strategy to champion the values that have served the Indo-Pacific so well: (1) respect for sovereignty and independence of all nations; (2) peaceful resolution of disputes; (3) free, fair, and reciprocal trade based on open investment, transparent agreements, and connectivity; and (4) adherence to international law, including freedom of navigation and overflight."[34] This explanation obviously implies that FOIP is primarily targeting China. Further, Congress demonstrated its support for FOIP through the passage of the Better Utilization of Investments Leading to Development (BUILD) Act and the Asia Reassurance Initiative (ARIA) Act in 2018, which both have an aspect of countering against China's expanding influence in the region.[35]

In light of these documents and policies, the essence of U.S. FOIP strategy mirrors U.S. diplomacy toward China. U.S. foreign policy toward China has evolved over the years; for a long time since the two countries' diplomatic normalization, it had been an "engagement" approach as the United States looked to reap economic benefits of China's vast economy. The United States had expected that China's authoritarian regime would inch toward democracy throughout economic development. While there was growing alarm about China's military expansion, the United States had attempted to "hedge" such risks, believing that China's democratization would diminish the concerns over time. Based on such erroneous

---

[33] Department of Defense, *Indo-Pacific Strategy Report: Preparedness, Partnerships, and Promoting a Networked Region* (Washington, DC: United States Department of Defense, June 1, 2019), 7–12, https://media.defense.gov/2019/Jul/01/2002152311/-1/-1/1/department-of-defense-indo-pacific-strategy-report-2019.pdf.

[34] Department of State, *A Free and Open Indo-Pacific: Advancing a Shared Vision* (Washington, DC: United States Department of State, November 4, 2019), 6, https://www.state.gov/a-free-and-open-indo-pacific-advancing-a-shared-vision.

[35] Wang Yiwei, "Can US' Asia Reassurance Initiative Act contain China?," *Global Times*, January 21, 2019, https://www.globaltimes.cn/content/1136474.shtml; and Andrew Chatzky and James McBride, "China's Massive Belt and Road Initiative," *Council on Foreign Relations*, January 28, 2020, https://www.cfr.org/backgrounder/chinas-massive-belt-and-road-initiative.

assumptions in hindsight, the mainstream policy of the United States toward China had been to engage China in the global economy through conciliatory measures such as backing the entry of China into the World Trade Organization.

However, since the second term of the Obama administration in 2013, the U.S. approach had shifted from engagement to "competition." This was because, first, unfair practices of Chinese companies and China's nationalistic trade and industrial policies came to be seen increasingly intolerable by U.S. business communities. Second, the Xi Jinping regime inaugurated in 2012 rolled back the democratization and transparency of Chinese Communist Party's political system that had been promoted under the previous regimes, even strengthening political and social control. Third, the foreign policy of China had become increasingly oriented toward great powers and aggressive expansionism. In 2014, President Xi advocated the "Chinese Dream," a vision of the great revival of the Chinese nation and the realization of a powerful country, launching the BRI, a global infrastructure development strategy. The Xi regime also announced "Made in China 2025" in 2015, and declared its intention to become a "strong" country espousing "socialism with Chinese characteristics" at the National Congress of the Chinese Communist Party in 2017. Both clearly demonstrated China's ambition of becoming a great power. The U.S. establishment was disappointed by these China's behaviors, and came to view China as a "competitor," resulting in the U.S.'s strong stance against China.[36]

In addition to the fundamental change of the U.S. approach toward China, the Trump administration took aim at trade imbalances, particularly massive imports from China to appeal to voters who had been economically hurt by trade liberalization. This policy further toughened American attitude toward China in its public opinion and lawmakers. The Trump administration's strategy was clarified by the 2017 NSS, which

[36] For understanding the shift in U.S. policy toward China, see for example: Hal Brands and Zack Cooper, "After the Responsible Stakeholder, What? Debating America's China Strategy," *The National Security Review*, Vol 2, Iss 2 (February 2019), http://dx.doi.org/10.26153/tsw/1943; Melanie Hart and Kelly Magsamen, "Limit, Leverage, and Compete: A New Strategy on China," *Center for American Progress*, April 3, 2019, https://www.americanprogress.org/issues/security/reports/2019/04/03/468136/limit-leverage-compete-new-strategy-china/; and Hal Brands and Jake Sullivan, "China Has Two Paths to Global Domination," *Foreign Policy*, May 22, 2020, https://foreignpolicy.com/2020/05/22/china-superpower-two-paths-global-domination-cold-war.

officially positioned China as a "strategic competitor" and "revisionist power" that challenges the influence and interests of the United States The U.S.'s FOIP has been formulated in the course of such a policy shift with respect to China over the past years.

## Indo-Pacific Strategy of India and Australia: Emphasis on Inclusiveness

The "Indian Maritime Security Strategy" released by the Indian Navy in 2015 had pointed out a shift in the world from the Euro-Atlantic to the Indo-Pacific.[37] The concept of the Indo-Pacific for India, however, became a full-fledged vision through Prime Minister Modi's speech at the Shangri-La Dialogue in 2018.[38]

India has traditionally been cautious about using the phrase of Indo-Pacific because it did not want recognition as a member of a coalition of Western nations against China. This attitude was indicated by India's initial response to the Quad, of which original concept was presented by Prime Minister Abe's "Confluence of the Two Seas" speech in August 2007 and supported by Prime Minister Singh along with the Vice President Cheney and Australian Prime Minister Howard.[39] Australia then

---

[37] Indian Navy, *Ensuring Secure Seas: Indian Maritime Security Strategy* (New Delhi: Indian Navy, October 2015), Foreword iii, https://indiannavy.nic.in/sites/default/files/Indian_Maritime_Security_Strategy_Document_25Jan16.pdf.

[38] Ministry of External Affairs, India, *Prime Minister's Keynote Address at Shangri La Dialogue.*; and Darshana M. Baruah, "India in the Indo-Pacific: New Delhi's Theater of Opportunity," *Carnegie Endowment for International Peace*, June 30, 2020, https://carnegieendowment.org/2020/06/30/india-in-indo-pacific-new-delhi-s-theater-of-opportunity-pub-82205.

[39] Before Abe's speech in 2007, the four countries' maritime cooperation had been realized in the joint response of the four countries to the 2004 Indian Ocean tsunami disaster. President Biden noted this as an origin of the Quad at the Quad summit meeting on March 12, 2021. See: White House, *Remarks by President Biden, Prime Minister Modi of India, Prime Minister Morrison of Australia, and Prime Minister Suga of Japan in the Virtual Quad Leaders Summit* (Washington, DC: White House, March 12 2021), https://www.whitehouse.gov/briefing-room/speeches-remarks/2021/03/12/remarks-by-president-biden-prime-minister-modi-of-india-prime-minister-morrison-of-australia-and-prime-minister-suga-of-japan-in-virtual-meeting-of-the-quad. Also, the first meeting of the initial Quad was held in May 2007 in the informal format on the occasion of the ASEAN Regional Forum (ARF) meeting in Manila. For understanding the initial Quad, see: Patrick Gerard Buchan and Benjamin Rimland, "Defining the Diamond: The Past, Present, and Future of the Quadrilateral Security Dialogue," *Center for Strategic*

participated in Malabar, a joint maritime military exercise by Japan, the United States, and India in September 2007. However, in response to criticism from China, Singh quickly claimed that the Quad carried "no security implication."[40] Abe said in retrospect that Singh's support for the Quad was actually lukewarm.[41] Following Abe's resignation and Australia's leadership transition from Howard to Rudd, the Quad lost its momentum. Australia decided not to participate in Malabar in 2008, resulting in the termination of the Quad cooperation.

However, since 2017, the Quad was revived at working level, leading to the first foreign ministers' meeting in 2019. The second foreign ministers' meeting was held in October 2020 where they agreed to gather on a regular basis. Australia then participated in Malabar in November 2020 for the first time since 2007. Shortly after the Biden administration was inaugurated in January 2021, the foreign ministers' teleconference was held in February, followed by the first summit meeting held online in March. According to the joint statement released after the meeting, the leaders declared that they were "united in a shared vision for the free and open Indo-Pacific," and determined to "strive for a region that is free, open, inclusive, healthy, anchored by democratic values, and unconstrained by coercion."[42] The leaders also agreed to hold an in-person summit by the end of 2021. As India and Australia were invited to the G7 summit meeting scheduled for June 2021, there is a good chance that the in-person summit would be held on this occasion.

What are the factors that have encouraged India to actively participate in the Indo-Pacific and the Quad in contrast to its cautious stance to the Quad in 2007? First, the threats of China have been becoming significantly imminent in recent years. India has been highly wary of China's infrastructure development in the Indian Ocean and Pakistan

---

and *International Studies*, March 16, 2020, https://www.csis.org/analysis/defining-diamond-past-present-and-future-quadrilateral-security-dialogue; and Tanvi Madan, "The Rise, Fall, and Rebirth of the Quad," *War on the Rocks*, November 16, 2017, https://warontherocks.com/2017/11/rise-fall-rebirth-quad.

[40] Brahma Chellaney, "This Quartet Has a Future," *The Times of India*, July 18, 2007, https://timesofindia.indiatimes.com/edit-page/LEADER-ARTICLE-This-Quartet-Has-A-Future/articleshow/2212192.cms.

[41] Shinzo Abe, "*Jiyu de Hirakareta Indo Taiheiyo ni Miru Senryakuteki Shiko* (Strategic Thinking in a Free and Open Indo-Pacific)," 95.

[42] White House, *Quad Leaders' Joint Statement: "The Spirit of the Quad"*.

through its "String of Pearls" strategy and BRI.[43] Further, after years of border conflicts, India and China engaged in two months of stand-offs and skirmishes in the border region of the Dokram Plateau in 2017. In 2020, the two countries had military clashes in the border region of Ladakh, resulting in fatalities for the first time since 1975. Since then, India has drastically sharpened its vigilance against China by military preparedness and economic measures centered on restriction on imports and investments from China.

Second, the political philosophy of Modi, who was sworn in as prime minister in 2014, has been influential to India's foreign policy. Modi has placed much emphasis on economic growth led by economic liberalization, and actively promoted cooperation with the United States, Japan, and other Western countries. As a passionate nationalist, he has also emphasized a resolute stance in confronting China's security threats. Such Modi's approaches are different from India's traditional non-aligned diplomacy and socialist policies.

India, on the other hand, has not adopted FOIP in the same way as the United States and Japan. Although Modi has demonstrated his strong attachment to the West, Delhi has still maintained its traditional foreign policy of "strategic autonomy." That is why he always states that the Indo-Pacific region should be a "free, open, inclusive region" and that "India does not see the Indo-Pacific region as a strategy or as a club of limited members, nor as a grouping that seeks to dominate."[44] The word "inclusive" indicates that the Quad should not exclude other countries including China. Presumably, due to India's insistence on "inclusiveness," the joint statement released after the Quad summit meeting in March

---

[43] India has never joined the support for BRI in the joint communique of the Shanghai Cooperation Organization summit meetings unlike other member states, nor sent its delegation to either of the two Belt and Road Forums in 2017 and 2019. Responding to a question about India's absence in the 2017 Forum, Indian government spokesman emphasized the importance of good governance in connectivity projects and announced India's concern about BRI's projects in Pakistan. See Ministry of External Affairs, India, *Official Spokesperson's Response to a Query on Participation of India in OBOR/BRI Forum* (New Delhi: Ministry of External Affairs, India, May 13, 2017), https://mea.gov.in/media-briefings.htm?dtl%2F28463%2FOfficial_Spokespersons_response_to_a_query_on_participation_of_India_in_OBORBRI_Forum.

[44] Ministry of External Affairs, India, *Prime Minister's Keynote Address at Shangri La Dialogue*; and White House, *Remarks by President Biden, Prime Minister Modi of India, Prime Minister Morrison of Australia, and Prime Minister Suga of Japan in the Virtual Quad Leaders Summit*.

2021 included phrases "a region that is free, open, inclusive, healthy, anchored by democratic values, and unconstrained by coercion" and "a free, open, inclusive, and resilient Indo-Pacific."[45]

India's considerations for the relationship with China originates from concerns about the risk of military conflict with China and strong economic ties between the two countries. China is India's biggest trade partner and exporter to India in 2020. At the same time, India's trade deficit with China is substantial, and its over-reliance on Chinese products has been a serious problem. In recent years, India has pursued restriction on imports from China to foster domestic industry.

Australia made it clear that the Indo-Pacific was the most important diplomatic concept in its 2017 Foreign Policy White Paper. Like India, Australia had been cautious about cooperation in the Quad because of Australia's dependance on Chinese economy. With the development of the Chinese economy since 2000, Australia's exports of natural resources and agricultural products to China have significantly increased. Accelerated further by China-Australia Free Trade Agreement's entry into force in 2015, China has grown into Australia's largest trading partner and importer, playing an indispensable role for Australia's economic development.

Australia, on the other hand, has become increasingly wary of growing Chinese investment in important sectors such as infrastructure and land and interference in Australian politics, and therefore implemented countermeasures such as tightening restrictions on foreign investment in 2016 and banning political donations from abroad in 2018. In 2020, China reacted violently to the Morrison administration's insistence on investigations into the origin of COVID-19, imposing a series of restrictions on imports of agricultural products and coal from Australia. This feud has significantly deteriorated the two countries' relationship and Australians' attitude toward China. According to the poll in 2020, only 23% of Australians trust China to act responsibly in the world.[46]

The rise of the Chinese threat and the deterioration of the diplomatic relations has encouraged Australia to place greater importance on the Indo-Pacific and to actively engage in the Quad. Having said that,

---

[45] White House, *Quad Leaders' Joint Statement: "The Spirit of the Quad"*.

[46] Lowy Institute, *Poll 2020: Relations with the US and China, Trust in Global Powers* (2020), https://poll.lowyinstitute.org/charts/trust-in-global-powers.

given the importance of China for its economy, Canberra still needs to stabilize this relationship. That is why, although FOIP could work as a strategic concept to counter China, Australia does not desire to flatly exclude China. Its ultimate goal is to create a rules-based Indo-Pacific region which does not critically antagonize China.

ASEAN adopted the "ASEAN Outlook on the Indo-Pacific" at its 2019 summit meeting.[47] ASEAN's vision of Indo-Pacific cooperation is to pursue dialogue and cooperation with the aim to promoting development and prosperity of all countries in the region and ASEAN emphasizes that it should play a central role. It does not indicate that China should be contained, but rather places an emphasis on inclusiveness to avoid exclusion of specific countries, namely China. Here, the objective of the "Indo-Pacific" is to alleviate tensions with China in contrast with FOIP.

## Prospects of FOIP and the Quad: Mutually Complementary Function

As mentioned above, Japan, the United States, India, Australia, and ASEAN have had different approaches to the Indo-Pacific. Although they share the term, "free and open Indo-Pacific" or "Indo-Pacific," the goals and policies of each country are not exactly the same. The biggest factor that divides their approaches is each country's relationship with China. As noted earlier, the Trump administration viewed China as a "strategic competitor" and a "revisionist state" that challenges U.S. power, influence, and interests, and developed FOIP as a means of countervailing such threats. The Biden administration has also clearly stated that China is "the greatest geopolitical challenge of the twenty-first century" and that, unlike the threats posed by Russia and Iran, China is "the only country" that can "seriously challenge the stable and open international system" and "all rules, values, and relationships that make the world work the way

---

[47] Association of Southeast Asian Nations, *ASEAN Outlook on the Indo-Pacific*.

we want it to."[48] Therefore, there will be highly likely no fundamental change in U.S. policy toward China.

In contrast, while Japan, Australia, India, and ASEAN, recognize the need to cope with China's security threats and unfairness in economic policies and practices, they have attempted to avoid provoking China to stabilize the relationship, given China's dominant military power and economic influence. While it would be preferable if the United States could deter China's aggressive behaviors by taking a hawkish stance, the countries would be concerned about the retaliation if they cooperate with such U.S. policy. India's traditional diplomacy of strategic autonomy and Japan's constitutional constraints on military use would be an obstacle for collective security among the four countries. China has criticized the Indo-Pacific strategy and the Quad because they aim at building a "new North Atlantic Treaty Organization (NATO)" in the region,[49] but there is no such possibility, considering the above-mentioned reality.[50]

If FOIP or the Quad will not develop into a military alliance, what will be their prospects? Will they end up merely a symbolic institution for message sharing? It is true that FOIP and the Quad are not expected to rapidly enhance military cooperation among the four countries. However, they could be effective platforms for policy coordination to deal with China's threats for the following reasons: First, while the United States regards China as a "competitor," it does not aim for regime change in China, nor does it adopt "containment" policy as it once did against the Soviet Union.[51] Given China's economic and military power, the stability

[48] White House, *Interim National Security Strategic Guidance* (Washington, DC: White House, March 3, 2021), https://www.whitehouse.gov/briefing-room/statements-releases/2021/03/03/interim-national-security-strategic-guidance; and Department of State, *A Foreign Policy for the American People* (Washington, DC: United States Department of State, March 3, 2021), https://www.state.gov/a-foreign-policy-for-the-american-people.

[49] Ministry of Foreign Affairs of the People's Republic of China, *Wang Yi: U.S. "Indo-Pacific Strategy" Undermines Peace and Development Prospects in East Asia* (Beijing: Ministry of Foreign Affairs of the People's Republic of China, October 13, 2020), https://www.fmprc.gov.cn/mfa_eng/zxxx_662805/t1824140.shtml.

[50] Michelle Ye Hee Lee and Joanna Slater "Meeting of Leaders Signals the 'Quad' Grouping will Become Central Part of the U.S. Strategy in Asia," *The Washington Post*, March 13, 2021, https://www.washingtonpost.com/national-security/quad-diplomacy-counter-china/2021/03/12/9317aee8-8299-11eb-ac37-4383f7709abe_story.html.

[51] Richard Fontaine and Ely Ratner, "The U.S.-China Confrontation Is Not Another Cold War. It's Something New," *The Washington Post*, July

of its regime, and the deepening economic interdependence between China and other countries, such a goal and policy are not feasible at least through external pressure (though the possibility of self-destruction through internal dissent should not be denied).[52] The United States aims at competition with China in the areas of military, technology, and global influence to uphold values and rules that the United States desires. That means, if such a goal can be achieved, even cooperation with China is unlikely to be ruled out.

In other words, the United States and China are neither in total confrontation, nor the world is divided into two blocks. In this sense, describing the U.S.–China relationship as a "new Cold War" or "all-out decoupling" provides an inaccurate image. To the contrary, the total trade between the United States and China amounted to $560 billion in 2020, down only 3% from 2016 even during the war-on-trade period, and U.S. exports to China increased by 8% in 2020.[53] Foreign direct investments in China reached $163 billion, up to 4% from the previous year even during the pandemic period, ranking first in the world in 2020.[54] Goldman Sachs has also been expanding its investments in China.[55] Decoupling is expected to advance only to the extent that technology and supply chains of critical goods are related due to U.S. policy to exclude China in these fields. Accordingly, the United States would not expect the framework of FOIP to play a role to "contain" China, while such a role would be also difficult for other allies and partners to accept.

Second, countries related to FOIP and the Quad other than the United States strongly desire United States presence in the Indo-Pacific. The United States could place substantial pressure on China, which is

2, 2020, https://www.washingtonpost.com/opinions/2020/07/02/us-china-confronta tion-is-not-another-cold-war-its-something-new.

[52] Zack Cooper and Hal Brands, "America Will Only Win When China's Regime Fails," *Foreign Policy*, March 11, 2021, https://foreignpolicy.com/2021/03/11/america-chinas-regime-fails.

[53] U.S. Census Bureau, *Trade in Goods with China* (Washington, DC: U.S. Census Bureau), https://www.census.gov/foreign-trade/balance/c5700.html.

[54] United Nations Conference on Trade and Development, *Investment Trends Monitor* (Geneva: United Nations Conference on Trade and Development, January 2021), https://unctad.org/system/files/official-document/diaeiainf2021d1_en.pdf.

[55] Scott Murdoch "Goldman Sachs Shifts to Full Ownership of China Securities Joint Venture," *Reuters*, December 8, 2020, https://www.reuters.com/article/us-goldman-sachs-china-idUSKBN28I0F0.

what other countries need but are unable to realize. The phrase "secure and prosperous Indo-Pacific" used by Biden's team instead of "FOIP" raised some concerns among Japanese intellectuals because they thought it would send a signal of a U.S. commitment setback.[56] Presumably at the request of the Suga administration, the Biden administration has since started to use FOIP.

Third, FOIP and the Quad are not only meant to counter China directly or militarily, but also serve as a framework for regional and global cooperation among relevant countries in a broader sense. In the Quad's first summit meeting in March 2020, the leaders agreed on the partnership for vaccine manufacturing and delivery, climate change, and important technology without mentioning ever "China" in the joint statement or fact sheet.[57] These areas were not conventionally regarded as security issues, but their importance has been growing in terms of economic security. The Quad summit meeting has provided an opportunity to strengthening multilateral cooperation in such fields.

For the above-mentioned reasons, it would be beneficial for all countries involved in FOIP and the Quad that: (1) The United States demonstrates a strong commitment to the Indo-Pacific, increasing deterrence and pressure on China; (2) other countries support such an approach, simultaneously managing their relations with China; and (3) all countries pursue multilateral cooperation in not only the field of conventional security, but also of economic security. If the United States and other relevant countries share this understanding, FOIP and the Quad will continue to function and develop as a mechanism for coordinating the policies of the countries.

The most important factor is the U.S.'s continued commitment. Therefore, other countries need to make every effort to keep the United States in the region. As mentioned earlier, the United States is expected to play the vanguard role in countering and pressuring China since other countries are vulnerable to China's aggressive behaviors. Given such

---

[56] Charles Crabtree, "Let's Keep It the "Free and Open" Indo-Pacific," *The Tokyo Foundation for Policy Research*, February 8, 2021, https://www.tkfd.or.jp/en/research/detail.php?id=798.

[57] White House, *Quad Leaders' Joint Statement: "The Spirit of the Quad."*; and White House, *Fact Sheet: Quad Summit* (Washington, DC: White House, March 12, 2021), https://www.whitehouse.gov/briefing-room/statements-releases/2021/03/12/fact-sheet-quad-summit.

differences in position and interests, other countries are expected to play a complementary role as effectively as possible. For example, the Quad's current joint military exercises should be continued and even intensified. Cooperation in economic security such as technology and supply chains should be further strengthened. Moreover, with the Quad at the core, it would make sense to expand cooperation to other Indo-Pacific countries such as ASEAN, South Korea, the EU, or the U.K.

## POLICY RECOMMENDATIONS: MULTI-LAYERED COALITIONS OF DEMOCRATIC COUNTRIES

This paper concludes with recommendations for cooperation in the framework of FOIP and the Quad and beyond. As already discussed, the driver for FOIP and the Quad cooperation is China. The rise of new superpower and its growing competition with a traditional superpower have forced Indo-Pacific countries to consider how to deal with this new reality. A possible solution is a functional approach to partnership and cooperation. The two great powers are in competition with each other in a variety of areas, including military, security, economy, and global influence. The essence of the competition—what the goal should be, how it should be achieved, and what countries should be involved—varies in different areas.

Regarding areas of cooperation, on the military and security front, it will be necessary to thoroughly deter China so that the sovereignty of Indo-Pacific countries will not be infringed. On the economic front, negotiation and compromise should not be excluded if China's economic policies and practices become fairer and more transparent. On the technology front, as far as crucial and emerging economic security technologies such as telecommunication, semiconductor, cyber security, and AI, are concerned, considering China's dual-use policy, it should be significantly important to defend against China's threats and slow down China's technological progress. Further, it should also be important for the United States and other democratic states to promote multilateral cooperation toward development of such important technologies. The same applies to the issue of supply chain. Indo-Pacific countries are diverse in their political and economic systems; their relations with China also have their own characteristics. Not all countries can completely agree on the policies that the United States pursues toward China. Forcing Indo-Pacific countries to choose between the United States and China would place them in a quandary, undermining the solidarity of Indo-Pacific countries as a consequence.

Regarding participants in cooperation, the Biden's team announced its intention to host a "global summit for Democracy."[58] However, the question regards which countries to invite and what themes to discuss. In the Indo-Pacific region, Vietnam and post-coup Myanmar are clearly not democratic countries. Thailand and Cambodia are at the very least in a dubious situation considering their oppressive governance. There is no doubt that Taiwan would be a highly controversial issue. Dividing Indo-Pacific countries by such selection would not be appropriate for countries involved in FOIP and the Quad to pursue their policies jointly toward China. Accordingly, it would be more appropriate to take a functional approach. That means, the Quad should be the core group, and, depending on the area of cooperation, other countries should be invited. This would create multi-layered coalitions of like-minded democratic countries. Major possible areas of cooperation are: military and security; technology; supply chain; governance (democracy and human rights); and economic development assistance.

First, regarding military and security, the issues to be addressed are free navigation in the Indo-Pacific, respect for every country's sovereignty, and regional stability. As the United States has the most effective military capacity to contain China's aggression in the South and East China Seas, the United States should emphasize its commitment and clarify a red line to prevent China from expanding its threatening activities toward Indo-Pacific countries. Other countries are required to provide full-support to the U.S.'s initiatives. Joint maritime military exercises should not only be continued and strengthened, but also attempt to involve appropriate ASEAN countries, the EU, and the U.K. The Trump administration's excessive pressure on allies for burden-sharing of military bases through bilateral negotiations could have undermined the trust of allies. Such sensitive issues for recipient countries' domestic politics should be deliberately discussed taking into account their external implications. Also, the U.S. could present an overall strategy for military deployment in the

---

[58] Biden Harris, *The Power of America's Example: The Biden Plan for Leading the Democratic World to Meet the Challenges of the 21st Century*, https://joebiden.com/americanleadership; and Joseph R. Biden, Jr. "Why America Must Lead Again," *Foreign Affairs* (March/April 2020), https://www.foreignaffairs.com/articles/united-states/2020-01-23/why-america-must-lead-again.

Indo-Pacific region to relevant allies so that all parties could pursue a fair solution.

Second, regarding technology and supply chain, the Trump administration implemented various measures centered on export controls and investment restrictions, and the Biden administration is likely to succeed most of the measures after its review.[59] In contrast to the Trump administration's unilateral approach, the Biden administration emphasized the need for multilateral cooperation. In this field, other countries are facing similar challenges to the threat of Chinese military technology and dependence on China for critical goods. Thus, the countries have a great deal of interests in common. Accordingly, multilateral talk should be pursued, and the Quad should play a core role. The "T-12," a concept of a framework for tech cooperation among 12 countries (G7 excluding Italy, plus Sweden, Norway, Israel, South Korea, Australia, and India), also deserves consideration.[60]

Third, governance (democracy and human rights) is an area where democratic groups centered on the Quad could make the most of its potential. The countries should seek to express a coordinated message on issues in China such as Xinjiang Uyghur Autonomous Region, Tibet, and Hong Kong. Democratic countries such as South Korea, the EU, and the U.K. could be included in this cooperation. As the U.K. invited South Korea, India, and Australia to the G7 summit meeting in June 2021, some argue that a "D10" group of 10 democracies should replace G7 with the addition of these three countries. This approach is more practical than Biden's democracy summit.

Finally, economic development assistance is an area where Japan has actively promoted in the Indo-Pacific region mainly through infrastructure projects, but it should be further enhanced in the Quad and FOIP framework in the same way that the Blue Dot Network functioned.[61]

[59] White House, *Executive Order on America's Supply Chains* (Washington, DC: White House, February 24, 2021), https://www.whitehouse.gov/briefing-room/presidential-act ions/2021/02/24/executive-order-on-americas-supply-chains.

[60] Jared Cohen and Richard Fontaine, "Uniting the Techno-Democracies: How to Build Digital Cooperation," *Foreign Affairs*, November/December 2020, https://www.foreignaffairs.com/articles/united-states/2020-10-13/uniting-techno-democracies.

[61] Department of State, *Blue Dot Network* (Washington, DC: United States Department of State), https://www.state.gov/blue-dot-network.

The Quad's cooperation for manufacturing and deployment of COVID-19 vaccines agreed on the summit meeting should be highly evaluated as an appropriate model.

## Conclusion

The rise of China and its competition with the United States are the most important geopolitical factors in the twenty-first century. No country in the world, especially in the Indo-Pacific region, can be distant from this two superpowers' competitive coexistence or avoid considering how to deal with this issue. FOIP, the Indo-Pacific, and the Quad are outcomes of this global trend.

As the United States, Japan, India, Australia, ASEAN, and Europe have their own agendas and interests, each of them discusses its own concept of Indo-Pacific. Its substance is multifaceted, and the goals of each country are not exactly the same. However, there are many areas of overlap, especially with respect to the issue of China, thus it has the potential to function effectively as a mechanism for coordinating the policies of each country. The key to its successful coordination is the U.S.'s continued commitment in the region, which need to be supported by each country's efforts for mutually complementary cooperation.

As the United States and China are competing over dominance in various areas, allies and partners of the United States are likely to form multi-layered coalitions. FOIP's vision and the Quad framework have a great potential to play a central role for these coalitions. Key issues for these coalitions will be military and security, technology, supply chain, governance (democracy and human rights), and economic development assistance. The four democratic countries, the United States, Japan, India, and Australia should wield strong leadership. In particular, Japan is expected to play the leading role for this cooperation, considering its historically solid alliance with the U.S., broad and stable partnership with India, Australia, and Southeast Asian countries as well as long-term experience of managing relations with China.

# Conclusion

In 1989, Samuel Kim, Professor at The Woodrow Wilson School at Princeton wrote what was at the time, one of the most seminal book volumes on Chinese foreign policy entitled, *"China and The World: New Directions in Chinese Foreign Relations."* For the first time in modern history Samuel wrote, "China has finally joined the world becoming a full-fledged member of the global political system."[1] Moreover, author Steven Levine noted, "The greatest danger to Sino-American relations may come from a general inattention to the necessity of keeping the overall relationship in a state of good repair. China has rarely if ever been at the center of U.S. attention for more than brief periods at a time."[2] That was 32 years ago. Today, China is consistently at the center of U.S. attention and the United States and China is the most important bilateral relationship in the World. Collaboration on a host of transnational issues can either garner great progress or in a worst case scenario, conflict, which could lead to unprecedented loss of life and economic prosperity. This collaborative volume supports the view that the United States and China should be intentional about identifying areas of cooperation which ultimately impact regional and global economies. It is helpful to remember that at the height of the Cold War rivalry between Russia and the United States,

---

[1] Edited by Samuel Kim, *China and The World: New Directions in Chinese Foreign Relations*, (Westview Press, 1989), 3.

[2] Ibid, 105.

the two superpowers while they couldn't agree on which nation could attain nuclear supremacy, nonetheless forged a relationship to end Polio. In the 1960s, the United States and the former Soviet Union threatened to destroy each other up with nuclear weapons. It almost led to an all-out war of mutually assured destruction (MAD). However, during the midst of this, Russian and American scientists—experts in virology—also collaborated on at least two vaccines that helped to eradicate the world of Polio. Secretly, senior virologists from the United States and Russia were also collaborating to develop vaccines, specifically against polio and smallpox, two of the major infectious diseases afflicting mankind till then. Today most kids are given an oral polio vaccine, which came directly out of the U.S.–Russian collaboration, according to the open-access peer-reviewed *Public Library of Science (PLOS) Journal of Neglected Tropical Diseases*.

It is critically important that we understand, appreciate, and cherish our common history of humanity and strive to repeat it particularly in light of a global pandemic. What this means for U.S.–Sino relations is that when you unleash the industrious, innovative, and entrepreneurial potential of these two nations working toward a common objective, you build trust. So, if there is consensus about anything from the United States and China high level talks in Anchorage, Alaska, in March of 2021, or U.S. Deputy Secretary of State Wendy Sherman's meeting with Chinese officials in July of 2021, it is that America and China need more communication, trust, and mutual understanding not less. There is so much that the United States and China can accomplish if they could be more focused discussions on areas of mutual shared interest such as joint development of technology in improving the enviornment, global health issues, transnational crime and the list goes on. In the next decade, history, science, and data have proven that the question will not be if the international community will face future global pandemics & environmental decay but when. The United States and China have a strategic, geopolitical, and moral imperative to identify ways to collaborate but this should not only fall on the responsibilities of states. Eighteenth-century Scottish philosopher and economist Adam Smith in his concept of the invisible hand argues that "social benefit and economic order are the result of the self-interested actions of individuals rather than the consequences of some formal plan."[3] The same should be said of the relationship between Washington and

---

[3] Adam Smith, "An Inquiry into the Nature and Causes of the Wealth of Nations" Volume 1, *Oxford University Press*, 1976.

Beijing. When states cannot set aside politics, it is up to individual people supporting non-profit organizations, and leading institutions like The National Committee on U.S.–China Relations and others to continue to foster dialogue and enhance mutual trust and understanding. This is why study abroad programs at both the high school and college levels coupled with other professional exchanges are so critically important and must be funded.

China's rise in the global arena for many represents a big shift for Chinese leaders, who for decades took care not to challenge the U.S. as the world's leader and followed the slogan Deng Xiaoping set decades ago: "Keep a low profile and bide your time."

Some senior Chinese officials privately—often called the U.S. *Lao Da*, or Big Boss., China's rise, however, to others represents an imperial over-reach. How can or should the Chinese government justify spending so much resources abroad when so many ordinary citizens in China struggle? However, another view in the Chinese leadership is that China's rise should not be feared by the West but more importantly viewed within the totality of the historical context of U.S.–China relations. Mr. Liqun Jin, President of the Asian Infrastructure Bank (AIIB) who began to be involved in the bilateral dialogues between China and the United States from the early 1980s, expressed guarded optimism in the evolvement of the bilateral relationship between these two most powerful nations in this world. *"The normalization of the diplomatic relationship put an end to the post-Korean War hostility, which was far more virulent than what is experienced today. There had been very limited official communication and conspicuous absence of people-to-people exchanges all the way until the icebreaking visit by President Nixon in 1972. For all the ostentatious acrimony these days, the trade and cross-border investment continue to go strong, and it seems that the so-called decoupling as touted by some American politicians will be spurned by businesses as it is prohibitively costly."*

*It is high time to reboot US-China relations. Neither of these two nations can afford to foreclose their ties simply because of the mutual mistrust or the presumed design on the each other. China's ascent on the steep curve of science and technology is unlikely to be thwarted. Indeed, this should incentivize the Americans who have faith in competition to further their state-of-the-art technologies. The US should not worry over an ever-growing a strong China, a peace-loving and non-expansionist nation. There is a broad space for China-U.S. collaboration way beyond climate change and anti-terrorism.*

*The bilateral relationship should not be defined by ultranationalism and populism; rather it is rational and reasonable thinking that should guide the forward-moving of the two nations.*

President Xi wants to project an image of strength and to convey to the world that China's time has arrived. "China can already look at the world on an equal level," he told the annual legislative sessions in Beijing in early March of 2021, a remark widely interpreted in Chinese media as a declaration that China no longer looks up to the United States.[4]

From America's standpoint, it often describes China as a strategic rival. In 2021, The U.S. Senate Foreign Relations Committee has proposed over $100 million for ongoing and new programs to support local media, build independent media, combat Chinese disinformation inside and outside China, invest in technology to subvert censorship, and monitor and evaluate these programs.[5] This is part of a unprecedented bipartisan bill issued jointly by both the Senate and The House of Representatives known as The Strategic Competition Act of 2021.[6] On May 17th the Senate voted (86–11) and passed this bipartisan bill which is the most important legislation passed thus far aimed at China. The cornerstone of this act is a whopping $100 billion in funding for the National Science Foundation to create a new technology directorate and if enacted would enable The Biden Administration to marshall efforts to counter a rising global China.[7] Moreover, the American public's increasingly negative view of China, largely stemming from exposure to the issues in Xinjiang, Tibet, and Hong Kong and blame directed at China due to COVID19,

[4] Lingling Wei and Bob Davis, "China's Message to America: We're Equal Now," *Wall Street Journal*, April 12, 2021, https://www.wsj.com/articles/america-china-policy-biden-xi-11617896117.

[5] Chairman Menendez Announces Bipartisan Comprehensive China Legislation, *Chairman Press*, April 8, 2021, https://www.foreign.senate.gov/press/chair/release/chairman-menendez-announces-bipartisan-comprehensive-china-legislation.

[6] "Strategic Competition Act 2021." https://www.foreign.senate.gov/imo/media/doc/DAV21598%20-%20Strategic%20Competition%20Act%20of%202021.pdf.

[7] Andrew Desiderio, "Senate advances a rare bipartisan deal on countering China," Politico, May 17th, 2021. https://www.politico.com/news/2021/05/17/senate-bipartisan-deal-countering-china-489152.

have further pushed the Biden Administration to take a tough stance against Beijing.[8]

Clearly the United States and China are positioning themselves for competition, but who really wins and loses in this competition? More importantly, who ultimately bears the costs of this competition? As the United States and China strive to both compete and cooperate on various bilateral issues it is critically important to implement codes of conduct to avoid any kind of military conflict. General Clint Hinote, the U.S. Air Force's top strategist, puts it this way, "It's clear that the United States and China have many interests in common, and we should work together where we can to pursue those interests. Some Chinese interests are not shared by the United States or China's neighbors in Asia. In these areas, we will compete vigorously. As we compete, however, we must find ways to steer the competition away from military conflict. There will be no winners in a war between the United States and China, as any victory would be pyrrhic at best, with unmatched economic costs and terrible bloodshed. We simply cannot let that happen." Both nations ultimately bear responsibility to ensure the peace and tranquility that the Asia–Pacific region has enjoyed over the last seven decades.

Just to underscore how much competition dominates the current narrative in U.S.–Sino relations, on May 26th, 2021, Kurt Campbell, U.S. coordinator for Indo-Pacific affairs at the National Security Council, described Sino–U.S. ties as entering a different phase of competition. "The period that was broadly described as engagement has come to an end; the dominant paradigm is going to be competition."[9] China's response was swift as Foreign Ministry Spokesman Zhao Lijian shot back, " China-US relations will naturally experience some competition, which is prevalent among other major-country relations, but it is wrong to define the relationship with competition because it will only lead to confrontation and conflict." To put it blunt, the United States must never lose sight nor forget cooperation. Some such as Fu Ying a former vice foreign minister of China have even gone so far as to propose that the

---

[8] Cheng Li, "Biden's China strategy: Coalition-driven competition or Cold War-style confrontation?" May 2021. https://www.brookings.edu/research/bidens-china-strategy-coalition-driven-competition-or-cold-war-style-confrontation/.

[9] "Biden's Asia czar Kurt Campbell says era of engagement with Xi's China is over," Straits Times, May 26th, 2021. https://www.straitstimes.com/world/united-states/us-says-looking-at-quad-meeting-in-fall-focused-on-infrastructure.

United States and China develop a relationship of "coopetition" (cooperation + competition).[10] Meaning that within the realm of competition a set of rules of engagement are identified. For example, during the 1990s, Beijing and Washington created a consultation dialogue around maritime security. Subsequently they established guidelines for dealing with unplanned encounters in the air and at sea and developed a hotline to convey critical information during a crisis. Today, almost twenty years later, a similar framework is needed, more than ever to build trust and mutual understanding between America and The People's Republic of China. To ignore, defy, or ill-define rules of engagement serves only to engender unpredictability, mistrust, and obfuscate communication. More importantly, the stakes of mismanaging the US–China relationship have never been higher.

The often irreconcilable tensions have increasingly driven the world into two trade and investment systems; will nations be forced to choose between stronger ties to America or be wooed by the economic incentives from the China-led Regional Comprehensive Economic Partnership (RCEP) or The Belt & Road Initiative? Will countries feel the continued pressure of two IT and internet systems defined by divergent visions or standards of the United States and China particularly on issues like telecommunications or 5G? In global financial markets, how will states react to potentially two financial and currency systems, one denominated in U.S. dollar and the other in *Renminbi*? Moreover in the realm of alliances how will countries react to political and military blocs like the Quad comprised of the United States, Australia, India, and Japan on one hand and China, Russia, and Iran on the other? To engage on these critical issues new leadership from the United States and China will be essential. China and the United States in sending new Ambassadors, Nicholas Burns and Qin Gang underscores how these individuals will engage at the highest levels of diplomacy during a time of increased tensions. A Bostonian at heart and at 65, having served as a former Undersecretary of State and Ambassador to both NATO and Greece, Burns brings almost three decades of government experience to the Ambassadorial post. Qin Gang was born in Tianjin and at 55 is the youngest of China's current vice ministers of Foreign Affairs and is being

---

[10] Fu Ying, "China and U.S. Can Have Cooperative Competition," The New York Times, November 24th, 2021. https://www.nytimes.com/2020/11/24/opinion/china-us-biden.html.

groomed to play an important role in China's foreign policy establishment. He is an experienced diplomat having most recently served as the Ministry of Foreign Affairs director of the Protocol Department and director-general of the Information Department as well as spokesperson. Ambassador Burns and Ambassador Gang's leadership will be required to navigate effectively their respective domestic bureaucracies. This will be essential to ensure that China and the United States can and must cooperate on maintaining stability in global financial markets, digital security, anti-money laundering, artificial intelligence governance, climate change, and global health issues as some of the core quintessential bilateral issues.

China has a revered history of over 5,000 years and has achieved significant cultural, economic, and social milestones. As of 2021, America has a significant shorter history of 245 years, but one that has embraced innovation, capitalism, institutions, and democratic values and a global financial system which has sustained a level of global order for several decades. China seeks to disrupt the current global order to establish standards that are more aligned with its values, norms, and best practices. A foundational principle is that the failures and successes of the past do not define the realities of tomorrow. It is up to the United States and China; senior leaders, teachers, engineers, essential workers, and yes ordinary citizens to reimagine and chart a better future not just for each individual nation but for all of global humanity.

# INDEX

CPSIA information can be obtained
at www.ICGtesting.com
Printed in the USA
LVHW080739081121
702733LV00003B/177